Mastering Social Studies Skills

FOURTH EDITION

Gerard J. Pelisson

AMSCO SCHOOL PUBLICATIONS, INC.
315 Hudson Street • New York, N.Y. 10013

About the Author

Gerard J. Pelisson taught social studies in New York City high schools for more than 20 years. In addition, he coordinated teacher training and student development programs for the High School Division of the New York City Board of Education. Mr. Pelisson is the co-author of *The Castle on the Parkway*, a history of DeWitt Clinton High School in New York City (Hutch Press, 2009). He is also the author of *Mastering United States History Skills* (Amsco).

Reviewers

Beth Berns Morrison, Social Studies Teacher, Eastchester Middle School, Eastchester, New York

Courtney Bradshaw, Social Studies Teacher/Dean, CIS 303, The Leadership and Community Service Academy, Bronx, New York

Cover Design: Sierra Graphics, Inc. and Delgado and Company, Inc.
Cover Photos: Colorful keyboard next to computer screen: Ralph Mercer/Getty Images; Young man at computer, main image: Hitoshi Nishimura/Getty Images; Globe with magnifying glass: ULTRA.F/Getty Images; Land mass with dark water: Harvey Lloyd/Getty Images; Foward and Search buttons: ©Masterfile-RF; Compass Rose: ©iStockphoto.com/DNY59; Blue keyboard: ©iStockphoto.com/hjalmeida
Art: Hadel Studio
Composition and Interior Design: Sierra Graphics, Inc.
Contributing Editor: Joan Kinne

Please visit our Web site at: **www.amscopub.com**

When ordering this book, please specify:
either **R 757 W** *or* MASTERING SOCIAL STUDIES SKILLS, SOFTBOUND

ISBN: 978-1-56765-683-1

Table of Contents

Preface

Mastering Social Studies Skills offers in one volume a comprehensive approach to the most important skills needed in Social Studies. This workbook combines traditional Social Studies skills with those that were once taught only in an English class or a Mathematics class, but that are also important for successful work in Social Studies.

The eight units of the book are organized as follows:

Unit One stresses reading comprehension by teaching students how to distinguish between main ideas and details, how to determine the sequence of events, and how to separate fact from fiction and opinion.

Unit Two works to improve writing skills, beginning with writing simple sentences and working up to essays and summaries that make every word count.

Unit Three teaches students how to find information in printed resources and on the Internet, how to understand it, and how to remember it.

Unit Four develops the skill of analysis as applied to reading tables, charts, and graphs and interpreting photographs, drawings, and cartoons.

Unit Five introduces the skills of map reading, including how to recognize landforms and water forms on a map, how to use directions to locate places on a map, and how to interpret map keys.

Unit Six teaches students how to locate exact places on a map using latitude and longitude. Latitude is also used to teach climate zones, and longitude is used to teach time zones.

Unit Seven extends map skills to interpreting population, relief, rainfall, climate, vegetation, land use, and product maps.

Unit Eight develops skills in taking a test and answering constructed-response questions (CRQs) and document-based questions (DBQs).

All reading selections, writing exercises, maps, and illustrations reflect as closely as possible the kinds of materials students are likely to encounter in their Social Studies classes and textbooks. While the contents of this workbook are mostly related to topics taught in Regional Studies courses, the skills are applicable to work in any Social Studies course.

Each chapter of this book:

- assumes that students are starting with little knowledge of the skill to be taught.
- is written to be understood by students who usually have difficulty comprehending what they read.
- asks questions so that students can see if they are understanding a skill as it develops. (Answers and their explanations are given in each chapter. By checking their answers with the ones given, students see immediately if they are learning the skill.)
- contains numerous exercises, giving students multiple chances to demonstrate their understanding of each skill.

Mastering Social Studies Skills can be used at the beginning of a term to teach all the skills at once or to supplement any standard textbook throughout the term. The 31 chapters in the workbook can be used as full class lessons taught by the teacher or as self-study lessons that enable students to work independently at their own pace.

The book can also help prepare students for standardized tests and minimum competency examinations in Social Studies. Students who master the skills in this book will have a much greater chance of doing well in all their Social Studies classes.

For their advice and assistance in developing one or more of the editions of this book, the author wishes to thank Sidney Langsam, Irwin Pfeffer, and Angelo Purcigliotti, former Assistant Principals; and Sara Goodblatt and Edward F. Schwartz, former Social Studies teachers (all of New York City high schools).

Gerard J. Pelisson

UNIT ONE

Reading Skills

Chapter 1

Using Details to Find the Main Idea

A skill is the ability to do something well. One of the most important Social Studies skills is reading. In this chapter, you will learn how to become a better reader by developing the skill of picking out the most important idea in a selection or story.

After you have finished reading a selection, you should be able to tell what it is all about. In other words, you should be able to use the information in the selection to find the *main idea*.

The information in a selection is called the *details*. They are the people, places, and events that appear in a selection. One detail in the following selection is that crops can be grown on only 15 percent of the land in Japan. Another detail states that Japan has to feed about 128 million people. Look for these and other details as you read the selection.

> Japan is a country of more than 3,000 islands. Most of its land is made up of steep hills and mountains. This rugged landscape makes it difficult to find good farmland. Crops can be grown on only 15 percent of the land. Yet Japan has to feed about 128 million people. So it is important to use every piece of land that is good for farming.
>
> rugged: rough, uneven

Place a check mark (✓) next to the correct answers to the questions.

1. Much of Japan is

   _____ (*a*) good farmland.

   _____ (*b*) made up of flat land and rolling hills.

   _____ (*c*) covered by steep hills and mountains.

Which answer did you choose? The second sentence in the selection tells you that the answer to question 1 is (*c*).

2. The population of Japan is roughly

   _____ (*a*) 15 million.

   _____ (*b*) 128 million.

   _____ (*c*) 150 million.

1

Which answer did you choose? The word *population* (number of people) does not appear in the paragraph. But the paragraph does state that Japan has to feed about 128 million people. This is another way of saying that the population is 128 million. Therefore, the answer to question 2 is (b).

Paying attention to the details is important. But it is not enough just to remember the details. They were put in the reading selection for a purpose. They support the main idea, or what the selection is all about.

The main idea is often found in the first sentence. But any sentence in the selection may contain the main idea. Or it may not be found in any of the sentences in the selection. To find the main idea in this case, you have to think about what all the sentences in the selection mean together. Answer the following question.

3. The main idea of the selection is that

_____ (a) Japan has plenty of land on which to grow food.

_____ (b) the rugged landscape of Japan makes it difficult to find good farmland.

_____ (c) the Japanese do not eat very much.

Which did you choose? Is there a sentence in Paragraph 1 that can help you to pick (a), (b), or (c)? Yes, the sentence "This rugged landscape makes it difficult to find good farmland." states the same idea as choice (b). This is an example of one sentence in the selection giving the main idea. Most of the other sentences give only details that support the main idea. Choices (a) and (c) are not supported by any details in the paragraph. Therefore, the answer to question 3 is (b).

So far, you have learned about a reading selection of only one paragraph expressing only one main idea. In fact, that is what a *paragraph* is: a group of sentences that expresses one main idea. But many reading selections consist of more than one paragraph. The main idea of each paragraph adds up to the main idea of the entire selection.

Read the following selection, which includes the paragraph you just read about the rugged landscape of Japan. Then answer the questions about paragraphs 2 and 3 and the entire selection.

Paragraph 1

Japan is a country of more than 3,000 islands. Most of its land is made up of steep hills and mountains. This rugged landscape makes it difficult to find good farmland. Crops can be grown on only 15 percent of the land. Yet Japan has to feed about 128 million people. So it is important to use every piece of land that is good for farming.

Paragraph 2

The most important crop in Japan is rice. But large fields of potatoes, soybeans, and grains such as wheat and barley can also be seen throughout Japan. On hillsides in some parts of the country, tea plants are a common sight. Some types of fruit are also grown.

Paragraph 3

Because Japanese farmers need most of their land for growing crops, not enough land is left over for raising large herds of cattle, sheep, and pigs. As a result, meat is rarely found on most Japanese dinner tables. Some food is <u>imported</u>, but it is not enough to meet Japan's needs. To get more food, the Japanese look to the sea that surrounds their island nation. The many kinds of fish living in the sea provide Japan with a large supply of food. Without this food from the sea, the Japanese would not have enough to eat.

<u>imported</u>: brought into a country

4. The main idea of Paragraph 2 is that

_____ (a) rice is the most important crop in Japan.

_____ (b) most farmers in Japan raise tea plants.

_____ (c) Japanese farmers grow many different kinds of crops.

Which answer did you choose? Is there any sentence in Paragraph 2 that tells you the main idea of the paragraph? No, each sentence tells you only about the different kinds of crops grown in Japan. By putting all those details together, you can say that many crops are grown in Japan. Therefore, the answer to question 4 is (c).

5. The main idea of Paragraph 3 is that

_____ (a) the Japanese do not like to eat meat.

_____ (b) meat is rarely found on most Japanese dinner tables.

_____ (c) the Japanese would not have enough food for everyone if they did not have fish to eat.

Which answer did you choose this time? Choice (a) is not supported by any information in Paragraph 3. Choice (b) gives a detail found in the second sentence. But that detail is not the main idea of the entire paragraph. Choice (c) states that the Japanese would not have enough food for everyone if they did not have fish to eat. Most of the sentences in Paragraph 3 support that idea. Therefore, the answer to question 5 is (c).

6. You have read all three paragraphs of the selection on Japan. Which one of the following groups of words states the main idea of the entire reading selection?

_____ (a) How the Japanese Catch Fish

_____ (b) How the Japanese Provide Food for Themselves

_____ (c) How the Japanese Farm Their Land

Which answer did you choose? All three paragraphs deal with how the Japanese provide food for themselves. Therefore, the best answer to question 6 is (b).

No one is born knowing how to read or how to pick out important ideas in a selection. All of us have to learn these skills through much practice. The following exercises will give you more practice in finding details in a reading selection and using them to find the main idea.

Using What You Have Learned

A. Place a check mark next to the correct answers to questions 1 to 6.

1. Reading skill is the ability to

___ (a) read fast.

___ (b) understand what you read.

___ (c) write down what you read.

2. The names, places, and events in a reading selection are called

___ (a) phrases.

___ (b) ideas.

___ (c) details.

3. If a classmate asks you what a reading selection is about, she wants to know

___ (a) all the information in the selection.

___ (b) the most interesting detail in the selection.

___ (c) the main idea of the selection.

4. A paragraph is

___ (a) a group of sentences that expresses one main idea.

___ (b) a group of sentences without important details.

___ (c) another term for main idea.

5. The main idea of a paragraph

___ (a) is always stated in the first sentence.

___ (b) is never stated in the paragraph.

___ (c) may be stated anywhere in the paragraph or not at all.

6. When a selection is made up of more than one paragraph, the main idea of the selection is

___ (a) usually supported by details in every paragraph.

___ (b) always found in the first paragraph.

___ (c) never stated in any of the paragraphs.

B. Reading for Details. Read the following selection. Then answer the questions to see how good you are at finding details.

Soccer Finds a Home in the United States

Before the 1970s, few American teenagers had ever heard of soccer. This is surprising since soccer is one of the oldest and most popular sports in the world. In many countries in Europe, South America, Africa, and Asia, soccer is the national sport. It is so popular in some countries that huge soccer stadiums have been built to hold as many as 200,000 fans.

No one knows for sure where or when the game of soccer started. The Chinese played a game like it 2,500 years ago, and so did the Romans almost 2,000 years ago. But the modern game of soccer seems to have started in England. From there the game spread to other countries in Europe. In the late 1800s, European traders and sailors spread the sport all over the world.

Today, soccer is truly an <u>international</u> game. Every four years, teams from more than 100 countries compete in the World Cup championships. Hundreds of millions of people watch these championship matches on television, making them the most popular sporting events in the world.

Soccer did not begin to become popular in the United States until the mid-1970s. Since then, it has become the fastest-growing college and high school sport. In the United States today, more than 15 million boys and girls under the age of 18 play soccer. One of the oldest and most popular sports in the world has finally found a place in American life.

<u>international</u>: involving two or more nations

Place a check mark next to the correct answers to questions 1 to 5.

1. It is thought that a game like soccer was played
   ___ (a) 2,500 years ago.
   ___ (b) 5,200 years ago.
   ___ (c) 12,500 years ago.

2. Soccer as we know it started in
   ___ (a) England.
   ___ (b) Brazil.
   ___ (c) China.

3. The World Cup championships are held
   ___ (a) every year.
   ___ (b) every two years.
   ___ (c) every four years.

4. Soccer first became popular in the United States in the
   ___ (a) late 1800s.
   ___ (b) mid-1970s.
   ___ (c) early 2000s.

5. How many boys and girls in the United States under the age of 18 play soccer?
   ___ (a) almost 10 million
   ___ (b) 12 million
   ___ (c) more than 15 million

C. **Using Details to Find the Main Idea.** Read the following selection. Then on the lines following it, give the main idea and three details that support the main idea.

> Southwest Asia/North Africa (also known as the Middle East) contains some of the busiest trade routes in the world. For this reason, Southwest Asia/North Africa is often called the "Crossroads of the World." One of the most important trade routes in the region is the Suez Canal. This human-made waterway connects the Mediterranean Sea and the Red Sea. Since the canal opened in 1869, ships from many parts of the world have passed through it carrying every kind of cargo. By using the Suez Canal, ships sailing between South Asia and Western Europe shorten the trip by as much as 5,000 miles. Without the canal, ships would have to sail all the way around Africa.
>
> trade route: course of travel used to transport goods
> cargo: goods or produce (crops, food) being transported, usually on a ship, plane, train, or truck.

Main Idea:

_____

Supporting Details:

_____

_____

_____

D. Finding the Main Idea of a Long Selection. Read the following selection. Then answer the questions that follow it.

Paragraph 1

Transportation is important to the people of South America. Modern ways of traveling can be seen in every country of this large continent. Modern boats move up and down the rivers. Railroads and airlines connect major cities. In fact, more than 50 airlines now fly to and from the major cities of South America. Land travel is almost impossible in the large sections of South America that are covered with rain forests and high mountains. The coming of the airplane has made traveling easier over these rugged areas.

Paragraph 2

The automobile is probably the fastest-growing way of traveling in South America. South Americans want automobiles for the same reasons that the people of the United States want them. Automobiles are easy to use. They allow people to live far from where they work. Moreover, they make it easier for people to take trips. Throughout the continent, there are more than 2,708,000 miles of roads. Of these, only 350,200 are paved. But more roads are being paved every year to meet the growing use of automobiles.

Paragraph 3

Even though there are many modern ways of traveling in South America, not everyone can use them. For many people there, the most common way of traveling is by foot or by boat. Travel by train, bus, or automobile is almost impossible in the high mountains and in many areas of the rain forests. Some areas of South America have no roads at all. In these areas, pack animals and oxcarts are used to carry people and goods. The old ways of traveling are still useful in this rugged land.

transportation: way of traveling
modern: new, up-to-date
major: important, great

Place a check mark next to the correct answers to questions 1 to 4.

1. The main idea of Paragraph 1 is that

___ (*a*) South America has many rain forests and high mountains.

___ (*b*) South America has many railroads that connect the major cities.

___ (*c*) South America has many modern ways of traveling.

2. The main idea of Paragraph 2 is that

___ (*a*) automobiles are easy to use.

___ (*b*) the automobile is the fastest-growing way of traveling in South America.

___ (*c*) South America has more than 2,708,000 miles of roads.

3. The main idea of Paragraph 3 is that

___ (*a*) some areas of South America have no roads at all.

___ (*b*) it is difficult to use trains, buses, and automobiles in the high mountains.

___ (*c*) the old ways of traveling—by foot, pack animals, and oxcarts—are still useful.

4. The main idea of the entire reading selection is that

___ (*a*) the automobile is the fastest-growing way of traveling in South America.

___ (*b*) the most common way of traveling in South America is by foot.

___ (*c*) South America has many modern ways of traveling, but it also has many old ones.

5. Make up a title that will help you remember the main idea of this reading selection.

_____

_____

E. Finding the Main Idea of a Long Selection. Read the following selection. Then answer the questions that follow it.

Paragraph 1

My name is Victor Orlovsky. When I was a youngster in the late 1970s, the Soviet Union still existed. My teachers would brag how the Soviet Union was the most important country in the world. I was very proud to learn so many wonderful things about my country. We were a <u>military</u> power the equal of the United States. Our space program had put the first human being in space. Every four years, our athletes were among the top medal winners at the Winter and Summer Olympics. Russian music and <u>literature</u> were admired around the world. The list of accomplishments seemed endless.

Paragraph 2

By the late 1980s, I was old enough to understand that my country had many problems. The Soviet system was based on the Communist idea that the government should own and control farms, businesses, and industries. But under this system, the people had little <u>prosperity</u>. Stores often had shortages of food and long lines. Families lived in small apartments, often sharing them with other families. Another serious problem was that many of the <u>ethnic</u> people living under the Soviet flag wanted their freedom. Little by little, I came to understand that the Soviet Union was not only a country. It was also an empire. It controlled by force other countries that had their own history and way of life. All these problems finally led many people, including me, to demand an end to communism—even if that meant an end to the Soviet Union itself.

Paragraph 3

I am still proud of my country, but today this means that I am proud to be Russian. Russia had been the leading one of the 15 <u>republics</u> of the Soviet Union. It became an <u>independent</u> republic with the breakup of the Soviet Union in 1991. Like most Russians, I yearn for the day when Russia will be a truly <u>democratic</u> country. We need better-paying jobs and better living conditions. Trade with other countries must improve. The more than 100 ethnic groups living in Russia must learn to live in peace. Religious freedom and equality must be guaranteed. Newspapers must have freedom of the press. Above all, we need to make sure that our problems do not lead us back to communism. If we succeed in keeping Russia on the road to prosperity and true democracy, I will have much to be proud of. In addition, my country will again be one of the most important in the world.

<u>military</u>: having to do with soldiers, weapons, or war
<u>literature</u>: the writings of respected authors
<u>prosperity</u>: wealth, riches
<u>ethnic</u>: having to do with a religious, racial, or national group
<u>republic</u>: form of government in which the people elect representatives to run the government
<u>independent</u>: free, on one's own
<u>democratic</u>: having free elections of government leaders and/or representatives

Place a check mark next to the correct answers to questions 1 to 4.

1. The main idea of Paragraph 1 is that

    ___ (*a*) the Soviet Union still exists.

    ___ (*b*) in his youth, Victor was proud of the Soviet Union.

    ___ (*c*) Russian music and literature are admired around the world.

2. The main idea of Paragraph 2 is that

    ___ (*a*) there were always food shortages in the Soviet Union.

    ___ (*b*) many problems led many Soviet people to call for an end to the Soviet Union.

    ___ (*c*) Communist ideas needed more time to see if they could improve the lives of the people in the Soviet Union.

3. The main idea of Paragraph 3 is that

____ (*a*) Russia today is one of the most important countries in the world.

____ (*b*) the breakup of the Soviet Union caused more problems than it solved.

____ (*c*) Russia has many problems to solve before it can bring about real prosperity and democracy.

4. The main idea of the entire reading selection is that

____ (*a*) Victor did not support the end of Communist rule in the Soviet Union.

____ (*b*) Victor is proud to be Russian.

____ (*c*) Victor's pride in his country has not stopped him from seeing its many problems.

5. Make up a title that will help you remember the main idea of this reading selection.

_____

_____

Chapter 2

Arranging Events in Sequence

A Social Studies reading selection often tells about many events, or things that happened. If these events are not described in the correct order in the selection, you might have difficulty understanding what the selection is about. The following example shows how strange a story seems when the events are not in the correct order.

"At 8 o'clock I left the house. I woke up at 7 o'clock this morning. I got dressed and arrived at class at 9 o'clock. Soon the bus to go to school came along, and I got on."

Confusing, isn't it? Most of the events are in the wrong order. For a story or a reading selection to make sense, the events described have to be placed in the order in which they happened. The first event usually comes at the beginning. Then the second event follows. This continues all the way to the last event, which usually appears at or near the end of the selection. Putting events into their correct order is also called "arranging events in the proper sequence."

In the following selection about the Dutch and British in South Africa, all the events are in the correct order. As you read the selection, watch for words or phrases like "first," "in the early 1800s," "later on," "soon," and "in the end." These "time" words and phrases will help you follow the sequence of events.

The first settlers from Europe, the Dutch, arrived in South Africa in 1652. They established a small trading post at the southern tip of the African continent. This settlement came to be called Capetown. In the early 1800s, the British also became interested in South Africa. They took control of Capetown and forced the Dutch to move farther north. Later on in the 1800s, gold and diamonds were discovered in the new territory where the Dutch had settled. When the British heard about these discoveries, they pushed north into the Dutch territory. The British now wanted to control this area because it was rich in gold and diamonds. Soon a war started between the British and the Dutch. In the end, the British defeated the Dutch, and South Africa became a British possession.

establish: to set up
territory: an area of land
possession: land or territory owned by another country

Did you follow the sequence of the story? To see how well you remember the order of events in the selection, answer the following questions.

1. Which words in the selection indicate, or point to, the start of the first event?

_____ (a) The first settlers

_____ (b) In 1652

_____ (c) The Dutch

Which answer did you choose? In a selection, you may see words or phrases such as "in the beginning," "at the start," or "first." These are often used to indicate the first event in a sequence. The first event in the above selection is stated in sentence one, "The first settlers from Europe, the Dutch, arrived in South Africa in 1652." The words "the first settlers" suggest the first event or beginning of the sequence. Therefore, the answer to question 1 is (*a*).

2. Which words indicate the start of the second event?

_____ (*a*) Soon

_____ (*b*) Later on

_____ (*c*) In the early 1800s

Which answer did you choose? The second event in the sequence is that the British became interested in South Africa. Are there any words in the selection that indicate the start of the second event? Yes, the words "in the early 1800s" in the fourth sentence introduce this event. Dates are often used to introduce an event in a selection. Therefore, the answer to question 2 is (*c*).

3. Which words show the start of the third event in the sequence?

_____ (*a*) In the early 1800s

_____ (*b*) Later on in the 1800s

_____ (*c*) Soon a war started

Which answer did you choose? The third event in the sequence is that gold and diamonds were discovered in the Dutch territory. The words "later on in the 1800s" in the sixth sentence show the start of the third event. Therefore, the answer to question 3 is (*b*).

4. When the British heard about the discovery of gold and diamonds, they pushed north into the Dutch territory. Which word is used to show the start of the next event?

_____ (*a*) Later

_____ (*b*) Soon

_____ (*c*) After

Which answer did you choose this time? The next event is that a war started between the British and the Dutch. This event is introduced by the word "soon" in the ninth sentence. Therefore, the answer to question 4 is (*b*).

The word "soon" is important for two reasons. First, it tells you that another event is about to happen. Second, the word "soon" tells you that the coming event happened only a short time after the event you just read about.

5. Which word or words indicate the start of the last event in the sequence?

_____ (*a*) Later

_____ (*b*) Soon

_____ (*c*) In the end

Which answer did you choose? In a selection, you may see words such as "at last," "finally," or "in the end." These words are often used to indicate the last event in a sequence. The last event in the above selection is stated in the tenth sentence, "In the end, the British defeated the Dutch, and South Africa became a British possession." The words "in the end" tell you that you are about to read the final event in the sequence. Therefore, the answer to question 5 is (*c*).

So far in this chapter, you have seen that events can be arranged in sequence to tell a story. How well do you remember the sequence of the selection about the Dutch and British in South Africa? The main events of the selection are stated below, but this time they are in the wrong order. Read the five statements carefully. Then read how to put them into the proper sequence.

____ In the early 1800s, the British took control of Capetown and forced the Dutch to move north.

____ The first settlers from Europe to arrive in South Africa were the Dutch.

____ The British defeated the Dutch in a war and made South Africa a British possession.

____ Later on in the 1800s, gold and diamonds were discovered in the new territory where the Dutch had settled.

____ When the British heard about the discovery of gold and diamonds in the Dutch territory, they moved into the territory.

How can you arrange these five events in their proper sequence? After each event, write the numbers of the sentences in which it appears in the selection. For example:

____ In the early 1800s, the British took control of Capetown and forced the Dutch to move north. **4, 5**

Do this for each event. After you have found the sentences in which each of these events appears, look for the event with the lowest numbers after it. The event with the lowest numbers came first in the selection and in the sequence. Put the number 1 in front of that statement. The statement with the second lowest numbers after it should have the number 2 placed in front of it. This continues all the way to the statement with the highest numbers after it. That statement came last in the selection and in the sequence. It should be given the number 5.

When you have finished, your answer should look like this.

__2__ In the early 1800s, the British took control of Capetown and forced the Dutch to move north. **4, 5**

__1__ The first settlers from Europe to arrive in South Africa were the Dutch. **1**

__5__ The British defeated the Dutch in a war and made South Africa a British possession. **9, 10**

__3__ Later on in the 1800s, gold and diamonds were discovered in the new territory where the Dutch had settled. **6**

__4__ When the British heard about the discovery of gold and diamonds in the Dutch territory, they moved into the territory. **7**

In this chapter, you have learned to arrange events in their proper sequence. The following exercises will give you more practice in using this important Social Studies skill.

USING WHAT YOU HAVE LEARNED

A. Read the following selection about India. Try to remember the proper sequence of the events it tells about.

The British first became interested in India in the 1600s, establishing trading posts as early as 1612. By the late 1800s, most of India was under British rule. Shortly thereafter, trouble broke out when the Indian people began to demand the right to govern themselves.

In time, the British allowed the Indians to have a small role in the government. But the Indians were not pleased with this because they wanted to be completely independent.

Not all Indians agreed on how independence should be achieved. Many followed Mohandas Gandhi, who led a peaceful struggle for freedom. Others thought only violence and force would end British rule. There was also the question of how to deal with religious differences. While most Indians were Hindus, there was a large minority of Muslims. The Muslims did not want to be controlled by the Hindus. As a result of all of this, fighting erupted as different political and religious groups tried to achieve independence in their own way.

At last, the British gave up, and India was given its independence in 1947. To avoid further fighting, India was divided into two independent countries—India, controlled by Hindus, and Pakistan, controlled by Muslims.

independent: free, on one's own
minority: a part that is less than half of the whole
political: having to do with government

A-1. Place a check mark next to the correct answers to questions 1 to 5.

    1. Which word indicates the start of the sequence of events in the reading selection?

        ___ (*a*) first

        ___ (*b*) after

        ___ (*c*) then

    2. Which words indicate the start of the second event in the sequence?

        ___ (*a*) Shortly thereafter

        ___ (*b*) In time

        ___ (*c*) By the late 1800s

    3. What happened shortly after the British took over India?

        ___ (*a*) The Indian people welcomed the British.

        ___ (*b*) Trouble broke out.

        ___ (*c*) India got its independence.

    4. The Indian people were not happy with their small role in the government. What did they do?

        ___ (*a*) They all turned to violence and killed the British.

        ___ (*b*) They all left India to live in other countries.

        ___ (*c*) Different groups tried to achieve independence in their own way.

    5. The British gave India its independence in 1947. This is the last event of the sequence. Which words indicate the start of the last event?

        ___ (*a*) In time

        ___ (*b*) By the late 1800s

        ___ (*c*) At last

A-2. Write the number 1, 2, 3, 4, or 5 next to each of the following statements to show the proper sequence in the selection.

    ___ By the late 1800s, most of India was under British rule.

    ___ Different political and religious groups tried to achieve independence in their own way.

    ___ The British first became interested in India in the 1600s.

    ___ The British allowed the Indians to have a small role in the government.

    ___ India became an independent country in 1947.

B. Read the following selection about Russia. Try to remember the proper sequence of the events discussed.

> At the start of World War I, in 1914, the Russian people expected their army to win battles easily. And early in the war, the army did well against Germany and the other Central Powers. But as the war

continued, defeats on the battlefield began to outnumber victories. By 1917, almost 2 million Russian soldiers had been killed, and over 4 million had been wounded. Food had become scarce for the soldiers as well as for the people back home.

The Russian people turned against the war and against their ruler, Czar Nicholas II. They blamed him for food shortages and other problems Russia faced. On March 8, 1917, riots erupted in St. Petersburg. A week later, on March 15, the Czar was forced to give up his throne.

A new government, first led by Prince Lvov and then by Alexander Kerensky, was determined to keep Russia in the war. But most Russians were no less determined to take their country out of the war.

Vladimir Lenin, the leader of a group called the Bolsheviks, promised peace. In November 1917, with the support of angry mobs, Lenin and the Bolsheviks seized control of the government. Four months later, Russia signed a separate peace treaty with Germany. For Russia, the war may have been over, but new hardships were on the way.

B-1. Place a check mark next to the correct answers to questions 1 to 5.

1. Which phrase indicates the beginning of the sequence of events in the selection?

   ___ (a) And early in the war

   ___ (b) At the start of World War I

   ___ (c) A week later

2. At the beginning of World War I, the Russian army did well on the battlefield. What words signal that defeats on the battlefield began to outnumber victories?

   ___ (a) But as the war continued

   ___ (b) By 1917

   ___ (c) On March 8, 1917

3. What event happened a week after riots broke out in St. Petersburg on March 8, 1917?

   ___ (a) World War I ended.

   ___ (b) The Bolsheviks came to power in Russia.

   ___ (c) The Czar was forced to give up his power.

4. The use of "first" and "then" in the third paragraph tells the reader that

   ___ (a) Prince Lvov and Alexander Kerensky shared power in the new government.

   ___ (b) Prince Lvov led the new government before Alexander Kerensky did.

   ___ (c) Prince Lvov's government was overthrown by Alexander Kerensky.

5. Which word or phrase indicates the start of the last sequence of events in the selection?

___ (a) With the support of angry mobs

___ (b) In November 1917

___ (c) Four months later

B-2. Make a list of the words in the reading selection that indicate the start of different events in the selection. One is already listed for you.

At the start _____   _____

_____   _____

_____   _____

_____   _____

B-3. Write the number 1, 2, 3, 4, or 5 next to each of the following statements to create a sequence of events that matches the sequence in the selection.

_____ Alexander Kerensky became the leader of the new Russian government.

_____ Czar Nicholas II was forced to give up power.

_____ Rising numbers of dead and wounded turned the Russian people against the war.

_____ Russia signed a separate peace treaty with Germany.

_____ Lenin and the Bolsheviks seized control of the government.

Chapter 3
Time Lines and Dates

When you study history, it is important to take notice of dates. Dates tell you when events took place and help you keep track of the sequence of events. Knowing the order in which events happened makes it easier to understand how one event may have influenced another.

Look at the following important events in Japanese history.

In 1638, the Japanese government closed Japan to most visitors from other countries.

In 1853, Commodore Matthew Perry of the United States visited Japan with many warships. As a result of this visit, Japanese leaders turned to making Japan a great military power.

In 1895, Japan moved toward becoming a world power by defeating China in a war.

Knowing the dates of these three events and their correct order is important. Remembering the proper order will help you understand better how each event influenced the one that followed.

Time Lines

One of the ways to remember the correct order of events is to use a *time line*. The time line at the bottom of the page starts with the year 1600 and ends with the year 1900. The three events you just read about took place between these years.

Read the statements that follow. In the space at the left of each statement, place the letter from the time line that represents,

or stands for, the period of the time in which the event took place.

_____1. Japan defeated China in a war.

_____2. The Japanese government closed Japan to most visitors from other countries.

_____3. Commodore Matthew Perry of the United States visited Japan.

If you put a **C** next to number 1, you are correct. Japan defeated China in 1895. The letter **C** represents the years between 1870 and 1900. The year 1895 is in this time period.

If you put an **A** next to number 2, you are correct. The Japanese government closed Japan to most visitors in 1638. The letter **A** represents the years between 1600 and 1810. The year 1638 is in this time period.

If you put a **B** next to number 3, you are again correct. Commodore Perry visited Japan in 1853. The letter **B** represents the years between 1810 and 1870. The year 1853 is in this time period.

As you saw in Chapter 2, dates make it easier to arrange events in sequence. Time lines help you see which events came first. Knowing how to use a time line will help you remember the correct sequence of events.

B.C. and A.D.

In a reading selection about history, you might see such dates as 300 B.C. or A.D. 300. These dates contain the same number, but

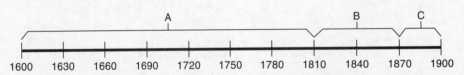

the letters B.C. and A.D. tell us that the two dates stand for different times.

B.C. means Before Christ.

A.D. means Anno Domini. Anno Domini are Latin words that mean "in the year of the Lord."

This way of writing dates was started hundreds of years ago. At that time, the Christian Church decided to change the calendar to show that it regarded the birth of its founder, Jesus Christ, as the most important event in the history of the world. So the year of Christ's birth became A.D. 1, or "in the year of the Lord 1." (Historians now believe that Jesus Christ was born four to six years earlier, but changing the calendar would cause many problems.)

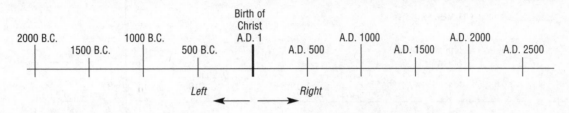

All dates that come after A.D. 1 are marked with the letters A.D., as you can see on the above time line. A.D. dates become higher as they go forward in history (to the right on the time line). Therefore, the year A.D. 1000 happened *after* the year A.D. 500.

All dates that come before A.D. 1 are marked with the letters B.C.—also shown on the above time line. B.C. dates become higher as they go backward in history (to the left on the time line). Therefore, the year 1000 B.C. happened *before* the year 500 B.C.

Now you know the difference between 300 B.C. and A.D. 300. By tradition, the letters B.C. come after the number in a date, while the letters A.D. come before the number in a date.

B.C.E. and C.E.

While B.C. and A.D. are still used in much of the world, a growing number of people prefer to use B.C.E. and C.E.

B.C.E. means Before the Common Era.

C.E. means Common Era.

The date 300 B.C.E. is 300 years before the start of the Common Era. It is the same year as 300 B.C. The date 300 C.E. is 300 years after the start of the Common Era. It is the same as A.D. 300.

Just like B.C., the letters B.C.E. and C.E. always appear after the number in a date.

Most of the time, the dates you see do not have letters before or after them. When there are no letters, the date is always A.D. (or C.E.). This means that 2000 is the same year as A.D. 2000 (or 2000 C.E.). A date showing B.C. or B.C.E. time always uses the letters B.C. or B.C.E.

The following rules will help you use B.C. and A.D. (or B.C.E. and C.E.) correctly.

1. To find out how long ago a B.C. (B.C.E.) date was, add the date to the present year.

2. To find out how long ago an A.D. (C.E.) date was, subtract the date from the present year.

Let us see if you can follow these rules.

1. Imagine that this is the year A.D. 2100. How many years ago was A.D. 1500?

_____ (a) 600 years

_____ (b) 1,500 years

_____ (c) 3,500 years

Which answer did you choose? You want to find out how many years ago an A.D. date was? To do this you must follow rule 2 and subtract 1500 from 2100. (Look at the time line below.) Therefore, the answer to question 1 is (a).

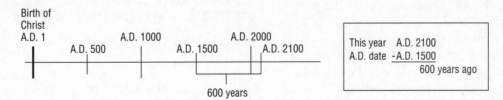

Let us try another example. The Suez Canal in Egypt opened in 1869. How many years ago was that? There are no letters before or after 1869, so it is an A.D. (or C.E.) date. Follow rule 2.

2. Imagine that this is the year 2100 C.E. How many years ago was 500 B.C.E.?

_____ (a) 600 years ago

_____ (b) 2,100 years ago

_____ (c) 2,600 years ago

Which answer did you choose? You want to find out how many years ago a B.C.E. date was. To do this, you must follow rule 1 and add the B.C.E. date to the C.E. date. (Look at the time line below.) Therefore, the answer to question 2 is (c).

Let us try one more example. How many years ago was 1000 B.C.E.? This is a B.C.E date, so follow rule 1.

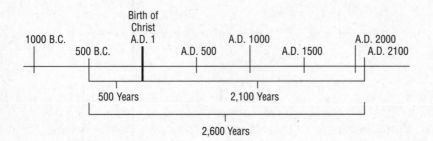

This year	2100 C.E.
B.C.E. date	+500 B.C.E.
	2,600 years ago

Centuries

You now know the meaning of dates such as 1400 B.C. or A.D. 1400 (1400 B.C.E or 1400 C.E.). But what if you see this date: 15th century? Do you know what period of time this date represents?

There are no letters after the date 15th century. Therefore, the date is A.D. (C.E.). But when did the 15th century take place? To find out, look at the chart on the right.

This chart is divided into *centuries*, which are periods of 100 years. The 100 years from 1 through 100 are called the first century. If an event happened any time between 1 and 100, we say it happened in the first century. For example, if an event happened in the year 25, we say it happened in the first century.

The 100 years between 101 and 200 are called the second century. If an event happened in the year 150, we say it happened in the second century.

This sequence of centuries continues from the years 201 to 300 (third century) all the way to the years 2001 to 2100 (the 21st century). Though not shown in the chart, the sequence could also run backward with centuries for B.C. (B.C.E.) years.

So what years does the 15th century represent? The chart shows that the 15th century includes the years 1401 to 1500.

Centuries Since A.D. 1 (1 C.E.)		
Century	*Years*	
First	A.D. 1 to A.D.	100
Second	A.D. 101 to A.D.	200
Third	A.D. 201 to A.D.	300
Fourth	A.D. 301 to A.D.	400
Fifth	A.D. 401 to A.D.	500
Sixth	A.D. 501 to A.D.	600
Seventh	A.D. 601 to A.D.	700
Eighth	A.D. 701 to A.D.	800
Ninth	A.D. 801 to A.D.	900
Tenth	A.D. 901 to A.D.	1000
11th	A.D. 1001 to A.D.	1100
12th	A.D. 1101 to A.D.	1200
13th	A.D. 1201 to A.D.	1300
14th	A.D. 1301 to A.D.	1400
15th	A.D. 1401 to A.D.	1500
16th	A.D. 1501 to A.D.	1600
17th	A.D. 1601 to A.D.	1700
18th	A.D. 1701 to A.D.	1800
19th	A.D. 1801 to A.D.	1900
20th	A.D. 1901 to A.D.	2000
21st	A.D. 2001 to A.D.	2100

Answer the following questions about centuries.

1. If an event happened in A.D. 639 (639 C.E.), in what century did it occur?

_____ (a) the sixth century

_____ (b) the seventh century

_____ (c) the eighth century

Which answer did you choose? Look at the chart. It shows that any event between the years 601 and 700 happened in the seventh century. Therefore, the answer to question 1 is (*b*).

2. If an event happened at the beginning of the 17th century, how many years ago did it happen?

_____ (*a*) about 17 years ago

_____ (*b*) about 300 years ago

_____ (*c*) about 400 years ago

Which answer did you choose? First look at the chart on page 18 to see that the 17th century covers 1601 to 1700. The same chart shows that we are now in the 21st century, which covers 2001 to 2100. The question does not give exact years, so your answer cannot be an exact number. This explains why all the choices start with "about." Because the event happened at the *beginning* of the 17th century and we are at the *beginning* of the 21st century, you can pick any year from the beginning of each century and subtract the earlier year from the later year. It is easier to subtract years that end in the same number, so let us pick 1602 and subtract it from 2002 to get 400 years. Therefore, if an event happened at the beginning of the 17th century, it happened about 400 years ago and the answer to question 2 is (*c*).

The following exercises will give you more practice in reading dates and using time lines.

USING WHAT YOU HAVE LEARNED

A. Read the following selection about Japanese history from 1894 to 1945. Pay careful attention to the dates when events occurred.

Japan Becomes a Powerful Country

By the 1890s, Japan was on the way to becoming one of the most powerful countries in the world. But first it had to solve a serious problem. Japan needed <u>natural resources</u>. Because there are few such useful materials in the island nation, Japan had to look to other countries for the resources it needed.

Japan first looked to nearby China. In 1894, the two countries went to war. The following year, China was defeated by Japan and had to pay Japan $165 million. The money could buy resources. Other nations of the world now realized that Japan was gaining power.

Nine years later, Japan went to war again. This time it turned against Russia in the Russo-Japanese War. At the end of this war, in 1905, Japan received land from Russia. Five years later, in 1910, Japan <u>seized</u> control of Korea.

When World War I ended in 1918, Japan was on the winning side. Germany was one of the losers in the war. As a result, in 1920 Japan was given a number of islands that had belonged to Germany.

The <u>population</u> of Japan grew <u>rapidly</u> during the 1920s. By 1930, there were 64 million people crowded onto the islands of Japan. Once again Japan looked for countries that could provide it with natural resources.

In 1931, Japanese soldiers invaded Manchuria, which is part of northern China. The Japanese took control of this area and renamed it Manchukuo. But Japan was not finished expanding. In 1937, it attacked several other areas of China.

The United States tried to stop this expansion by Japan. Starting in 1940, the United States refused to sell scrap iron and oil to Japan because it believed that Japan was using these materials to prepare for future wars. Japan became angry with the United States. On December 7, 1941, the Japanese attacked the U.S. naval base at Pearl Harbor in the Hawaiian Islands.

This was the beginning of World War II for the United States. For four years, it fought hard against Japan (and other enemy powers). Then, in 1945, the United States dropped two atomic bombs on Japan. Soon afterward, Japan gave up.

natural resources: materials found on or in the earth that are used to benefit humans. Examples are water, trees, animals, gold, iron ore, oil.

seized: took by force
population: the number of people living in a place
rapidly: quickly, with great speed
expanding: growing larger

Use this time line to answer the questions.

A	B	C	D	E	F
1890–1899	1900–1909	1910–1919	1920–1929	1930–1939	1940–1949

Look back at the reading selection to find out what year each of the following events took place. Then in the space at the left of each sentence, put the letter from the time line that represents the period of time when each event occurred. The first one is done for you.

C 1. World War I ended.

_____ 2. Japan seized control of Korea.

_____ 3. China paid Japan $165 million.

_____ 4. Japan fought Russia in the Russo-Japanese War.

_____ 5. Japan attacked Pearl Harbor in the Hawaiian Islands.

_____ 6. Japanese soldiers invaded Manchuria.

_____ 7. The United States refused to sell oil to Japan.

_____ 8. Japan was given islands that had belonged to Germany.

_____ 9. Japan attacked China a second time.

_____ 10. Atomic bombs were dropped on Japan.

B. Place a check mark next to the correct answers to questions 1 to 10.

1. The letters B.C. after a date mean
   ___ (a) Before Christ.
   ___ (b) Before the Common Era.
   ___ (c) Before the Christian Era.

2. The letters A.D. before a date stand for the phrase
   ___ (a) After Death.
   ___ (b) Any Date in the Common Era.
   ___ (c) Anno Domini (in the year of the Lord).

3. The year 700 B.C. can also be written
   ___ (a) 700 C.E.
   ___ (b) A.D. 700.
   ___ (c) 700 B.C.E.

4. The year 500 B.C.E. happened
   ___ (a) before 300 B.C.E.
   ___ (b) after 300 B.C.E.
   ___ (c) at the same time as 300 B.C.E.

5. How long ago was 200 B.C.? You find the answer by
   ___ (a) subtracting 200 B.C. from the present year.
   ___ (b) adding 200 B.C. to the present year.
   ___ (c) adding 200 B.C. and A.D. 200 together.

6. The year 1222 can also be written
   ___ (a) 1222 B.C. or 1222 B.C.E.
   ___ (b) A.D. 1222 or 1222 C.E.
   ___ (c) the 12th century.

7. How long ago was 1000 C.E.? You find the answer by
   ___ (a) subtracting 1000 C.E. from the present year.
   ___ (b) adding 1000 C.E. to the present year.
   ___ (c) adding 1000 B.C.E. and 1000 C.E. together.

8. The 14th century covers the years
   ___ (a) 401 to 500.
   ___ (b) 1301 to 1400.
   ___ (c) 1401 to 1500.

9. The first century A.D. covers the years
   ___ (a) A.D. 101 to A.D. 200.
   ___ (b) A.D. 1 to A.D. 100.
   ___ (c) 1 B.C. to A.D. 1.

10. How long ago was the beginning of the 12th century?

    ___ (*a*) about 12 years ago

    ___ (*b*) about 800 years ago

    ___ (*c*) about 900 years ago

C. Time Line

C-1. Completing a Time Line. Complete the dates on the time line below and on the list of events that follows. For each date, decide whether the letters B.C. and A.D. or the letters B.C.E. and C.E. should be used. Put the letters you choose in the correct place, either before or after the number in the date.

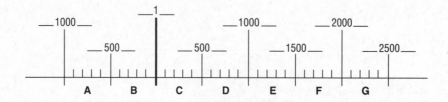

(The letters **A** to **G** on the above time line show where the events listed **A** through **G** below fit on the time line.)

List of Events

A. Growing of corn began in eastern North America, _____ 800 _____

B. First section of the Great Wall of China completed, _____ 214 _____

C. Gupta ruler united northern India, _____ 320 _____

D. Muhammad fled from Mecca to Medina, _____ 622 _____

E. Rule of Mansa Musa over the Mali Empire began, _____ 1312 _____

F. Catherine the Great became Czarina of Russia, _____ 1762 _____

G. The United Nations began the International Decade for a Culture of Peace and Non-Violence for the Children of the World, _____ 2001 _____

C-2. Using a Time Line. Place a check mark next to the correct answers to questions 1 to 4 and write the answer to question 5 on the line provided.

1. Each letter (**A** to **G**) along the bottom of the time line represents

    ___ (*a*) 100 years.

    ___ (*b*) 500 years.

    ___ (*c*) 1,000 years.

2. How many years passed between the flight of Muhammad from Mecca to Medina and the beginning of the rule of Mansa Musa of Mali?

    ___ (*a*) 622 years

    ___ (*b*) 690 years

    ___ (*c*) 1,312 years

3. How many years passed between the completion of the first section of the Great Wall of China and the uniting of northern India by the Gupta ruler?

＿＿ (*a*) 106 years

＿＿ (*b*) 214 years

＿＿ (*c*) 534 years

4. Mansa Musa could not have known of

＿＿ (*a*) Catherine the Great.

＿＿ (*b*) the Great Wall of China.

＿＿ (*c*) Muhammad.

5. About how many years ago was corn first grown in eastern North America?

＿＿＿＿＿＿＿＿

Chapter 4
Separating Fact From Fiction and Opinion

The things you read in books, newspapers, and magazines—and even on the Internet—can be described as fact, fiction, or opinion.

A *fact* is something that is true or something that happened. A fact can be proved to be true.

The word *fiction* applies to stories that are made up and, thus, are not true. Sometimes the word fiction merely means the opposite of fact. People ask, is that fact or fiction? But the word fiction also describes a kind of literature. A novel or short story is a work of fiction because it tells a "made up" story.

An *opinion* is something that a person believes to be true or is how a person feels about something. An opinion cannot be proved to be fact or fiction. If it could, it would no longer be an opinion.

Here is a fact:

Vladimir Lenin and the Bolsheviks seized control of the government of Russia during the October Revolution of 1917.

This statement is a fact because *every* part of it is true.

Here is an example of fiction:

[Read your own name] and the Bolsheviks seized control of the government of Russia during the October Revolution of 1917.

Surely, you did not lead the Bolsheviks to victory in 1917! But notice that this statement of fiction contains a fact: People called Bolsheviks did seize control of the government of Russia during the October Revolution of 1917. So even when a story mentions real people and real events, it is considered fiction if any part of the story is made up.

Here is an example of opinion:

If Vladimir Lenin had never lived, there would have been no October Revolution of 1917.

But Lenin did live. There is no way to prove that without him there would have been no October Revolution of 1917. This is why the statement is an opinion.

Very often people use the same facts to form different opinions. This is known as *interpreting facts*. Different people may interpret facts in different ways. Someone might say that a certain event was the best thing that could have happened. Another person might say that the same event was the worst thing that could have happened. When it cannot be proved to be the "best" or the "worst," you are talking about an opinion.

Imagine that students in a Social Studies class had a lesson on imperialism in Africa. Their teacher told them that during the 19th century, several powerful countries of Europe took over and claimed ownership of areas of Africa. This was known as European *imperialism* in Africa. The students were then asked to write a report evaluating the effects of that imperialism on Africa.

The reports all contained many of the same facts and events. But the students were divided in their opinions about the effects of imperialism in Africa. Read the following reports carefully to see how two students used the same facts to form different opinions.

Student A

In the 19th century, some European countries took control of large areas of Africa. They were interested in Africa mainly for its wealth. But the Europeans also introduced new ways of doing things. Many Africans welcomed European <u>culture</u>. For the first time, modern medicine was used in Africa. Modern machines were put to work on farms and in factories. Some Africans were taught to read and write. When the African nations received their independence, it was the European-educated Africans who became the leaders of their new nations. In the end, the European control of Africa helped Africans more than it hurt them.

Student B

The European countries that took over Africa in the 19th century were concerned only with making themselves rich. Any good they did was only an excuse to take Africa's wealth. Many Africans were killed, and many others were forced to work for the Europeans. The Europeans introduced modern medicines, but they also brought diseases that the Africans had not known before. Even though the Europeans opened schools, they did much to destroy African culture. The Africans were forced to see the world through European eyes. The Europeans changed Africa forever.

<u>culture</u>: the common way of life of a large group of people or a nation

As you read, you should have seen that each student agreed on certain facts. Here are some of them:

- European countries took control of areas of Africa in the 19th century.
- The Europeans introduced modern medicines to Africa.
- The Europeans educated some Africans.

Go back and find these three facts in each report.

You also should have noticed that each student interpreted facts and events differently. Let us see how well you picked up these different interpretations.

Answer the following questions:

___ 1. Which student said that European control of Africa helped Africans more than it hurt them?

Which report did you choose? Student A made this statement in the last sentence of the report. You may wonder why it is considered an opinion. Isn't there enough information to prove that this statement is fact

or fiction? The tricky word in the statement is "more." Most people agree that the Europeans did good things and bad things in Africa. The disagreement comes with whether the Europeans did more good things or more bad things. This is why the statement is an opinion.

___ 2. Which student said that European control of Africa changed Africa forever?

Which report did you choose? Student B made this statement in the last sentence of the report. The statement would be a fact if it said only that European control of Africa changed Africa. But the word "forever" makes the statement an opinion. Forever, as it is used in the statement, has to do with the future, and no one knows the future. Therefore, the whole statement must be seen as an opinion.

The following selection contains some of the facts you read in the reports of students A and B. As you read it, decide whether the whole selection should be called fact, fiction, or opinion.

I remember the first day I went to school in my village in Kenya. The English had opened the school and I was one of the lucky children chosen to attend. One day, a doctor came to the school with a big needle. He told us that the needle contained modern medicine that would keep us from getting ill. Some of my classmates cried when the needle was put into their arms. As we got older, some of us cried for more serious reasons. The English killed people in my village who wanted the English to go back to England. I appreciated the chance to go to school, but I too wanted the English to go home.

Is this selection fact, fiction, or opinion? The answer is, it depends. If the selection had been written by someone who lived in Kenya at the time the English took control, it could be fact. A document created by someone who experienced the events in the document is called a *primary source*. On the other hand, the person telling the story may have been invented by the writer. This selection could be a paragraph in a novel or short story. Even though the story contains facts, if the storyteller is a made-up person, then you have to call the whole selection a work of fiction.

The following exercises will give you more practice in understanding the differences among fact, fiction, and opinion.

USING WHAT YOU HAVE LEARNED

A. The following selection is about going to school in China. After you have read the selection, try to separate the facts from the opinions.

Going to School in China

Before the Communists took control of China in 1949, few Chinese people went to school. Today, most Chinese young people have the chance to receive a formal education.

Schooling for Chinese boys and girls begins at the age of three. They go to kindergarten until they are seven years old. Starting school at such a young age is a good idea. It helps the children learn how to act with other children in an orderly way.

Primary education begins at the age of seven and lasts for five years. In the primary schools, students work very hard. They study mathematics, science, music, art, and the Chinese language. Primary schools in China are much better than primary schools in the United States.

Secondary education consists of three years of junior middle school followed by two to three years of senior middle school. The subjects in the middle schools include politics, the Chinese language, mathematics, history, geography, farming, biology, chemistry, physical education, music, and art. Unfortunately, formal education for most Chinese ends with graduation from the junior middle school.

Some students who graduate from the junior middle school attend secondary technical schools. There they receive training for three or four years in such fields as farming, forestry, medicine, or fine arts.

Universities and colleges admit students who have graduated

from senior middle school and who have passed a national entrance examination. The students do not have to pay to attend a university or college. This is a wise policy because deserving students are not deprived of higher education just because they are poor. Universities offer study in many subjects. Colleges, by contrast, provide courses in one field or a few closely related fields.

In recent years, university and college students have also benefited from exchange programs with schools in the United States and other countries. Chinese students learn about the countries in which they study. At the same time, students who remain in China have the opportunity to meet exchange students from other countries.

Chinese students appreciate the opportunity to go to school. They realize that a good education will help them and their country as well. Perhaps the Chinese value their education more than any other people on Earth.

Each of the following statements is based on the selection you just read. If the statement is a *fact*, put an **F** in front of it. If the statement is an *opinion*, put an **O** in front of it. It is important to remember the meanings of fact and opinion. Not everything you read will be a fact.

_____ 1. Before 1949, few Chinese went to school.

_____ 2. Today, most Chinese young people have a chance to receive a formal education.

_____ 3. It is a good idea for children to start school at the age of three.

_____ 4. Chinese students start primary school when they are seven years old.

_____ 5. Primary schools in China are much better than primary schools in the United States.

_____ 6. Secondary education consists of junior middle schools and senior middle schools.

_____ 7. Unfortunately, formal education ends for most Chinese with graduation from junior middle school.

_____ 8. Students must pass a national entrance examination before they are admitted to a university or college.

_____ 9. It is a wise policy that deserving students do not have to pay to go to college.

_____ 10. The Chinese value their education more than any other people on Earth.

B. The following two selections deal with cutting down the rain forest in Brazil. The persons who wrote the selections used the same facts, but they reached different conclusions. Read each selection carefully.

Selection 1

Brazil is a large country with a land area of 3,286,470 square miles. Yet most of Brazil's population of 187 million live near the <u>coast</u>. The <u>vast</u> inland areas of the country are covered by rain forest and inhabited mainly by indigenous peoples, animals, and insects. The government has already cleared some of the rain forest and built cities in its place. More of the rain forest should be cleared and more cities built. Large numbers of Brazilians who now crowd the coastal cities, such as São Paulo and Rio de Janeiro, could move into these new cities. The rain forest should not be left just to indigenous groups, animals, and insects.

Selection 2

Destroying the rain forest of Brazil will do more harm than good. It is true that most of Brazil's 187 million people live near the coast and that in some cities, such as São Paulo and Rio de Janeiro, conditions are very crowded. But the answer to this problem is not to cut down the rain forest. The rain forest affects weather all over the world, especially in North America. Forests cool the Earth. If the rain forest is destroyed, the Earth will become warmer. The destruction of the rain forest will also mean the end of a way of life for the indigenous peoples who live in it. Such great changes may even kill the indigenous peoples. Let us not help some people while doing harm to others.

coast: land next to the sea   vast: large, covering a great area
inhabited: lived in   indigenous: original, first
destruction: the act of destroying or damaging something

B-1. As you read each selection, you should have seen that both writers agreed on certain facts. List two facts on which both writers agreed.

1. _____

_____

2. _____

_____

B-2. Can you remember the different opinions reached by the two writers? Place the number of the correct selection on the answer line at the left of each question.

____ 1. Which selection stated that destroying the rain forest will do more harm than good?

____ 2. Which selection stated that the rain forest should not be left to indigenous groups, animals, and insects?

____ 3. Which selection stated that more of the rain forest should be cleared and more cities built?

____ 4. Which selection stated that clearing away the rain forest might kill the indigenous peoples?

____ 5. Which selection stated that the answer to overcrowded cities is not to cut down the rain forest?

B-3. Place a check mark next to the correct answers.

1. Which statement best describes the opinion of the person who wrote Selection 1?

_____ (*a*) Brazil has a land area of 3,286,470 square miles.

_____ (b) The destruction of the rain forest will mean an end to the way of life of the indigenous peoples who live there.

_____ (c) The clearing of the rain forest will solve the problems of overcrowding in Brazil's cities.

2. Which statement best describes the opinion of the person who wrote Selection 2?

_____ (a) Most of Brazil's 187 million people live near the coast.

_____ (b) The destruction of the rain forest will have no effect on weather conditions around the world.

_____ (c) The rain forest should not be cleared to benefit some people while harming others.

C. When World War II began in 1939, the United States was not involved. Not until December 8, 1941, did the United States enter the war. This was one day after Japan attacked the U.S. naval base at Pearl Harbor in Hawaii. In August 1945, after nearly four years of fighting, the United States dropped two atomic bombs on Japan. Several days later, Japan surrendered, and World War II was over. The following two selections deal with the dropping of the two atomic bombs on Japan.

Ms. Ruiz

In August 1945, the United States dropped two atomic bombs on Japan. President Harry Truman gave the order to drop the bombs on the cities of Hiroshima and Nagasaki.

This was the worst thing that the United States ever did. In war, soldiers are supposed to fight only soldiers. Only <u>military</u> targets are supposed to be attacked, but these Japanese cities were not military targets. Thousands of <u>civilians</u> were killed without reason.

This was a foolish attack by a nation that should have known better. Because our soldiers were defeating the Japanese soldiers, there was no reason for the United States to kill innocent people. It would have been only a matter of time before Japan surrendered. Dropping the atomic bombs was not needed to win the war.

Mr. Vesey

President Harry Truman ordered the atomic bombs dropped on the Japanese cities of Hiroshima and Nagasaki in August 1945. He believed that this would stop the fighting.

World War II had dragged on for four years. Many lives had been lost on both sides, and there was no sign that Japan was ready to surrender. President Truman believed that if the war continued, many more lives would be lost.

To drop the atomic bombs was not an easy decision for President Truman to make. He knew that thousands of civilians would be killed, but he thought that he would be saving lives by ending the war quickly.

No one is happy that the United States took this action, but it was something that had to be done.

<u>military:</u> having to do with soldiers, weapons, or war
<u>civilians:</u> people not in the military

C-1. As you read each selection, you should have seen that both writers agreed on certain facts. The following are two facts on which they agreed:

- The atomic bombs were dropped on Hiroshima and Nagasaki.
- Thousands of civilians were killed.

List two other facts on which Ms. Ruiz and Mr. Vesey agreed:

1. _____

_____

2. _____

_____

C-2. Can you remember the different opinions reached by Ms. Ruiz and Mr. Vesey? Place an **R** in front of the opinions expressed by Ms. Ruiz. Place a **V** in front of the opinions expressed by Mr. Vesey.

____ 1. Which person called the dropping of the bombs a foolish attack?

____ 2. Which person said that in war only military targets are to be attacked?

____ 3. Which person probably supported Truman's belief that in the long run, more lives would be saved by dropping the bomb?

____ 4. Which person said that our soldiers were already defeating the Japanese soldiers?

____ 5. Which person said there was no sign that the Japanese would surrender?

C-3. Place a check mark next to the correct answers.

1. Which statement best describes the opinion of Ms. Ruiz?

____ (a) Hiroshima and Nagasaki were not military targets.

____ (b) Dropping atomic bombs on Japan was wrong and unnecessary.

____ (c) Soldiers should be allowed to kill civilians during a war.

2. Which statement best describes the opinion of Mr. Vesey?

____ (a) By 1945, many lives had been lost in World War II.

____ (b) President Truman made a difficult decision.

____ (c) The United States had to drop the atomic bombs on Japan to end the war.

D. Fact, Fiction, or Opinion? Read the following selection. Then answer the questions after it.

The Time: The Early 1500s

High in the Andes Mountains of South America, a young girl brought water to her father and older brother who were digging up the crop of new potatoes. She was surprised to find them doing more talking than work.

"They will never be able to conquer us," the boy said to his father.

"If our people do not stop fighting one another," said the father, "we will be too weak to keep them out."

"What are you talking about?" asked the girl, handing her father and brother small containers of water.

"Nothing," said the father, taking a drink of his water. "You are too young to worry about such things."

But the boy went on. "Father, you forget that we are a mighty empire. We stretch for many miles along these mountains. We have millions of people to fight off the invaders."

"What invaders? asked the girl.

"People from way beyond the mountains," said the boy, drinking his water. "They call us Incas, and they call themselves Spanish."

"I have an idea," said the girl. "Why don't we cut down the bridges we built between the mountains? That will keep them away."

The father smiled at his daughter, but he knew that if the invaders were smart enough to travel so far, they would be smart enough to cross a few mountains.

Place a check mark next to the correct answer to question 1 to 4.

1. All of the following statements contain one or more facts. Which statement contains a fact that is NOT given in the selection?

___ (a) The Spanish gave the Incas their name.

___ (b) The Incas grew potatoes high in the Andes Mountains of South America.

___ (c) The Spanish gained control of the land that had once been the Inca Empire.

2. Which one of the following statements from the selection is an opinion?

___ (a) "They will never be able to conquer us."

___ (b) "They call us Incas, and they call themselves Spanish."

___ (c) "Father, you forget that we are a mighty empire."

3. The entire selection would be considered fiction if

___ (a) the time—the early 1500s—had not been stated.

___ (b) the three people in the story were made up.

___ (c) no quotation marks (" ") had been used.

4. The entire selection would be a primary source if

___ (a) it were written by a real person who was present during the scene.

___ (b) it stated what happened to the Incas after the arrival of the Spanish.

___ (c) the names of the people in the story had been given.

5. What would you call the entire selection—fact, fiction, or opinion? Explain.

_____

_____

Writing Skills

Chapter 5

Writing Sentences and Paragraphs

In Unit One, you learned how to improve your reading skills. Just as it is important to read well, it is also important to write well. Your success in taking tests, taking notes, or writing reports depends on the quality of your writing. Being able to express yourself clearly and correctly is a necessary Social Studies skill.

In this chapter, you will learn how to answer a question in sentence and paragraph form. (A paragraph is a group of sentences that express one main idea.)

Study the following questions and sample answers. You will see that a single-sentence answer doesn't tell the reader very much. But a three- or four-sentence paragraph both informs and interests the reader.

One way to write a one-sentence answer is to repeat part of the question in your answer. Then add one or two facts to finish the sentence. Here is an example of a possible one-sentence answer.

Why do few people live in the Sahara, a desert in Africa?

One-Sentence Answer

Few people live in the Sahara, a desert, because of the lack of water and the heat.

You could also answer the same question in more than one sentence. The more information you give, the more your reader will know about living in the Sahara. Here is the question again. This time it has been answered in a paragraph.

Why do few people live in the Sahara, a desert in Africa?

Paragraph Answer

Few people live in the Sahara, a desert, because of the lack of water and the heat. Without rain, it is difficult to grow food. The burning heat makes living in the desert very uncomfortable.

The paragraph you just read contains three sentences. Each gives a reason why few people live in the Sahara. Now the reader knows more than he or she would if the answer were only one sentence.

Look at the next example of a question that has been answered in one sentence and in a paragraph.

Why do the people of the island nation of Japan look to the sea for food?

One-Sentence Answer

The people of Japan look to the sea for food because it contains a great supply of fish.

Paragraph Answer

Japan is an island nation. It cannot grow enough food to feed its people. So Japan turns to the sea to find food. The waters around Japan provide the country with a great supply of fish.

Once again, a question has been answered in two different ways. The one-sentence answer is correct. But it is the paragraph answer that shows the reader you have a greater knowledge of Japan. The more you know, the longer your paragraph can be.

Being able to write good sentences and paragraphs is an important Social Studies skill. The following exercises will give you more practice in developing this skill.

USING WHAT YOU HAVE LEARNED

A. Read the following selection. Then answer each question in one sentence. The first question has been answered as an example.

Cows Are Sacred in India

Most of the people in India practice the Hindu religion. This religion teaches that killing cows is wrong. To the Hindus of India, therefore, the cow is a sacred animal.

More than 200 million cows live in India, and many of them move freely through the countryside and the city streets. Sometimes they eat food that the people need, and some of them carry diseases. But the Hindus are still opposed to killing them.

Despite these problems, cows are useful to the Indians. Cows serve as work animals on farms. Food is made from their milk, and their dung (manure) is used as fuel. Cows in India help the people and, at the same time, cause harm.

sacred: holy

---

1. What religion do most Indians practice?

Most Indians practice the Hindu religion.

2. Why don't the Hindus kill cows?

_____

_____

3. How many cows are there in India?

_____

_____

4. What harm do the cows in India cause?

_____

_____

5. How are cows useful to the Indians?

_____

_____

_____

B. Read the following selection. Answer the question after the selection in both a single sentence and a paragraph.

Rivers Are Important to the Growth of Cities

What do St. Louis in the United States, Cairo in Egypt, Manaus in Brazil, and Nanjing in China all have in common? All of them are cities built near rivers.

Since very early times, people have realized the importance of rivers. Early humans settled near rivers to be sure of having fish for food and water to drink. Rivers were used for washing clothes and for bathing. When people learned to farm, rivers were used to irrigate the land. The same rivers were then used to send crops quickly and easily to other places.

As more and more people settled in one place along a river, a town would develop. Some towns became stopping places for those who carried products up and down the river. These places grew larger and turned into cities.

Today, rivers continue to be important to many cities. They provide food and drinking water and carry away dirt and garbage. Rivers are still used to send goods from one place to another. The next time you look at a map of the world, notice how many important cities have been built near rivers.

irrigate: to bring water to

1. Why have rivers been important to the growth of cities?

ONE-SENTENCE ANSWER

_____

_____

_____

_____

PARAGRAPH ANSWER (three sentences)

_____

_____

_____

_____

_____

_____

_____

_____

_____

C. Read the following selection. Then answer the question in a paragraph.

Operations Without Pain

Imagine sticking a needle into your body to stop pain. You would think that the needle would cause pain. But thousands of years ago, the Chinese developed a method of killing pain by using needles. This method is called acupuncture. Needles are stuck into the body at certain places to numb the part of the body that hurts. Doctors can then operate freely without causing any pain to their patients.

Doctors from many parts of the world have traveled to China to see the use of acupuncture in operations. They watched many operations, including open-heart surgery, during which the patients remained awake but felt no pain. Some patients who had minor operations were able to walk out of the operating room right after their operations.

No one knows why acupuncture is successful. But it does seem to work. People all over the world are becoming more interested in this very old Chinese method of killing pain.

method: a way of doing something
acupuncture: using needles to stop pain or cure disease
numb: to cause to have no feeling or pain
minor: less important, less serious

1. How does acupuncture help patients?

PARAGRAPH ANSWER (three sentences)

_____

_____

_____

_____

_____

_____

_____

_____

_____

D. Read the following selection. Then answer the question in a paragraph.

Religion in Southwest Asia

Southwest Asia is the birthplace of three major religions—Judaism, Christianity, and Islam. For centuries, their presence in the region has been a source of inspiration, but it has also resulted in distrust and, sometimes, war.

Judaism is the oldest of the three religions, dating back more than 5,000 years. It is the religion of most of the people of Israel. Christianity dates back 2,000 years. Today in the region, only Lebanon has a large Christian population. Islam dates back nearly 1,400 years. It is the major religion of nearly all the countries of Southwest Asia.

Religion has greatly influenced all aspects of life in Southwest Asia. Laws are based on the Bible, the holy book of Judaism and Christianity, and on the Koran, the holy book of Islam. Religious ceremonies mark the important events in a person's life. For example, Jews celebrate their 13th birthday with a religious ceremony known as a Bar Mitzvah for a man and a Bat Mitzvah for a woman. The style of dress and the foods people eat often reflect religious teachings. Art, too, reflects religious teachings. For example, strict Islamic teachings do not allow artworks to show a human form. Many Christian churches, on the other hand, encourage paintings and statues of Jesus Christ and other religious figures.

The shame is that members of these three religions have not always been able to live in peace with one another. Over the centuries, so-called "religious" wars have brought death and destruction. The hope is that the children of today and tomorrow will be inspired by their religion to love their neighbor.

region: area of land marked by some common geographic features
aspects: parts, areas, sides

1. How has religion played an important part in the development of Southwest Asia?

PARAGRAPH ANSWER (five sentences)

_____

_____

_____

_____

_____

_____

_____

_____

_____

Chapter 6
Expressing an Opinion

An important part of Social Studies is the discussion of *current* (present-day) problems in the world. These problems may include dirty air or water, war, poverty, crime, and poorly run government. You may be asked in your Social Studies class to write your opinion about one of these issues in a paragraph.

In Chapter 5, the paragraphs you wrote were concerned mainly with giving correct information. This information was often supplied by a reading selection that contained someone else's ideas.

In writing an opinion, you are giving your own ideas about a current problem. You may gather ideas and facts from various sources. But your paragraph should contain your own thoughts and opinions. A paragraph written to present a personal point of view is called an essay.

One major problem facing the United States and the world today is air pollution.

The boxed paragraph at the bottom of the page is an essay about air pollution. It expresses, or states, the opinion of one person about how to deal with this problem.

This short essay is one person's opinion about the problem of air pollution. Do you agree or disagree with this opinion? Write your own essay to tell how you would deal with the problem of air pollution.

Your essay should contain two basic parts:

1. Information learned from other sources—books, television, radio, the Internet, newspapers, parents, friends, teachers.
2. Your own ideas and opinions about the information learned.

It is a good idea to think out your essay before you write it. After all, an essay starts in the mind, so let it stay in the mind for a while. Then begin to write.

How I Would Deal With Air Pollution

I hope that someday we will be able to put an end to the terrible problem of air pollution. But we have to be careful not to destroy America while trying to clean it up. I know that cars, buses, and factories are major causes of pollution. But we can't stop making cars and buses or close down all the factories in America. Right now giving Americans jobs is more important than clean air. Let's build America today. We can worry about air pollution tomorrow.

How I Would Deal With Air Pollution

_____

_____

_____

_____

_____

_____

_____

_____

_____

_____

_____

What you have written is your opinion about how to deal with the problem of air pollution. Some people may agree with you. Some may disagree. Some may even argue that you are wrong. Can we really say that a person's opinion is wrong? Of course! An essay must be based on logical thinking and correct information.

Imagine that your essay on air pollution contained this wild sentence: "I would deal with air pollution by sending everyone to live on the moon." Such an idea may be your opinion, but it is not a logical answer to the problem. Sending everyone to the moon would be impossible.

Suppose you had written this sentence: "All air pollution is caused by factories." This may be your opinion, but you could not support this statement with facts. Cars, buses, airplanes, and many other things also cause air pollution.

You might have included this opinion: "Automobile companies can cut down on air pollution by providing cleaner burning engines. They would put less dirty exhaust into the air." This opinion can be supported by facts. Automobile companies have long been working to develop cleaner burning engines. Of course, cars are only one part of the problem of air pollution. But this opinion is based on a realistic answer to part of the problem of air pollution.

We all have a right to our opinions. But in an essay, we must present a logical point of view that is based on facts. The exercises starting on page 42 will give you practice in expressing your own ideas in essays.

Making the Most of Every Word in an Essay

A good essay uses words wisely. It contains words that accurately express the writer's ideas. It does not say in many words what can be said in a few words.

Here's how to make the most of every word you write in an essay.

1. Use the Most Accurate Word

Some of the great writers in history have admitted that sometimes it took them a whole day to write one paragraph. Why? They wanted each word to be the perfect word.

You may never use a whole day to write an essay, but you should try to make every word the perfect one. You should use words that accurately say what you mean to say.

a. The Wrong Word

In writing an essay, use only words whose meanings you know. Do not try to impress a reader by using big words that you do not fully understand. You do not want to mislead or confuse the reader.

Do you know the difference between *emigrate* and *immigrate*? If you think they mean the same, you could end up writing a sentence that makes no sense.

Emigrate means to *move away from* a country.
Immigrate means to *come into* a country.

The scientist Albert Einstein *emigrated from* Germany to the United States in 1933.
The scientist Albert Einstein *immigrated to* the United States from Germany in 1933.

Collaborate means to *work with* some one.
Corroborate means to *show* something *to be true.*

On your own paper, write a sentence using *collaborate* and a sentence using *corroborate.*

b. Words With More Than One Meaning

Be careful with words that sometimes mean the same thing and sometimes do not.

Warm can mean *muggy.*
Warm can mean *friendly.*
Muggy does not mean *friendly.*

The Congo has a *warm* climate most of the year.
You can substitute *muggy* but not *friendly* for *warm.*

The president is a *warm* and honest leader.
You can substitute *friendly* but not *muggy* for *warm.*

Outstanding means *special.*
Outstanding means *unpaid.*
Special does not mean *unpaid.*

On your own paper, write two sentences that contain the word *outstanding.* In the first sentence, you should be able to substitute the word *special* for *outstanding.* In the second sentence, you should be able to substitute the word *unpaid* for *outstanding.*

c. Words of Exaggeration

Be careful about calling someone or something the best or the worst, the biggest or the smallest, or the richest or the poorest. If you want to write that a particular country has the largest oil tankers in the world, be sure that is true. Otherwise, write that the country has some of the largest oil tankers in the world.

Do not say that something is true of all people in a group unless it is true of every person in that group. Here is one way to decide what term you should use to show how many people you are talking about:

All people—100 percent of people
Nearly all people—90 to 99 percent of people
Most people—more than 50 percent of people
Many people—26 to 50 percent of people
Some people—1 to 25 percent of people
Few people—1 to 5 percent of people
No one—0 percent of people.

On your own piece of paper, write a sentence accurately using each of the terms.

Here are four more phrases you have to be careful about:

I know *I believe* *I feel* *I think*

Which three of these phrases are closest in meaning? The first one—*I know*—says that you are certain. The second, third, and fourth phrases mean you are not certain. You are expressing an opinion. *I believe, I feel*, and *I think* are phrases that are often substituted for one another.

On your own piece of paper, write a sentence using each of the four phrases.

2. Use Only the Words You Need

a. Unnecessary Phrases

It is often difficult to find the right words to begin an essay. As a result, some students might begin with:

I am writing this essay to say that global warming is a serious problem.

The reader knows you are writing an essay. You do not have to say it. Begin your essay with:

Global warming is a serious problem.

b. Unnecessary Words

In the following sentence, pick out the words that add little to the meaning and, therefore, are unnecessary.

I truly believe that we have a very serious economic problem in this country.

What is the difference between *I truly believe* and *I believe*? There is no difference, and so there is no need to use the word *truly*.

What is the difference between *very serious* and *serious*? There are issues that are more *serious* than others. But most of the time it is enough to say that an issue is *serious*. You do not need *very*.

c. Unnecessary Multiple Words

It is fine to use more than one word to describe something. But do not choose words that mean the same thing.

Read the following sentences:

The war is important and necessary if we are going to defend freedom.

It was the most thrilling and exciting time of my life.

In the first sentence, *important* and *necessary* mean the same thing. In the second sentence, *thrilling* and *exciting* mean the same thing.

Let us see how much you have learned. The following essay is poorly written. On your own paper, rewrite the essay, making the most of every word.

I would like to start my essay by saying that the United States should do more to help poor and underprivileged children in so many parts of the world. I know that most Americans are willing to pay higher taxes to help poor people. But many Americans fear that their financial aid will not go to help the poor. Instead, it will end up in the pockets of government officials who are corrupt and dishonest. In some countries, the leaders live in very large palaces while nearly all the people are left to roam the garbage dumps for the niceties of life.

Governments of free and prosperous countries should corroborate in an effort to put pressure on corrupt governments to change. News agencies should continue to report on countries suffering from extreme and severe poverty. How do we get these things to happen? If enough of us ordinary citizens demand action, our government will be forced to respond. If we shout from the rooftops, news agencies will cover the story. Let us show the world that Americans are an immensely generous and giving people.

A. Read the following selection.

> ### Tigers in Danger
>
> Most people get to see tigers only in a zoo. Someday it may be the only place to see them. It is becoming harder and harder to find tigers in their natural surroundings, where they live naturally. Why are they disappearing? The answer is simple. They are being killed off rapidly, mostly for their fur.
>
> All tigers are endangered <u>species</u>. This means that they are in danger of becoming <u>extinct</u>—that is, of dying out entirely. Two of the most endangered species are the Siberian and Sumatran tigers. Only 430–520 of the Siberian tigers and 400–500 of the Sumatran tigers exist in the wild.
>
> Governments, wildlife groups, and individual citizens are trying to save endangered species in various ways. One method is to raise them in zoos. Another is to keep hunters out of the animals' natural surroundings. Another is to make it <u>illegal</u> to kill an endangered species. But more must be done—because once a species is gone, it is gone forever.
>
> <u>species</u>: a class of living things having common qualities
> <u>extinct</u>: a species that no longer exists
> <u>illegal</u>: against the law

Do you think that more should be done to save the tigers from extinction? Write an essay expressing your opinion on this issue.

PARAGRAPH ANSWER (three sentences)

_____

_____

_____

_____

_____

_____

B. Read the following selection.

Should English Be the Official Language of the United States?

It might come as a surprise to many Americans that English is *not* the official language of the United States. It is not the language required by law to be used in this country. Nevertheless, English is the most widely used language in the United States. This is true in every area of society, from television and publishing to the operation of schools and the running of the government. When the United States came into existence in 1776, most Americans spoke English. Thereafter, nearly all immigrants who came to this country, or their children, learned to speak English. As more states were added to the Union, English became the most widely used language in those states too.

Today, some Americans fear that the United States is slowly dividing into a country with different language regions. They want English to be made the official language. They argue that there are areas of large cities where Spanish is heard more often than English. In cities such as Miami, some Americans have difficulty getting jobs because they do not speak Spanish. The arrival of large numbers of Asian immigrants is also a concern for supporters of English. They want to know if these groups from Asia will demand that their languages be accepted in place of English.

English supporters believe that this country has been successful because the millions of people who came from Europe, Africa, Asia, and Latin America in years past learned to speak English. They believe that by encouraging the use of any language other than English, we will see problems arising similar to those faced by Canada. There English-speaking and French-speaking Canadians are at odds with each other. A worse situation exists in India, where 14 different main languages are used.

There are, however, many Americans who want to encourage the ethnic differences in the United States. Concerning Spanish, they remind us that great parts of the American Southwest and Florida heard the Spanish language long before English was ever heard. Those who speak languages other than English fear that their cultures will be lost. They believe that American society would be enriched by allowing people to maintain their original languages. The many-languages supporters remind us that other ethnic groups, such as the Italians, have come to this country and lived in communities in which their native language was widely spoken. The people who oppose making English the official language are concerned that those who do not speak English might be denied their rights, such as the right to vote. Finally, this group argues that no harm will be done if the various ethnic groups use their native languages, for nearly all of them will also eventually learn to speak English.

official language: one that a government must use
immigrants: people who come to live in a country that is not their original home

---

Do you think English should be made the official language of the United States? Write an essay expressing your opinion about this question.

YOUR OPINION (four or five sentences)

_____

_____

_____

_____

_____

_____

_____

C. Pick any current problem facing the United States or the world. You may have read about this problem in a book or a magazine or have seen a television program about it. Write an essay expressing your opinion about how to deal with this problem.

YOUR OPINION (four or five sentences)

_____

_____

_____

_____

_____

_____

_____

Chapter 7
Writing a Summary

Have you ever read something and just a short time later forgotten what it was all about? It is not possible to remember everything you read. But what if you were to take notes while you were reading? What if you were to write down the highlights—the important points? If you did this, you could remember what you had read by going over your notes.

When you take notes on what you read, you are *summarizing*. You are reducing many sentences to one or two sentences or a few phrases. The sentences or phrases you write down will help you recall the entire selection.

In Chapter 1, you learned how to find the main idea of a reading selection. The main idea is what the selection is all about. A good summary states the main idea of a selection, but usually adds more information. If you can find the main idea, you have the start of a good summary.

Read Selection A about the importance of oil in the world. Then see how the selection is summarized in one sentence.

Summary A states the main idea of Selection A. One sentence summarizes a reading selection containing six sentences. But Selection A contains many facts that you may need to remember. To include them, another sentence or a few phrases are needed. A more complete summary might look like this:

Summary A

The world depends on the oil of Southwest Asia for many uses:
—fuel for cars, trucks, planes, buses, and ships
—plastic goods, electrical power, and heat

Now you have a better idea of what information is contained in Selection A. A few phrases added to the summary sentence make it easier to remember what is in the entire selection.

Notice that this summary contains the same opinion that is found in the selection.

Selection A

Southwest Asia is the world's leading producer of oil. The United States, Western Europe, East Asia, and other parts of the world need the oil found in Southwest Asia. Oil is used for fuel in cars, trucks, buses, airplanes, and ships. It is also used to make plastic and to produce electrical power to run factories. Homes and office buildings are heated by oil. Much of the world depends on the oil produced in Southwest Asia.

Summary A

The world depends on the oil of Southwest Asia for many uses.

You should not add your own opinion to a summary. It should contain only the opinion of the person who wrote the selection.

Notice also that this summary was not copied word for word from the reading selection. You should write a summary in your own words. Then you can be sure you understand the main idea and the facts of the selection.

Here is another reading selection about oil in Southwest Asia. Read the selection and the one-sentence summary that appears after it. This time add to the summary phrases that will help you remember the entire selection.

Selection B

The first large deposits of oil in Southwest Asia were discovered in Iran in 1908. At that time, the countries of Southwest Asia did not have the money or the skill needed to take the oil out of the ground. So they allowed American and European companies to drill for the oil. These companies decided how much oil would be produced and how much to charge for the oil. The countries of Southwest Asia received only a small amount of money for the oil found on their land. In the 1950s, these countries began to demand more money for their oil. Within a short time, the countries of Southwest Asia gained control of their oil resources. Now they decide how much oil to produce and how much to charge for it.

Summary B

Control of Southwest Asian oil resources has passed from American and European companies to the countries of Southwest Asia.

_____

_____

_____

_____

_____

_____

_____

_____

_____

_____

If the phrases you have written help you remember more information from Selection B, you have written a good summary. Here is an example of what you could have written.

Summary B

Control of Southwest Asian oil resources has passed from American and European companies to the countries of Southwest Asia.

—after oil discovered in 1908, Southwest Asian countries allowed foreign companies to take it out of the ground

—small amount of money paid to Southwest Asian countries by foreign companies

—Southwest Asian countries demanded

more money, and after the 1950s, took
_____

control of oil production and pricing
_____

Sometimes the reading selection you are asked to summarize may contain more than one paragraph. When this is the case, it may be impossible to summarize the entire selection in just one sentence or a few phrases.

You may need several sentences or phrases to summarize each paragraph.

The following reading selection contains three paragraphs. You have already read the first two paragraphs in Selections A and B. Now read all three paragraphs. Notice that Paragraphs 1 and 2 have been summarized. For Paragraph 3 write a summary that includes one sentence stating the main idea and at least two phrases. Use the information in Paragraph 3 to help you.

Oil Changes the World

Paragraph 1

Southwest Asia is the world's leading producer of oil. The United States, Western Europe, East Asia, and other parts of the world need the oil found in Southwest Asia. Oil is used for fuel in cars, trucks, buses, airplanes, and ships. It is also used to make plastic and to produce electrical power to run factories. Homes and office buildings are heated by oil. Much of the world depends on the oil produced in Southwest Asia.

Paragraph 2

The first large deposits of oil in Southwest Asia were discovered in Iran in 1908. At that time, the countries of Southwest Asia did not have the money or the skill needed to take the oil out of the ground. So they allowed American and European companies to drill for the oil. These companies decided how much oil would be produced and how much to charge for the oil. The countries of Southwest Asia received only a small amount of money for the oil found on their land. In the 1950s, these countries began to demand more money for their oil. Within a short time, the countries of Southwest Asia gained control of their oil resources. Now they decide how much oil to produce and how much to charge for it.

Paragraph 3

By raising the price of their oil, the Southwest Asian oil-producing countries have become very wealthy. Some of this wealth has been spent by the rulers, who replaced their camels and tents with fancy, large cars and air-conditioned palaces. Recently, the rulers have begun to spend more money for the good of their people. Many of the countries now provide their people with free health care and free education. Large cities with modern housing have been built. For years, the oil of Southwest Asia brought changes to the rest of the world. Now the money made from oil is changing the lives of the people of Southwest Asia.

Summary of Paragraph 1

The world depends on the oil of South-West Asia for many uses:
  —fuel for cars, trucks, planes, buses, and ships
  —plastic goods, electrical power, and heat

Summary of Paragraph 2

Control of Southwest Asian oil resources has passed from American and European companies to the countries of Southwest Asia.
  —after oil discovered in 1908, Southwest Asian countries allowed foreign companies to take it out of the ground
  —small amounts of money paid to Southwest Asian countries by foreign companies
  —Southwest Asian countries demanded more money, and after 1950s, took control of oil production and pricing

Summary of Paragraph 3

_____

_____

_____

_____

_____

_____

_____

How you finished this summary was up to you. All that matters is that your summary helps you remember the main ideas and important facts contained in a longer reading selection.

Here are a few important points to remember when you are writing a summary:

1. Your summary should be much shorter than the reading selection.
2. Your summary should contain the main ideas of the reading selection.
3. Your summary should not contain your opinion. It should contain only the opinion of the person who wrote the selection.
4. Your summary sentences and phrases should not be copied word for word from the selection. Write a summary in your own words. Then you can be sure you understand the main ideas of the selection.

The next time you are reading something for school, make a summary of what you read. It will help you do better in school. The following exercises will give you practice in writing good summaries.

USING WHAT YOU HAVE LEARNED

A. Read the following selection. Then complete the summary that has been started. Use the information in the selection to help you.

A Great City With a Big Problem

All my life I have lived in Mexico City, the capital and largest city of Mexico. It is a city of beautiful avenues and fine buildings, a city alive with music and sports. Schools, museums, and libraries of every kind enrich the lives of the people. It is a city where people of different racial and ethnic backgrounds have learned to live in peace.

There is, however, one major problem. The city is too crowded. Believe me, I love my neighbors—but there are just too many of them. About 9 million people live in Mexico City proper. When you add in the surrounding areas, the population jumps to 20 million. The city's rapid growth has resulted in serious air pollution, water shortages, and major traffic jams.

You are, of course, invited to visit my great city—as long as you promise not to stay too long.

SUMMARY

According to the writer, Mexico City is a great city with a big problem.

—capital and largest city of Mexico

—beautiful avenues and fine buildings

_____

_____

_____

_____

_____

_____

_____

B. Read the following selection. Then write your own summary.

Asian Goods Have a Big Market in the United States

If you own a television set, a radio, a DVD or CD player, look at where it was made. There is a good chance that it was made in Asia. If your family owns a car, a computer, or a camera, it may also have been made in Asia. The same is probably true for some of the clothes you wear. Asia is one of the major <u>industrial</u> areas of the world today, and the United States is one of its biggest customers.

China leads all other countries in Asia in selling goods to the United States. U.S. imports from China are valued at nearly $325 billion. They include computers, household goods and furniture, toys and sporting goods, clothing, video equipment, and footwear. Recent concerns over the health risks of some Chinese products have not stopped the growing American demand for Chinese goods.

Japan is the second-largest Asian seller of goods to the United States. U.S. imports from Japan are valued at nearly $145 billion. Then comes South Korea with U.S. imports from there valued at $48 billion. The list goes on: Taiwan, $39 billion; Malaysia, $33 billion; India, $24 billion; Thailand, $23 billion; Singapore, $19 billion; Indonesia, $15 billion; Vietnam, $11 billion; and the Philippines, $9 billion.

Years ago, Americans bought Asian goods because they were cheaper than goods made in the United States. Today, this is still true for some products. But Americans buy Asian goods because, for the most part, they are made well. It seems that Americans cannot get enough of them.

<u>industrial</u>: having to do with factories and machines; manufacturing

_____

_____

_____

_____

_____

_____

_____

_____

_____

_____

C. Read the following selection. Then write your own summary.

An African Kingdom of the Past

Far into the 20th century, Africa south of the Sahara was still a mystery to most Americans. In most U.S. schools, studying the history of the area used to be limited to European imperialism in Africa. It was as if Africa south of the Sahara had no history of its own.

Only in the 1960s did American schools begin to teach about the great civilizations that once existed in Africa south of the Sahara. One of those civilizations, located in West Africa, was Songhai. It extended both east and west of the Niger River and covered an area some 2,000 miles wide.

From the mid-1400s to the late 1500s was the time of Songhai's greatest strength. Its power and wealth came from trade. Every year, large groups of traders from Songhai rode on camels across the Sahara carrying gold and ivory. They returned with salt, jewelry, and cloth. Iron weapons helped the rulers of Songhai control the people of their very large territory.

One of Songhai's most important cities was Timbuktu, noted for its university. A visitor from North Africa wrote about the city in 1526: "Here are a great many doctors, judges, priests, and learned men." Although Songhai was taken over by invaders in the late 16th century, Timbuktu has continued to be famous.

civilization: a high level of culture, science, industry, and government

SUMMARY

_____

_____

Information Literacy Skills

Chapter 8
Using a Textbook

Imagine what it would be like if you knew everything. If you were asked any question, you could come up with the answer immediately.

The truth is that no one knows everything or is born with a knowledge of every subject. You know things because you learn about them. That is why you go to school—to learn important and interesting subjects that will help you throughout your life. In school you also learn where to find answers to your questions.

The greatest source of knowledge is books. One of the most important books you use every day is your textbook. It can give you a lot of information if you know how to use it.

Table of Contents

Let us imagine that you are going to use a textbook titled *Africa* in your Social Studies class. You would like to know what this book is going to teach you about Africa. To find out, you could look through every page of the book, but this would take a long time. How can you find out quickly and easily what this book on Africa is all about? You could look at the *table of contents*, which is found within the first few pages of almost every book. A table of contents is a list of the main topics contained in a book.

In a textbook, the table of contents usually lists units and chapters. The units deal with the most important subjects covered in the book. Each unit is divided into several chapters. Each chapter covers a specific (certain) subject, which is part of the general subject of its unit. For example, a unit on United States geography might have separate chapters on each region of the country.

On page 53 is the table of contents for the textbook on Africa. Notice the number that is listed to the right of each chapter title. This number is the page on which the chapter begins. For example:

Chapter 3   Animals of Africa   12

This means that Chapter 3 begins on page 12.

In many textbooks, no page number is listed to the right of each unit title in the table of contents. This might mean that each unit begins on the same page as the first chapter of that unit. Thus, in the textbook on Africa, Unit One begins on page 3, Unit Two begins on page 25, and so forth.

AFRICA: Table of Contents

Answer the following questions using the table of contents.

1. The table of contents of the book Africa

_____ (a) lists every subject covered in the book.

_____ (b) lists only ten of the most important subjects in the book.

_____ (c) lists the important subjects in the book and the pages on which they are found.

Which answer did you choose? No table of contents lists every subject in a book. The purpose of a table of contents is to list the important subjects and the pages on which they are found. The table of contents of the book *Africa* does this. Therefore, the answer to question 1 is (*c*).

2. From the table of contents, you can be sure that the book *Africa* discusses the

_____ (a) different peoples of Africa.

_____ (b) influence of African culture in the United States.

_____ (c) kinds of clothing that Africans wear.

Which answer did you choose? The book *Africa* may deal with the subjects given in all three choices. But the table of contents lists only the different peoples of Africa. Therefore, the answer to question 2 is (*a*).

3. Chapter 5, "Africa's Past," is

_____ (a) five pages long.

_____ (b) ten pages long.

_____ (c) 15 pages long.

Which answer did you choose this time? The table of contents tells you that Chapter 5 begins on page 25 and Chapter 6 begins on page 35. By subtracting 25 from 35, you come up with 10. Therefore, Chapter 5 is ten pages long and the answer to question 3 is (b).

Index

Because you cannot find anything about African clothing in the table of contents does not mean that the topic is not mentioned in the book. Remember, the table of contents lists only the main subjects covered in the book. African clothing is surely discussed somewhere in the book. To find out by look-

ing through every page for the information would take a long time. How then can you find the pages in the book where African clothing is discussed? You can answer this question by using the *index* of the book. It is usually at the back of a book. Every subject in a book is listed in the index in *alphabetical order*. This means that the subjects are arranged in the order of the letters of the alphabet. Next to each subject, you can find the page number or numbers where the information can be found.

Here is a part of the index from the book on Africa. This example shows only subjects in the book that start with the letter C. Remember, however, that an index uses all the letters in the alphabet.

Use the index to answer the following questions.

1. Which pages in the book contain information about clothing in Africa?

_____ (a) 47, 112

_____ (b) 97, 99, 103

_____ (c) 20, 83, 113–116

Which answer did you choose? First, find the word "clothing" in the index. Remember,

the index is in alphabetical order. When you find "clothing," you will see numbers next to it. These numbers are the pages in the book that contain information about clothing in Africa. Next to the words "Clothing in Africa" in the index are the numbers 20, 83, 113–116. Therefore, the answer to question 1 is (c).

The information about clothing in Africa is found in three separate places in the book. The first place is on page 20. The second place is on page 83. The third place is on pages 113–116. The dash (–) between 113 and 116 stands for all the pages between 113 and 116. In this case, the dash stands for pages 114 and 115. So when you see a dash between pages in an index, you know it really stands for all of the pages between those listed.

2. Which one of the following subjects comes first in the index?

_____ (a) Churchill

_____ (b) Congo

_____ (c) Caravans

Which answer did you choose? Remember that the index is arranged in alphabetical order. Look at the choices to the answer to question 2. Caravans, starting with the letters Ca, comes before Churchill (Ch) and Congo (Co). Therefore, the answer to question 2 is (c).

Next to the word "Caravans" in the index are the numbers 8, 26, 90. You now know that these numbers stand for pages where information on caravans can be found. But there are other words on the same line as Caravans, 8, 26, 90. These words are "*See also* Animals." This means that by looking under Animals in the index, you can find more information about caravans.

The phrase "*See also* Animals" is called a *cross-reference* because it refers, or sends, you to another part of the book to find more information on the subject.

Notice that the name "Churchill" is listed in the index like this: Churchill, Winston. The person's name was really Winston Churchill. But a person's last name is more important than her or his first name. So the last name is written first, followed by a comma (,) and then the first name.

Notice also the word "Congo" in the index. There are no pages given after the word. Instead, you read "*See* Democratic Republic of the Congo and Republic of Congo." This means that you have to look elsewhere in the index. You would look under D for Democratic Republic of the Congo or R for Republic of Congo. For both listings, you would find pages.

3. The book *Africa* tells how strong European countries controlled weaker areas of Africa. These areas were considered to be colonies, or possessions. The system of control was called colonialism. Which pages in the book contain information on Portuguese colonialism in Africa?

_____ (a) 35–37

_____ (b) 41, 49

_____ (c) 54, 59

Which answer did you choose this time? In the index, would you look under P for Portuguese or under C for colonialism? In some books, you could look under either letter. In this book on Africa, the pages are given under C for colonialism. When you find colonialism in the index, you see that the information is divided into six parts. It looks like this:

> Colonialism, 35–49
> Belgian, 36
> British, 37–39, 43–44
> French, 39–40, 44–45
> German, 42
> Portuguese, 41, 49
> Spanish, 41

The main countries that had colonies in Africa are listed in alphabetical order. The pages listed next to each country contain information about its colonialism in Africa. Look under colonialism until you find "Portuguese." The pages next to Portuguese are 41 and 49. On these pages you can find information on Portuguese colonialism in Africa. Therefore, the answer to question 3 is (b).

Glossary

Another important part of many textbooks is the *glossary*. It is a list of difficult terms and their meanings in alphabetical order. A glossary is usually found at the back of a book just before the index. In the textbook *Africa*, the table of contents shows that the glossary starts on page 131. When you come across a difficult word in a book, look to see whether it is in the glossary. Knowing the meaning of every word will help you understand more clearly what you are reading.

Here is a glossary with some of the Social Studies terms from this book.

century period of 100 years
civilization high level of culture, science, industry, and government
culture the common way of life of a large group of people or a nation
endangered species type of living thing (a species) in danger of dying out
industrial having to do with factories and machines, manufacturing
natural resources materials found on or in the earth used to benefit humans
population total number of people living in a place

Answer the following questions using the glossary.

1. A glossary lists

_____ (a) every subject covered in a book.

_____ (b) difficult terms in the order in which they appear in a book.

_____ (c) difficult terms in alphabetical order.

Which answer did you choose? A glossary does not list every subject. Nor does it list difficult subjects in the order in which they appear, for that would make them too hard to find. A glossary lists difficult terms in alphabetical order. Therefore, the answer to question 1 is (c).

2. Why do you think a page number is usually not given next to each term in a glossary?

_____

_____

What did you write? Your answer could have included one or both of the following reasons. The first is that you probably know the page number already. If you have come upon a term in the text on a certain page, you know the page. You do not know the meaning of the term. That is why you go to the glossary. The second reason is that the term may appear many times in the text. There is not room in a glossary to list numerous pages after each term.

USING WHAT YOU HAVE LEARNED

A. Place a check mark next to the correct answers to questions 1 to 10.

1. The table of contents provides

___ (a) a list of every subject in a book.

___ (b) a list of important subjects in alphabetical order.

___ (c) an overall view of the major subjects in a book.

2. The table of contents is usually found in the

___ (a) first few pages of a book.

___ (b) middle of a book.

___ (c) back of a book.

3. The table of contents in a textbook is usually divided into

___ (a) units and chapters.

___ (b) books and volumes.

___ (c) pages.

4. Most every subject in a book is listed in the

___ (a) table of contents.

___ (b) index.

___ (c) glossary.

5. The index of a book is arranged

___ (a) like the table of contents.

___ (b) by page order.

___ (c) in alphabetical order.

6. The index is usually found in the

___ (a) front of a book.

___ (b) middle of a book.

___ (c) back of a book.

7. Which one of the following subjects would be listed before the other two in an index?

___ (a) World War II

___ (b) Woodrow Wilson

___ (c) women's rights

8. In an index example Pollution, 172–175, information on pollution can be found on

___ (a) lines 172 and 175.

___ (b) pages 172 and 175 only.

___ (c) pages 172, 173, 174, and 175.

9. The difficult words in a textbook are often explained in the

___ (a) index.

___ (b) glossary.

___ (c) table of contents.

10. The glossary in a book is usually found

___ (a) just after the table of contents.

___ (b) just before the index.

___ (c) in the middle of the book.

B. Study the following table of contents and index.

SOUTHWEST ASIA/AFRICA: Table of Contents

SOUTHWEST ASIA/AFRICA: Index

Place a check mark next to the correct answers to questions 1 to 10.

1. The book on Southwest Asia/Africa is divided into

   ___ (*a*) two units.

   ___ (*b*) four units.

   ___ (*c*) six units.

2. Unit Two deals with

    ____ (*a*) the land and people of Southwest Asia/Africa.

    ____ (*b*) Southwest Asia/Africa in modern times.

    ____ (*c*) the history of Southwest Asia/Africa.

3. The chapter on traveling in Southwest Asia/Africa begins on

    ____ (*a*) page 53.

    ____ (*b*) page 7.

    ____ (*c*) page 75.

4. The table of contents shows that this book

    ____ (*a*) deals with the importance of oil in Southwest Asia/Africa.

    ____ (*b*) contains homework assignments.

    ____ (*c*) contains many colored photographs.

5. If you come across a difficult word in this book, you can look up its meaning in the

    ____ (*a*) table of contents.

    ____ (*b*) glossary.

    ____ (*c*) index.

6. When a subject is not listed in the table of contents,

    ____ (*a*) there is no way to look it up.

    ____ (*b*) it is necessary to look through every page of the book to find it.

    ____ (*c*) you can most likely find it listed in the index.

7. The index in the book begins on

    ____ (*a*) page 3.

    ____ (*b*) page 89.

    ____ (*c*) page 93.

8. Information on the Aswan Dam can be found on

    ____ (*a*) page 6.

    ____ (*b*) page 35.

    ____ (*c*) page 40.

9. Which one of the following subjects is listed before the other two in the index?

    ____ (*a*) Kemal Ataturk

    ____ (*b*) Alexander the Great

    ____ (*c*) Animals

10. The index lists the pages for Saudi Arabia

    ____ (*a*) under A for Arabia.

    ____ (*b*) under S for Saudi Arabia.

    ____ (*c*) under C for Countries of Southwest Asia/Africa.

C. Study the following table of contents and index.

THE ASIAN WORLD: *Table of Contents*

THE ASIAN WORLD: *Index*

Place a check mark next to the correct answers to questions 1 to 9.

1. The book *The Asian World* is divided into

    ___ (*a*) two units.

    ___ (*b*) four units.

    ___ (*c*) five units.

2. Unit Two of the book deals with

    ___ (*a*) Russia and Central Asia.

    ___ (*b*) China and its neighbors.

    ___ (*c*) Japan.

3. Unit Four begins on

    ___ (*a*) page 54.

    ___ (*b*) page 93.

    ___ (*c*) page 121.

4. The table of contents shows that this book deals with the early history of

____ (a) Russia.

____ (b) Africa.

____ (c) the United States.

5. The chapter on the people of Japan is

____ (a) four pages long.

____ (b) six pages long.

____ (c) ten pages long.

6. Information on Kashmir can be found on

____ (a) page 148.

____ (b) page 101.

____ (c) page 72.

7. Which one of the following subjects is mentioned on more than one page in the book?

____ (a) Lena River

____ (b) Koran

____ (c) Mao Zedong

8. The book tells about Muslims in

____ (a) Russia and Central Asia only.

____ (b) India and Southeast Asia only.

____ (c) South Asia, Southeast Asia, Russia, and Central Asia.

9. In the index listing for Korea, the phrase "*See also* Manchuria" is called a cross-reference because

____ (a) it refers, or sends, you to another part of the book for more information on Korea.

____ (b) all the information in the book on Korea is found on four pages.

____ (c) it refers, or sends, you to another part of the book for more information on Manchuria.

10. Describe in your own words the differences between a table of contents and an index. (Answer in two or three sentences.)

_____

_____

_____

_____

_____

_____

_____

D. Study the following table of contents and index of the book *The Latin American World.*

THE LATIN AMERICAN WORLD: *Table of Contents*

THE LATIN AMERICAN WORLD: *Index*

D-1. Place a check mark next to the correct answers to questions 1 to 10.

1. This book *The Latin American World* is divided into

    ___ (*a*) four units.

    ___ (*b*) five units.

    ___ (*c*) ten units.

2. Unit Three deals with

    ___ (*a*) South America.

    ___ (*b*) Mexico and Central America.

    ___ (*c*) Mexico only.

3. The chapter on Puerto Rico begins on

    ___ (*a*) page 29.

    ___ (*b*) page 136.

    ___ (*c*) page 182.

4. Which one of the following is found in the front of the book?

    ___ (*a*) the table of contents

    ___ (*b*) the glossary

    ___ (*c*) the index

5. The table of contents shows that the book deals with

    ___ (*a*) Napoleon III's takeover of Mexico.

    ___ (*b*) the United States' interest in Latin America.

    ___ (*c*) the Panama Canal.

6. In the glossary beginning on page 205, you can expect to find

    ___ (*a*) a list of Social Studies terms with page numbers.

    ___ (*b*) an alphabetical list of difficult terms and their meanings.

    ___ (*c*) a list of the most important terms used in the book arranged in the order in which they appear.

7. The index in the book begins on

　　___ (a) page 4.

　　___ (b) page 205.

　　___ (c) page 213.

8. Which one of the following is listed before the other two in the index?

　　___ (a) Panama Canal

　　___ (b) Panama

　　___ (c) Pan-American Highway

9. If you look up oil in the index, you are told

　　___ (a) that the information is on pages 72 and 148.

　　___ (b) to see Natural Resources.

　　___ (c) that no information is given in the book.

10. The index shows that information on the natural resources of South America is on pages 69–81. This means that information can be found on

　　___(a) two pages.　　　___(b) ten pages.　　　___(c) 13 pages.

D-2. Look at the index and then fill in the correct page or pages where the following information can be found.

1. pampas _____

2. Bernardo O'Higgins _____

3. natural resources in Mexico _____

4. Patagonian Desert _____

5. Puerto Rican nationalism _____

Chapter 9
Using Reference Materials

Perhaps the most important source of information in your Social Studies class is your textbook. But it may not give you as much information on a certain subject, or topic, as you would like. To find more detailed information, you may need to use special *reference materials*.

Reference materials come in various forms. In this chapter, you will learn about the forms that are described as "print," "software," and "online."

Reference Materials in Print

When we speak of reference materials in print form, we usually mean books. Your school or public library will have a large number of reference books in an area of the library marked REFERENCE. Because many people use these reference books, you are not allowed to take them out of the library. Reference books contain a great deal of information on many topics. You usually do not read through them. Instead, you pick out only the information you need.

Encyclopedias

Let us suppose that you are reading about glaciers in your Social Studies class. You want to know more about them than what your textbook tells you. A good place to start your research is with an *encyclopedia* in print (book) form. Encyclopedias give detailed information on almost every subject.

All the subjects in an encyclopedia are arranged in alphabetical order. Because an encyclopedia contains so much information, it is usually divided into several books, or volumes. In the drawing on the right, you

can see an example of how an encyclopedia may be divided into volumes. Letters are printed on the *spine* (narrow end) of each volume. This way you know which volume to pick up when you are looking for a certain subject. For example, the first letter in the subject glaciers is *g*. You will find articles on glaciers and on all other subjects beginning with g in the volume with the letter *G* on the binding.

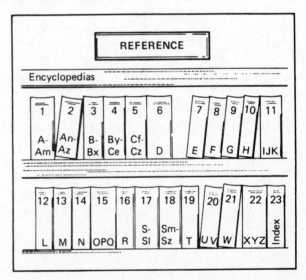

You can also see in the drawing that some letters need more than one volume while other letters share a volume. Notice also the special *index volume* (usually the last one, in this case Volume 23). It lists in alphabetical order all the subjects covered in the encyclopedia. The index gives the volume and pages where each subject can be found.

Many encyclopedia articles include maps, photographs, and useful facts and figures. Long articles are divided into sections, with each section dealing with a different aspect of the subject. In the *World Book Encyclopedia*, the article on glaciers is divided into an introduction, five smaller topics called subtopics, and lists of related articles and additional resources at the end. It also comes with photographs and drawings. The entire text of the article is printed in Exercise C of this chapter, on pages 74–76. The sections of the article are:

Glacier
Kinds of glaciers
How glaciers form
How glaciers move
How glaciers shape the land
Famous glaciers
Related articles
Additional resources

The headings of the different sections are in bold type to make it easier to see where they begin. The headings help you find information quickly. For example, if you want to know why glaciers move, you can go quickly to the subtopic "How glaciers move." If the article does not contain all the information you need, you can go to the section "Related articles." It lists other articles relating to glaciers that are found elsewhere in the encyclopedia. In the last section, "Additional resources," you can find the titles of books on glaciers. Your school or public library might have some of these books.

Almanacs

Another helpful reference book is an *almanac*. It contains useful, up-to-date facts and figures on a large number of subjects, including art, business, countries of the world, geography, education, industry, farming, religion, science, entertainment, and sports. Almanacs are published yearly to keep all their facts and figures up to date. Many encyclopedias are also updated yearly, but they are much more expensive than almanacs. The entire article on Switzerland from *The World Almanac and Book of Facts 2009* is printed in Exercise D of this chapter, on pages 77–78.

Atlases

An *atlas* is another helpful reference book. It is a book devoted mostly to maps. The maps can show the entire Earth or a small area of it. The maps also show boundaries, population, rainfall, heights of land features, natural resources, products, and other subjects.

Perhaps you want to locate Malaspina Glacier on a map. First, look at the index of the atlas. Here is a small section of the index from the Hammond *Medallion World Atlas*:

Malargue, Arg. 143/C4
Malartic, Que. 174/B3
Malaspina (glac.), Alaska 196/K3
Malaspina (str.), Br. Col. 184/J2
Malatya, Turkey 59/C2
Malatya (prov.), Turkey 63/H3
Malawi, 3/L6

Malaspina Glacier is the third entry. The abbreviation (glac.) is for glacier. This glacier is located in Alaska. Notice the indication 196/K3. The first number means that you are to look at the map on page 196 of the atlas. K and 3 are guidelines for locating the glacier itself. Along the top of the map on page 196 are letters from A to Q. Along the sides are numbers from 1 to 3. Find K and follow it down to the level of 3. In the area where these two meet, you will find Malaspina Glacier.

There are other items in this sample section of an index that are worth noting. A country appears by itself—Malawi. Cities and towns are followed by the names of larger areas in which they are located—Malatya, in the country of Turkey, Malartic, in the province of Quebec (Que.), Canada. A physical feature, such as a glacier, river, lake, or strait, is also indicated in parentheses.

In Units Five, Six, and Seven, you will learn more about using maps.

Dictionaries

Another important reference book is a *dictionary*, which is an alphabetical list of the words in a language and their meanings. For each word listed, a dictionary gives the spelling, the pronunciation, the part of speech, the various meanings, and the origin (where the word comes from).

Let us take a close look at a word in a dictionary. Here is what the paperback edition of *The American Heritage Dictionary* says about the word "current":

> **cur·rent** (kur′ ənt) *adj.* **1.** Belonging to the time now passing; now in progress. **2.** Commonly accepted; prevalent.— *n.* **1.** A steady and smooth onward movement, as of water. **2.** The part of any body of liquid or gas that has a continuous onward movement. **3.** A general tendency. **4. a.** A flow of electric charge. **b.** The amount of electric charge flowing past a specified circuit point per unit time. [<L. *currere*, to run.]

The entry first shows that "cur·rent" is divided into two *syllables* (parts). The respelling in parentheses (kur′ nt) shows how to *pronounce* the word. (You will find a key that indicates how to say each letter in the parentheses either on the same page as the word or in a guide to pronunciation in the front of the dictionary.) Next comes a *part of speech, adj.* for adjective. Later comes another part of speech, *n.* for noun. There are seven meanings, or definitions, of the word. (Make sure you know which meaning you want.) The L stands for Latin, so we know that the English word "current" comes from (<) the Latin word *currere*, meaning "to run."

Let us see what you have learned about reference material in book form.

1. Which reference book would be likely to give the most information on ocean currents?

    _____ (*a*) dictionary

    _____ (*b*) almanac

    _____ (*c*) encyclopedia

Which answer did you choose? A dictionary will give you the meaning of ocean currents. An almanac might list different ocean currents and their locations. But an encyclopedia would be the most likely to give you detailed information on ocean currents, along with maps and drawings. Therefore, the answer to question 1 is (*c*).

2. Which reference book in a library is most likely to have the latest population figures for Alaska?

    _____ (*a*) encyclopedia

    _____ (*b*) almanac

    _____ (*c*) atlas

Which answer did you choose? All of these reference books could give population figures for Alaska. But it is the most recently published reference book that will probably have the latest population figures. An almanac is less expensive than a set of encyclopedias and most atlases, so your library will most likely buy the latest almanac every year. Therefore, the answer to question 2 is (*b*).

Reference Materials on Software

Computers are another source of reference materials. The information you find in an encyclopedia in print form can also be found in an encyclopedia software program. That is also true for almanacs, atlases, and dictionaries. Computer reference programs can come on CDs (compact disks). Your school computer probably has reference programs already installed. Many people keep their home computer reference programs up-to-date by buying and installing software updates.

Computer reference programs offer information that a book cannot. For example, on some CD versions of encyclopedias, you can listen to the national anthem and major languages of nearly every country.

Computer reference programs usually allow you to copy material, including photographs and maps, for your own personal use. They also allow you to print the items. Just follow the directions on the screen.

Reference Materials "Online" on the Internet

If the computer you use is connected to the Internet, another valuable source of information is available to you. Many computers make the connection over a telephone or cable line. Thus, people say that they are "online" when their computers are connected to the Internet. To gain *access* (entry) to the Internet, the computer you use must be connected to an Internet Service Provider (ISP).

But what exactly does it mean to be connected to the Internet? The Internet is a worldwide network of computers that allows people to share information and ideas. People use special software programs to create Web sites that contain the information and ideas they want to share. The same programs help them to place their Web sites on the Internet. When you go online, you are able to access Web sites all around the world. Each Web site has a *home page* and usually additional pages. You move from one page to the next by clicking the links on a page.

Why may the access to a Web site be blocked? Web sites are operated by individuals or organizations that place whatever information and ideas they want to on their Web sites. They may block your access by requiring a password. In addition, parents, guardians, schools, and public libraries may program the computer you are using to block access to Web sites they feel are inappropriate for people under a certain age.

Even when you are allowed access to a Web site, you have to be alert. You should not type in any personal information like your full name, address, phone number or e-mail address. Once that information is put on the Internet, you do not know where it will end up. You do not know who may use it to cause you harm. Be alert!

Beyond safety, there is another reason to be alert. Because anyone can place information on the Internet, the information may be inaccurate. It may also be outdated. If a Web site gives you the population of China, you have to know the date when that information was gathered. You cannot believe information just because it is in a book, and you cannot accept everything on the Internet as fact. That is why a good researcher seeks out several sources of information.

Search Programs

You can find just about anything on the Internet. But when the Internet contains billions of pieces of information, how do you find exactly what you need to know? The answer is to use a *search program.*

The appearance or look of your opening Internet screen will vary, depending on whether you are in school, a public library, or home. However, that first screen will probably tell you how to get to a search program. It may even give you a way to start a search immediately. Whether you choose a special search program like Google or Yahoo! or the search program available on the first screen, the steps will mostly be the same.

On the opening screen of all search programs, you will find a blank search box and next to it the word "Search" or "Go" in a smaller box or underlined. In the blank box, type a word or phrase that must appear in all your search results. Let us say that you type in *glaciers*, as shown below. You then click on Search or Go.

The search program will list on a new screen all the resources it has that match your request. Each resource will offer a brief description, and the word "glaciers," if it appears in the description, will be in bold type. You can see what the screen of a search result looks like in Exercise E of this chapter on pages 79–80.

Here is an example of a listing:

What is a glacier?

Presently, **glaciers** occupy about 10 percent of the world's total land area, with . . . **Glaciers** can be thought as remnants from the last Ice Age, when ice covered . . .

nsidc.org/**glaciers**/questions/what.html–14k–Cached

This listing is a page of a Web site. The real Internet address of this Web page is given on the last line of the listing. To go to the page, you click on the link (the underlined group of words) on the first line. In this example, the page that opens will not be the home page. But you can go to the home page by clicking the link HOME near the top of the page.

Notice the underlined word Cached on the same line as the real address. Some search programs make a copy of every Web page they have. In this way, they have a copy of the page even when the page is no longer available on its original Web site. So when you click on the underlined link and nothing happens, you can click on the Cached link and the copy will open.

Near the top of the screen of results for glaciers, you could see the following:

```
1–10 of about 7,000,000 for glaciers
```

This means that the search has found about 7,000,000 Web pages containing the word "glaciers." Some of those pages will belong to the same Web site. The number of Web pages changes from day to day as pages are added to the Internet or removed.

The numbers 1–10 mean that the screen is showing only the first 10 results. The topic *glaciers* returned so many results that it will take many pages to show them all. At the bottom of the screen, you will see a string of links like the following:

```
1 2 3 4 5 6 7 8 9 10   Next
```

Notice that the number 1 is not underlined. That is because you already are on page 1 of the results. To see the next 10 listings, you click the link 2 or the link Next. As you click higher numbers or Next, the string of numbers will go higher until you come to the last page of listings. Here is what the string of links will look like when you are on page 9 of the results:

```
Previous   1 2 3 4 5 6 7 8 9 10 11 12
      13 14 15 16 17 18 19   Next
```

Just as you can click the link Next to go to page 10, you can click the link Previous to go to page 8.

Limiting Your Search

Before you choose the first Web site to visit, consider *narrowing* (limiting) your search. Perhaps you want to find only information on the Malaspina Glacier in Alaska. At the top and the bottom of the screen, you will see a box with your entry glaciers and next to it Search or Go.

Select and delete the word "glaciers." In its place, type in *Malaspina Glacier* and click on Search or Go.

When the next screen appears, you may see that the number of Web pages listed has gone down to about 18,500. The new list will show only those Web pages that contain the words *Malaspina* and *Glacier*. Most search programs will first list pages that show the words together one after the other. But you could see a Web page about Malaspina University in which the word glacier is used once or twice in passing. To ensure that your search program will list only Web pages on the Malaspina Glacier, place quotation marks around the two words, as shown below, and click on Search or Go.

```
"Malaspina Glacier"   ( SEARCH )  or  ( GO )
```

When the next screen appears, you may see that the number of listed Web pages has gone down to about 15,000. What exactly did the quotation marks do? They told the search program to list only those Web pages in which the words *Malaspina* and *Glacier* appear together and in that order.

Even with the quotation marks, you will come up with thousands of Web pages for Malaspina Glacier. You can further narrow your search by adding key words. Let us say that you want to know the exact location of the glacier in Alaska. You also want to know about the early explorers of the glacier. Put a space after "Malaspina Glacier" and type in +location. You must put a *plus sign* (+)

before any word you add to the box. Then put a space after +location and type in +explorer. When your search box looks like the following, click on Search or Go.

```
"Malaspina Glacier" +location +explorer        ( SEARCH )  or  ( GO )
```

This time the screen may list 70 Web pages because every page that contains "Malaspina Glacier" must also contain the words location and explorer.

You could still narrow the search more by adding other +words or by adding –words.

By placing a *minus sign* (–) in front of a word, you are telling the search program not to list any Web page that contains that word. For example, if you did not want any Web page that contained the word icebergs, you would type:

```
"Malaspina Glacier" +location +explorer –icebergs        ( SEARCH )  or  ( GO )
```

Your new list of results may be around 50. That is an easier number of results to handle than the original 18,500 for Malaspina Glacier. Look down the list until you come to a Web page that looks worthwhile. Then click on the underlined link and the Web page will appear on your screen. The opening Web page may not be the home page of the Web site. If you want to go to the Home page, click the link marked HOME. If you find the information you need, you can select the text, then copy and paste it into a computer file.

Let us see what you have learned about using the Internet for research.

3. What are two reasons given in this chapter why you should be alert when using the Internet?

   _____

   _____

What did you write? Earlier in the chapter, you read that you should not put personal information on the Internet. You never know into whose hands it may fall. You also read that information on the Internet may not be accurate and up-to-date.

4. Your search result page shows:

```
Previous    7 8 9 10 11 12 13 14 15
         16 17 18 19    Next
```

What are two ways you can go to page 14 of the search results?

   _____

   _____

What did you write? You can see that page 15 is not underlined. This means you are on page 15. Because you are on page 15, you can click the link Previous to go to page 14. You can also click the link 14.

5. Which one of the following entries in an Internet search program would result in the smallest number of Web pages?

   _____ (a) North America

   _____ (b) "North America"

   _____ (c) "North America" +glacier

Which answer did you choose? If you picked choice (a), your search result would give every page that contains the words *North* and *America*. It would also include pages that contain only *North* and pages that contain only *America*. The quotation marks around *North America* in choice (*b*) would produce only results that have the words *North America* together and in that order. Thus, choice (*b*) would produce fewer results than choice (*a*). Adding +glacier to "North America," as in choice (*c*), would produce even fewer results. The search would only give Web pages that contain the words North America together and in that order and the word glacier. Therefore, choice (*c*) is the answer to question 5.

The following exercises will give you more practice using reference materials.

USING WHAT YOU HAVE LEARNED

A. Which reference book would you look at first to find the following information? Write **E** for encyclopedia, **D** for dictionary, **AL** for almanac, or **AT** for atlas.

___ 1. the use of wood in African art

___ 2. a listing of the five longest rivers in the world

___ 3. various meanings of the word "history"

___ 4. a map showing the greatest number of cities in Algeria that can fit on the map

___ 5. the number of medals won by the United States in the last five Olympic games

___ 6. the building of the Panama Canal

___ 7. facts and figures on the number of immigrants entering the United States

___ 8. the life of Mohandas Gandhi

___ 9. the correct way to pronounce "illustrate"

___10. the location of the island nations of Tonga and Vanuatu and their distance from each other

B. Place a check mark next to the correct answers to questions 1 to 10.

1. An encyclopedia contains information

___ (*a*) on subjects usually not found in textbooks.

___ (*b*) on almost all subjects.

___ (*c*) only on special subjects.

2. The letter M on the spine of a volume of an encyclopedia means that

___ (*a*) the volume contains only subjects beginning with the letter M.

___ (*b*) M is the first letter of the last name of the author of the articles in that volume.

___ (*c*) the volume covers all subjects starting with the letters A to M.

3. A dictionary is a reference book that

___ (*a*) gives detailed information on many subjects.

___ (*b*) uses just pictures and no words.

___ (*c*) gives the pronunciation, meanings, and origin of words.

4. You would expect this year's almanac to

___ (a) give complete details on every subject.

___ (b) give up-to-date facts and figures on many subjects.

___ (c) have a longer index than last year's edition.

5. Among print reference books, you would most likely use an atlas first to find

___ (a) the location of different countries.

___ (b) the present ruler of a country.

___ (c) information on the military strength of a country.

6. To be online in computer talk is to

___ (a) have the most up-to-date software.

___ (b) be connected to the Internet.

___ (c) have your computer connected to another computer.

7. Which of the following is an example of a resource material in print form?

___ (a) the Web site of *Information Please* almanac

___ (b) the CD version of *Encyclopaedia Britannica*

___ (c) a paperback version of *The American Heritage Dictionary*

8. The personal information you put on the Internet

___ (a) is removed by law within 24 hours.

___ (b) may be seen by people you did not intend to see it.

___ (c) cannot be seen by anyone without your permission.

9. Assume that in an Internet search program, you first typed in "South Africa." By adding +Boer to your first search request, you would be

___ (a) broadening your search.

___ (b) narrowing your search.

___ (c) expanding your search.

10. If the first screen you open on a Web site is not the home page, how can you get to the home page?

___ (a) Click the link marked HOME.

___ (b) You cannot get to the home page.

___ (c) Begin a new search.

C. Read the following encyclopedia article on glaciers. Then answer the questions based on the article and on what you have learned about encyclopedias in this chapter.

Glacier is a large mass of ice that flows slowly under the influence of gravity. Glaciers consist of packed snow that has built up over many years. The snow's weight eventually compresses its lower layers into ice. Glaciers scrape the ground as they move over it, eroding old landforms and creating new ones. They range in thickness from several feet or meters to 10,000 feet (3,000 meters) or more. Glaciers form in the colder regions near the North and South poles and in mountainous areas. During periods called *ice ages*, glaciers can grow to cover large portions of Earth's surface.

Kinds of glaciers. Scientists classify glaciers according to size and shape. An *ice sheet* is a dome-shaped glacier covering an area greater than 19,300 square miles (50,000 square kilometers). The ice in an ice sheet flows slowly outward from one or more central domes. Faster moving glaciers called *outlet glaciers* flow outward from the edge of an ice sheet. Ice sheets can reach a thickness of more than 2 miles (3 kilometers). They often conceal the entire landscape beneath them except for the tallest mountain peaks, called *nunataks*. Huge ice sheets cover most of Antarctica and Greenland.

An *icecap* is a dome-shaped glacier that covers an area of 19,300 square miles (50,000 square kilometers) or less. Icecaps resemble ice sheets, with outlet glaciers flowing outward from a central ice dome. Icecaps occur in Iceland and Norway and on several Arctic islands.

In some high mountain areas, glaciers form in a cirque, a bowl-shaped hollow with steep walls. A relatively small glacier confined to a cirque is called a *cirque glacier*. A valley glacier is a long, narrow stream of ice that flows down a mountain valley. Valley glaciers occur in mountainous regions worldwide.

Different valley glaciers flowing downhill sometimes come together, much as the tributaries of a river merge. Unlike tributaries, however, each of the glaciers remains a separate mass and continues to flow on its own. Rock debris carried by the glaciers accumulates at the boundaries between them. Some valley glaciers flow out of mountains and onto flatter ground. No longer confined by valley walls, the ice spreads out to form a rounded lump called a *piedmont glacier*.

Scientists also classify glaciers by comparing the temperature of a glacier's ice with the ice's *melting point* the temperature at which it turns to water. Within a *temperate glacier*, the ice remains at or near its melting point throughout most of the year.

Temperate glaciers contain ample *meltwater* (water from melted ice). They are not frozen firmly to the ground. The ice in a *polar glacier* remains well below its melting point throughout the year. Polar glaciers contain little or no meltwater. Most polar glaciers are frozen to the ground and cannot slide over it. A single large glacier can stretch across different Climate zones or elevations that have different temperatures. One portion of such a glacier might be temperate, and another portion might be polar.

How glaciers form. Glaciers form in areas where some snow remains on the ground throughout the year. This snow accumulates in layers over hundreds or thousands of years. Eventually, the weight of the upper snow layers compresses the lower layers into tiny pellets of ice called *firn*. At greater depths, the weight further compresses firn into solid ice. As snow turns into firn and ice, the frozen mass becomes more dense. With enough pressure, the ice can begin to flow, and the mass becomes a glacier.

Meltwater plays an important role in the formation of most glaciers. As ice on the glacier's surface melts, meltwater seeps deep into the ice mass, filling open spaces between ice crystals and particles and then refreezing. Meltwater also reduces the friction between ice particles, speeding the internal movement of the glacier as well as the rate at which the glacier slips over the ground. An abundance of meltwater makes temperate glaciers move faster than polar glaciers.

Glaciers grow and shrink with seasonal variations in temperature and snowfall. Typically, lower air temperatures in winter and spring prevent a glacier from melting, and heavy snowfall causes it to grow. In summer and autumn, higher air temperatures can melt portions of a glacier, causing it to shrink.

In frigid regions, glaciers can shrink as they enter the sea. The ice on a glacier's leading edge, which floats, is pushed upward by seawater. Huge chunks of ice break off in a process known as *calving*. The chunks, called *icebergs*, are carried away by wind and ocean currents.

Glaciers also grow and shrink with changes in Earth's climate. During an ice age, lower air temperatures and increased snowfall cause glaciers to thicken and expand. During an *interglacial period*, higher air temperatures and lower snowfall cause glaciers to thin and retreat.

Glaciers covered vast areas of Asia,

Europe, and North America during the Pleistocene Epoch, a period in Earth's history from about 2 million to 11,500 years ago. Many ice ages occurred during that time. During the Pleistocene Epoch, the huge Laurentide Ice Sheet covered much of what are now Canada and the northern United States. Today, many valley glaciers around the world are retreating and thinning in response to a global warming trend that began in the late 1800's.

How glaciers move. Gravity causes the Ice in a glacier to move. From the surface down to a depth of about 130 feet (40 meters), the ice is brittle. This area can become stretched or compressed as the glacier changes its speed or moves over uneven or steep terrain. The ice often breaks, forming deep cracks called crevasses. At greater depths, the ice in a glacier flows like a thick plastic without breaking. At these depths, the pressure of the overlying layers causes ice crystals to change shape and regroup. These small changes in the individual crystals cause the entire ice mass to move internally.

Glaciers move over the ground at different speeds. Heat from the ground and friction causes some melting at the bottom of a temperate glacier. The meltwater lubricates the bedrock, causing the glacier to slide over the ground more quickly. Temperate glaciers typically advance only 1 inch (2.5 centimeters) or so a day, but, in steep terrain, such glaciers can move as much as 20 feet (6 meters) per day. Pressure from an icecap or ice sheet can push some outlet glaciers from about 30 to 100 feet (9 to 30 meters) per day. The various parts of a glacier can also move at different speeds. For example, the central and uppermost portions of a valley glacier flow the fastest. Friction with the valley walls and floor causes the sides and bottom of the glacier to move more slowly.

How glaciers shape the land. The impact of prehistoric glaciers can be seen in many modern landscapes. For example, the rolling terrain of the northern United States was shaped by glaciers that melted more than 10,000 years ago. Geologists believe ancient glaciers also carved long, narrow inlets called *fiords* in Norway and similar features found in Alaska, British Columbia, Maine, Newfoundland and Labrador, Greenland, and New Zealand.

Advancing glaciers create a variety of landforms by eroding, transporting, and depositing rock debris. Meltwater from glaciers can enter cracks in the bedrock. This water then freezes and expands, breaking away pieces of rock that are carried off by the glacier. Glaciers also scoop up rock debris and drag it along at their bases. This debris polishes, scratches, or grooves exposed bedrock as the glacier scrapes over it. Valley glaciers can carve sharp-bottomed,

V-shaped river valleys into gently curving, U-shaped valleys. An advancing glacier can shape a rocky knob into a formation called a *stoss-and-lee* feature. The side that faced the approaching glacier, called the *stoss* side, is smooth and gently sloping. The opposite side, called the *lee* side, is rough and steep.

A moving glacier transports and deposits till, angular rock fragments that range in size from gravel to boulders. Glaciers deposit till in uneven ridges known as moraines. A *ground moraine* forms under the glacier and features an irregular surface. Ridges called *lateral moraines* develop along the sides of a valley glacier. Where two valley glaciers come together, their lateral moraines merge to form a *medial moraine* where the two streams of ice meet. A *terminal moraine*, or *end moraine*, marks the farthest point of advance of a valley or piedmont glacier. A *recessional moraine* forms when a glacier that was retreating begins to advance or temporarily halts. Advancing glaciers can also deposit till in an oval-shaped hill called a *drumlin*.

Glaciers also shape the land as they thin and retreat. Meltwater flows over, under, and through the ice of a retreating glacier. Streams of meltwater carry rock fragments freed from the ice by melting. This process polishes and rounds the fragments and separates them by size, leaving fragments of different sizes in different deposits. An esker is a narrow, winding ridge of sand and gravel deposited by a stream of water flowing through a tunnel or crevasse in a melting glacier. Sometimes, large chunks of melting ice become buried by sediment. These chunks melt slowly, leaving behind a *kettle*, a circular or oval depression that fills with water. Streams draining a melting glacier transport sediment over a broad, flat area known as an outwash plain.

Famous glaciers. The French and Swiss Alps feature some of the world's best-known glaciers, including the Mer de Glace on Mont Blanc and the Aletsch Glacier near the Jungfrau. Europe's largest glacier, Vatnajokull in Iceland, covers 3,130 square miles (8,100 square kilometers). Jostedalsbreen in Norway, the largest glacier on the European continent, covers about 190 square miles (490 square kilometers). The largest North American glacier outside Greenland is the 1,930-square-mile (5,000-square-kilometer) Malaspina Glacier near Yakutat Bay in Alaska's Saint Elias Mountains. Other North American glaciers include those in Banff National Park in Alberta, Glacier National Park in Montana, and on Mount Rainier in Washington. Some other well-known glaciers are in the Andes Mountains of South America, the Himalaya of southern Asia, and the Southern Alps of New Zealand.

Joseph M. Moran

Related articles in *World Book* include:		Additional resources
Alaska (Glaciers)	Icecap	Gallant, Roy A. *Glaciers*. Watts, 1999. Younger readers.
Alps (How the Alps were formed)	Iceland (The inland plateau)	Knight, Peter G. *Glaciers*. Stanley Thornes, 1999.
Great lakes (How the lakes were formed)	Lake (How lakes are formed)	Sharp, Robert P. *Living Ice: Understanding Glaciers and Glaciation*, 1988. Reprint Cambridge, 1991.
Ice age	Moraine	
Ice formation	Pleistocene Epoch	
Iceberg	River (picture: a melting glacier)	

Place a check mark next to the correct answers to questions 1 to 10.

1. The definition of glacier is found in

___ (a) the first paragraph of the article.

___ (b) the subtopic **Kinds of glaciers**.

___ (c) every subtopic in the article.

2. Information on how glaciers differ in shape, size, and location can be found in the subtopic

___ (a) **Kinds of glaciers.**

___ (b) **How glaciers form.**

___ (c) **How glaciers shape the land.**

3. According to the article, glaciers shaped the rolling terrain of

___ (a) southern Italy.

___ (b) central Brazil.

___ (c) the northern United States.

4. The article states that meltwater

___ (a) seeps deep into the ice mass, fills in spaces, and refreezes.

___ (b) increases the friction between ice particles.

___ (c) makes temperate glaciers move more slowly than polar glaciers.

5. The largest glacier on the European continent is

___ (a) Mer de Glace.

___ (b) Jostedalsbreen.

___ (c) Malaspina.

6. According to the article, which one of the following factors has the most influence on the size of a glacier?

___ (a) sea level

___ (b) movement

___ (c) climate

7. Which related article would appear first in the encyclopedia?

___ (*a*) Ice age

___ (*b*) Iceberg

___ (*c*) Iceland

8. Which one of the **Related articles** would most likely discuss glaciers in Europe?

___ (*a*) Alaska (Glaciers)

___ (*b*) Alps (How the Alps were formed)

___ (*c*) Great Lakes (How the lakes were formed)

9. Who wrote the article on glaciers?

___ (*a*) Peter G. Knight

___ (*b*) Roy A. Gallant

___ (*c*) Joseph M. Moran

10. In which volume of an encyclopedia would you look for both the article Iceberg and the article *Jostedal Glacier*?

___ (*a*) the volume marked G

___ (*b*) the volume marked H

___ (*c*) the volume marked I J K

D. Read the selection below from *The World Almanac and Book of Facts 2009*. Then answer the questions that follow.

Switzerland
Swiss Confederation

People: Population: 7,581,520. **Age distrib.** (%): <15: 15.8; 65+: 16. **Pop. density:** 493.7 per sq mi, 190.6 per sq km. **Urban:** 73.3%. **Ethnic groups:** German 65%, French 18%, Italian 10%.

Principal languages: German, French, Italian, Romansch (all national & official). **Chief religions:** Roman Catholic 42%, Protestant 35%, Muslim 4%, none 11%.

Geography: Total area: 15,942 sq mi, 41,290 sq km; **Land area:** 15,355 sq mi, 39,770 sq km. **Location:** In Alps Mts. in central Europe. **Neighbors:** France on W; Italy on S; Liechtenstein, Austria on E; Germany on N. **Topography:** The Alps cover 60% of land area; the Jura, near France, 10%. Running between, NESW, are midlands, 30%. **Capital:** Bern, 337,000. **Cities (urban aggr.):** Zürich, 1,108,000.

Government: Type: Federal republic. **Head of state and gov.:** The president is elected by the Federal Assembly to a nonrenewable 1-year term. **Local divisions:** 20 full cantons, 6 half cantons. **Defense budget:** $3.78 bil. **Active troops:** 22,600.

Economy: Industries: machinery, chemicals, watches, textiles, precision instruments, tourism, banking, insurance. **Chief crops:** grains, fruits, vegetables. **Natural resources:** hydropower potential, timber, salt. **Arable land:** 10%. **Livestock:** cattle: 1.6 mil; chickens:

8 mil; goats: 75,000; pigs: 1.7 mil; sheep: 450,000. **Fish catch:** 2,636 metric tons. **Electricity prod.:** (2006): 60.5 bil kWh. **Labor force:** (1998): agric. 4.6%, industry 26.3%, services 69.1%.

Finance: Monetary unit: Franc (CHF) (Sept. 2008: 1.14 = $1 U.S.). **GDP:** $300.2 bil; **per capita GDP:** $41,100; **GDP growth:** 3.1%. **Imports:** $184.9 bil; Germany 27.3%, Italy 10.1%, U.S. 9.1%, France 8.1%, Russia 7.6%, UK 4.9%, Austria 4.1%. **Exports:** $202.8 bil; Germany 21.5%, U.S. 9.5%, France 8.6%, Italy 8.4%, UK 5.3%. **Tourism:** $10.6 bil. **Budget:** $143.1 bil. **Intl. reserves less gold:** 28.14 bil. **Gold:** 36.82 mil oz t. **Consumer prices:** 0.7%.

Transport: Railroad: Length: 3,007 mi. **Motor vehicles:** 3.9 mil pass. cars; 353,100 comm. vehicles. **Civil aviation:** 12.8 bil pass.-mi; 42 airports. **Chief port:** Basel.

Communications: TV sets: 457 per 1,000 pop. **Radios:** 979 per 1,000 pop. **Telephone lines:** 5 mil. **Daily newspaper circ.:** 371.7 per 1,000 pop. **Internet:** 4.6 mil users.

Health: Life expect.: 77.9 male; 83.7 female. **Births** (per 1,000 pop.): 9.6. **Deaths** (per 1,000 pop.): 8.5. **Natural inc.:** 0.11%. **Infant mortality** (per 1,000 live births): 4.2 **HIV rate:** 0.6%.

Education: Compulsory: ages 7–15. **Literacy:** 99%.

Major intl. organizations: UN and most of its specialized agencies, EFTA, OECD, OSCE. **Embassy:** 2900 Cathedral Ave. NW 20008; 745-7900. **Website:** www.ch.ch

Switzerland, the former Roman province of Helvetia, traces its modern history to 1291, when 3 cantons created a defensive league. Other cantons were subsequently admitted to the Swiss Confederation, which obtained its independence from the Holy Roman Empire through the Peace of Westphalia (1648). The cantons were joined under a federal constitution in 1848, with large powers of local control retained by each. Switzerland has maintained an armed neutrality since 1815 and has not been involved in a foreign war since 1515. It is the seat of many UN and other international agencies but did not become a full member of the UN until Sept. 10, 2002. Switzerland is a world banking center. Stung by charges that assets seized by the Nazis and deposited in Swiss banks in WWII had not been properly returned, the government announced, Mar. 5, 1997, a $4.7 bil fund to compensate victims of the Holocaust and other catastrophies. Swiss banks agreed Aug. 12, 1998, to pay $1.25 bil in reparations. Abortion was decriminalized by a June 2, 2002 referendum. The rightist Swiss People's Party (SVP) topped Oct. 2003 parliamentary voting and entered a coalition government. In referendums June 5 and Sept. 25, 2005, voters backed plans harmonizing travel, asylum, law enforcement, and labor policies with the EU; more rights for same-sex couples were also endorsed June 5. Campaigning on an anti-immigrant platform, the SVP made further gains in the elections of Oct. 21, 2007.

Source for data: *The World Almanac and Book of Facts*. Copyright © 2009 World Almanac Education Group.

1. What is the capital of Switzerland?

_____

2. What are the official languages of Switzerland?

_____

3. How is the president of Switzerland chosen?

_____

4. How may Switzerland's topography have protected it from invaders over the centuries?

_____

_____

5. According to the article, what banking issue "stung" the Swiss in the 1990s?

_____

_____

E. Study the following results of an Internet search for Web pages dealing with Siberia. Then answer the questions that follow based on the results and on what you have learned about the Internet in this chapter.

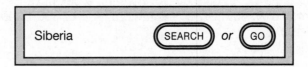

Results **21–30** of about **9,900,000** for **Siberia**

SIBERIA: CULTURE – ECONOMICS – BUSINESS

When a Westerner hears "**Siberia**", images of frozen tundra and prison camps come to mind. But things are changing even in this lost region. . . .
www.friends-partners.org/partners/**siberia**/ – Cached

Trans–**Siberia**.com

Trans–**Siberia**.com—all you need to know to help plan your journey across **Siberia** on the Trans–**Siberian** Railway including tours, books, advice and photos.
www.trans-**siberia**.com/ – Cached

About **Siberia** . . .

Siberia is an enormous area in north Asia spreading from the Urals in the west to mountainous ridges of the Okhotsk Sea coast in the east, from the Arctic . . .
www.sbras.ru/sicc/**siberia**_.htm – Cached

The Eskimo of **Siberia** – Index

Sacred-Texts Native American **Siberian** Inuit. The Eskimo of **Siberia**. by Waldemar Bogoras. [Leiden & New York, 1913]. Title Page · CONTENTS. I. — FOLK-TALES . . .
www.sacred-texts.com/nam/inu/eos/index.htm – Cached

WWF – Rare leopards captured by camera in east Siberia

Apr 25, 2008 . . . I didn't even know there were leopards in Siberia/Northern Asia. Animalsaver24, Member (April 26, 2008 at 14:21) . . .

www.panda.org/news_facts/newsroom/index.cfm?uNewsID=131901 – 23k – Cached

Siberian History Resources

Asian History research links for high school and college students.

www.snowcrest.net/jmike/siberia.html – 4k – Cached – Similar pages

Climate warning as Siberia melts

– earth – 11 August 2005 – New . . . Aug 11, 2005 . . . The world's largest frozen peat bog – a million square kilometres – is melting, according to Russian researchers just back from the area.

www.newscientist.com/article/mg18725124.500.html – 56k – Cached

A trip to Siberia

Impressions from my stay in Siberia Nov. 27 - Dec. 17, 2001.

mkolar.org/travel/Sibir/ – 5k – Cached

Siberia—Hell's Kitchen – New York Magazine Bar Guide

NOW CLOSED. NYC's best dive bar for meeting a celebrity. See the profile of this NYC bar at 356 W. 40th St. in Manhattan. Map of 356 W 40th St, New York, NY 10018

nymag.com/listings/bar/**siberia**/ – Cached

American Troops in Northern Russia and Siberia

In September 1917, the Russian Provisional Government asked the US for help in maintaining the Trans-Siberian railway. Two hundred eighty-five men from . . .

www.militaria.com/8th/WW1/**siberia**.html – Cached

Previous   1 2 3 4 5 6 7 8 9 10   Next

1. About how many matches altogether did this search find for Siberia?

_____

2. Why do you think that the words **Siberia** and **Siberian** are in bold in the search results?

_____

3. What is the page number of this screen of search results?

_____

4. Which Web page appears to contain information that was posted in April 2008?

_____

5. Which Web page would you most likely visit if you were planning to travel across the length of Siberia?

_____

6. How would you open the Web page of the entry **Siberian** History Resources?

_____

7. Which Web page would you most likely visit if you wanted to learn about the many cultures that live in Siberia?

_____

8. What are *two* ways in which you can get to the next page of research results for Siberia?

_____

9. Which Web page is NOT about the geographical area Siberia?

_____

10. If you placed the cursor one space after Siberia in the search box, then typed in— railway, and clicked on <u>Search</u>, which of the Web pages on the screen would least likely appear in the new results?

_____

11. You want to narrow your search on Siberia by finding Web pages on Siberia that mention Joseph Stalin and communism. How would you enter *Siberia, Joseph Stalin,* and *communism* in the search box?

_____

12. What is the real address of the Web page listed in the results as <u>American Troops in Northern Russia and **Siberia**</u>?

_____

13. What is the purpose of a link marked <u>cached</u>?

_____

14. When a real Web address ends in .com or .com/, that usually means it is the home page of a Web site. Therefore, which entry on the listing appears to be a home page?

_____

15. How would you start a new search on Antarctica?

_____

Chapter 10

Understanding and Remembering What Is Said

Being a good listener takes skill, especially if you want to understand and remember what is being said. To be a good listener, you need to concentrate on what is being said and interpret it correctly.

Concentration

Concentration is the act of keeping your mind on the thing you are doing at that moment. Athletes need to have good concentration. They cannot let the roar of the crowd distract them from their game. A surgeon in an operating room must have good concentration. So must someone operating a dangerous construction tool.

For most people, it is easy to concentrate when they are doing something they like to do. The real test comes when you have little interest in something the exact moment you are supposed to be doing it.

You know that it is important to get a good education. But sometimes you become *distracted*, meaning that you find it difficult to keep your mind on a lesson.

What are some of the things that could distract you during a classroom lesson?

_____

_____

Just about anything could be a distraction. It could be a worry you have about

something. Another student is trying to get your attention. There is noise in the hall outside your classroom. Someone's cell phone goes off. A bee flies in the classroom window.

The only one who can keep you from being distracted is you. Simply put, you have to develop ways to keep your mind on the topic.

Remember that the class you are in exists for your benefit. It exists to help you learn something you do not already know. You have just as much right as any other student to be in the class. In exchange for that right, you have the responsibility to be respectful of others and to pay attention to the lesson.

Here are some ways you can keep your mind focused on what the teacher is saying and on the questions and answers coming from other students:

1. Oddly enough, the first way takes place before you enter the classroom. If your teacher gives you a homework assignment to prepare you for the next day's lesson, be sure to do it. Starting a lesson with some idea of the topic will give you a head start in understanding what the teacher is saying.

2. Have a special word that you say to yourself when you are about to be distracted. The word could be "Later." So even when an important thing comes into your mind, tell yourself that you will think

about it later. "Diploma" is another word. It is a reminder that if you want to graduate, you had better stay on topic.

3. Make eye contact with your teacher. From time to time, you will need to look at the board or to look down to write notes in your notebook. Otherwise, keep your eyes on the teacher's eyes. It will keep you focused. The teacher will also be able to look into your eyes and judge whether you understand what is being said.

4. Think of the lesson as a contest. Everything in the world wants to distract you. Every noise, every other student, the teacher's voice, someone's coughing or sneezing, your emotions, cell phones, bees, worry—you name it! They are all in the contest to beat you. Give in to them, and they win. Tell yourself that you must win.

As you can see, concentration is a skill of the mind. It is an old saying but a true one: Control your mind or your mind will control you.

If you try hard to concentrate but do not succeed, you should talk to someone about your difficulty. Tell a teacher or counselor. Either one can direct you to people who are "skilled" in helping students to concentrate.

Interpretation

The second part of being a good listener is being able to interpret what is being said. You may know the term interpretation from studying a foreign language. In that sense, it means the translation of a word from one language, such as French, into another language. In this chapter, *interpretation* is the act of giving meaning to the words you are hearing and the ideas being expressed. In other words, the meaning may not be immediately obvious and you have to determine it.

Though it is a good idea to ask the teacher to explain something that you do not understand, do not rush to ask a question. Do not get angry or discouraged. Give the teacher time to explain and give yourself time to think about what is being said.

Here are some of the reasons why you will have to interpret what your teacher is saying:

Unknown Word or Phrase

You may hear a word or phrase you never heard before. You could ask the teacher to explain it. You could try to figure out what it means from how it is being used. You could write it down to find its meaning at the end of class. If you cannot spell it, write it down as it sounds.

Think about this statement:

For tens of thousands of years, cataracts have made travel on the Nile River difficult.

Even if you do not know what cataracts are, you can figure out some things. You just heard that the cataracts of the Nile have been around for tens of thousands of years. That probably means that they are not things made by people. They could be animals or insects. If not, they could be made by nature, maybe things in the river that block or slow down boats. For the moment, it is more important to know what they do than what they are exactly. When you look up the word later in a dictionary, you will see that cataracts are shallow stretches of water that are often rocky and that can move rapidly when running downhill. No wonder boat travel is difficult!

Words With Different Meanings

Words often have several meanings. Think about this statement:

China is a great country.

Does that mean that China is a large country, an important country, or a powerful country? Think of what else your teacher is saying about China and you will probably come up with why the word "great" was used.

Words That Sound Alike

Some words sound alike, but they are spelled differently and have different meanings. Think about these two statements:

1. His *descent* made the situation more difficult.

2. His *dissent* made the situation more difficult.

If your teacher just made either statement, you would not know whether you heard descent or dissent.

Here are the two statements again, but with more information:

1. We wanted him to stay up in the tree and scan the horizon for help. But he wanted to come down. His *descent* made the situation more difficult.

2. We hoped that he would agree with us and vote for the law. But he voted against it. His *dissent* made the situation more difficult.

Descent means "coming down." *Dissent* means "disagreeing." You will know which word your teacher meant only by listening to everything being said.

The Location of Words in a Statement

The order of words in a statement can change the meaning of the statement. Think about these two statements:

1. Bantu is spoken *only* in southeastern Africa.

2. *Only* Bantu is spoken in southeastern Africa.

The first statement tells you that southeastern Africa is the only part of the world where Bantu is spoken. The second statement tells you that no language other than Bantu is spoken in southeastern Africa. The placement of the "only" gives these two statements with the same words very different meanings. It should be pointed out that both statements are false.

The Inflection in a Voice

Inflection in a voice is the change in the sound of a word when it is spoken. For example, you say something and a person responds, "Right."

If "right" is said with sincerity, it probably means that the person agrees with you. But if the "right" is said in a mocking or funny voice, the person may be disagreeing with you.

The emphasis your teacher puts on certain words may affect the meaning of a statement. Think about the following statement:

The woman said she believes in democracy.

Written on the page, this statement seems simple enough. But when spoken, its meaning can by affected by the teacher's inflection. If the teacher emphasizes "said" in this statement or pronounces it in a mocking fashion, it might mean that the teacher does not believe that the woman really believes in democracy.

Fact or Opinion

Teachers have a difficult task when it comes to teaching controversial topics. They have a right to *express* their opinion. But they have a right to *teach* their opinion only when it is clear to the class that that is what they are doing.

Think about the following statements:

> In my opinion, the United States has caused many of Latin America's problems.
>
> The United States has caused many of Latin America's problems.

In the first statement, the teacher lets you know that the comment is an opinion. But is the second statement a fact or the teacher's opinion? Some people think that the second statement is a fact. Other people do not.

You want the knowledge a lesson has to offer. You may or may not want to agree with the opinions stated by the teacher or other students. Your task is to stay alert as to what is a fact and what is an opinion.

Note Taking: An Aid to Remembering

You have read in this chapter that if you understand what you are hearing, you are more likely to remember it. Still, it is impossible to remember everything. This is why you must take notes in class. Your notes should include more than what your teacher writes on the board. As you listen to what the teacher is saying, you will hear important facts and ideas that you should include in your notes.

The teacher will give clues as to what is important. If the teacher repeats something or spends a long time on it, it is probably important. The teacher might summarize the most important parts of the lesson just before the class ends. Likewise, the teacher might review the most important parts of a lesson at the beginning of the next day's lesson.

What should your notes look like? Do not try to write down everything the teacher is saying. Use key words and phrases when you do not have time to write sentences. Put stars next to the items that are most important. When it comes time to study for a test, the stars will remind you to go over those items thoroughly. Put question marks next to items you do not fully understand. Later, it will be easier to identify those items by the question marks. Above all, write notes that you will be able to read and understand the next day or next week.

Answer the following questions.

1. To concentrate is to

   _____ (a) do what you are doing.

   _____ (b) be distracted.

   _____ (c) remember what you hear.

Which answer did you choose? You have read in this chapter that concentration is the act of keeping your mind on what you are doing. Therefore, the answer to question 1 is (a).

2. Which one of the following is an example of interpreting what is being said?

   _____ (a) You let information come in one ear and go out the other.

   _____ (b) You concentrate on what is being said.

   _____ (c) You catch the humorous tone in the teacher's voice.

Which answer did you choose? You might think that the answer is (b). But interpretation is different from concentration. Concentration is keeping your mind on something. Interpretation is what your mind should be doing when it is concentrating. If you catch the humor in the teacher's voice, then you are using your interpretive skills. Therefore, the answer to question 2 is (c).

3. To remember what is said in a lesson, you should

   _____ (a) listen to what the teacher and other students are saying and not bother to take notes.

   _____ (b) concentrate on what is being said, interpret it correctly, and take notes on the important items.

   _____ (c) immediately ask the teacher or another student to explain an item that you do not understand.

What did you write? Choice (a) tells you not to take notes. Choice (c) tells you to ask the teacher or another student immediately to explain something you do not understand. From what you read in this chapter, neither choice would be a good idea. Choice (b) is a summary of this whole chapter and the answer to question 3.

Being a Good Listener Outside the Classroom

You should think of every classroom lesson as an opportunity to learn two things. The first is the topic of the lesson. It may be in history, geography, or English. The second is a skill, such as the one you are learning in this chapter. You may forget the subject matter over time. But if you practice being a good listener during every lesson, you will have a skill for life.

The following exercises will give more practicing in understanding and remembering what you have heard.

USING WHAT YOU HAVE LEARNED

A. Place a check mark next to the correct answers to questions 1 to 5.

1. Concentration is the act of

   ___ (a) remembering what you have heard.

   ___ (b) doing things that interest you.

   ___ (c) keeping your mind on the thing you are doing.

2. You are said to have poor concentration when you

___ (a) do not remember everything that is said.

___ (b) are easily distracted.

___ (c) do not understand what is being said.

3. Doing your homework for the next day's lesson will usually

___ (a) make it easier to understand the next day's lesson.

___ (b) confuse you during the next day's lesson.

___ (c) free you from having to pay attention during the next day's lesson.

4. The chief responsibility for becoming a good listener belongs to

___ (a) your teacher.

___ (b) a parent.

___ (c) yourself.

5. The most important part of taking good class notes is to

___ (a) write down everything the teacher says.

___ (b) write your notes in a way that you can understand them later.

___ (c) write notes only on the topics you do not understand.

B. Interpreting What Is Said

B-1. Figuring Out the Meaning of Words. Use the information in each statement to figure out the meaning of the word in *italics*. Then write what you think the meaning is.

a. The *preponderance* of evidence suggests that there really is a thing called global warming.

_____

b. The emperor was interested only in his own *aggrandizement* at the expense of his people.

_____

B-2. Choosing the Right Meaning of a Word. Each pair of statements contains the same word in *italics*. But the italicized word has a different meaning in each statement. Write what you think the italicized word means in the statement.

a. All *men* are created equal.   All *men* are expected to wear ties and jackets.

_____   _____

b. The people have the *right* to elect their rulers.   The people are *right* to demand lower taxes.

_____   _____

B-3. Words That Sound Alike. Read each of the following statements. Then explain what you think the *italicized* word means in that statement.

   a. The chief of the Masai tribe of Tanzania regarded the chief of the Kikuyu tribe in Kenya as his *peer*. But the Kikuyu chief thought of himself as having no equal.

   _____

   As the ship approached the *pier* in Cape Town, fireworks exploded over the city.

   _____

   b. We read in religious texts written thousands of years ago that *prophets* warned of hard times if the people did not repent of their sins.

   _____

   In today's world, *profits* seem to be the only thing that matters to businesses. The goal is to make money, and then make more money.

   _____

B-4. Watching Out for the Location of Words. The placement of the word in *italics* affects the meaning of each of the following statements. Explain what each statement is saying.

   a. The *damaged* train of bananas pulled into the station.

   _____

   The train of *damaged* bananas pulled into the station.

   _____

   b. The Ural Mountains touch both Europe and Asia as they extend north to south, forming a natural border between the two continents. On the other hand, the Himalaya Mountains can be found *only* in Asia.

   _____

   The man was wrong when he said that the Himalayas are the *only* mountains in Asia.

   _____

C. Listening and Note Taking

   1. How might maintaining eye contact with your teacher during a lesson help your concentration?

   _____

   2. What are two clues your teacher might give to show that the topic being discussed is important?

   _____

   _____

   3. How can you indicate in your notes that a topic is important?

   _____

   4. How can you indicate in your notes that you do not fully understand certain points that the teacher is making in class?

   _____

D. A Listening Exercise That Includes Taking Good Notes

Your teacher or an assigned person will read aloud the following selection. Your task is to listen carefully and take good notes on what is being said. Your teacher will then collect your notes. At a later date, your notes will be returned to you and you will be asked to explain what they say. It will be the teacher's choice whether you give your explanation just to the teacher or to part or all of the class. How well you explain what is in your notes will be an indication of how well you listened and took notes.

If I Were President

I hear many people say what they would do if they were president of the United States. Their ideas are usually simple. Blow up the enemy. Raise taxes. Reduce taxes. Pass a new law.

Lately, the talk is often about China. News stories tell of Chinese citizens put in jail without a trial for speaking out against the government. Americans strongly criticize the Chinese government for violating the rights of its people.

Should the United States carry on trade with a country that denies real freedom to its people? Many Americans say that we should stop importing goods from China until it becomes more democratic. They say that China will be forced to respect human rights if it wants to get our trade back.

That sounds simple enough! But other people think that being tough on China will not work and that it will hurt the United States. China has more than a billion people, the argument goes, and needs strict government control to maintain law and order. As for the trade, Americans will lose out on cheap imports. Like it or not, the United States buys a lot of Chinese goods. Buying them somewhere else will probably cost more money.

So what would I do if I were president? Stop trading with China in hope that the loss of American money will force the government to give its people more freedom? Trade with China in hope that trade exposes the Chinese people to the American way of life, and in time the people will demand more American-style freedom?

What to do? Be tough. Be patient. Maybe it's good I am not president.

Analysis Skills

Chapter 11
Charts

Have you ever wondered how many other families in the United States earn or receive about the same amount of money (income) as your family? One way to find out would be to read an article on family income. But this might take more time than you have. Also, you might have a difficult time finding the exact information you want. It would be easier and quicker to look at a *chart*, an arrangement of words and numbers that shows information in a clear and simple way.

The following chart divides families in the United States into six income groups. It shows the percent (%) of families in each group in 2007. A percent is a part of a hundred or of a total number.

Example: 10% of 50 = 5
10% of 100 = 10
25% of 100 = 25
25% of 200 = 50

U.S. FAMILY INCOME GROUPS IN 2007

Income Group	Percent of Families
$ 0–$19,999	12.1%
$20,000–$39,999	19.2%
$40,000–$59,999	17.3%
$60,000–$79,999	14.6%
$80,000–$99,999	11.0%
$100,000 and over	25.8%

1. What percent of families in 2007 made between $80,000 and $99,999?

_____ (a) 11.0 percent

_____ (b) 12.1 percent

_____ (c) 14.6 percent

Looking at the chart, you can see that on the same line as $80,000–$99,999 is 11.0%. Therefore, the answer to question 1 is (a).

2. To what income group does the largest percent of families belong?

_____ (a) $0–$19,999

_____ (b) $20,000–$39,999

_____ (c) $100,000 and over

Looking at the chart once again, you can see that the largest percent is 25.8%. On the same line as 25.8% is the income group $100,000 and over. Therefore, the answer to question 2 is (c).

3. What percent of families in 2007 had an income between $40,000 and $79,999?

_____ (a) 25.6 percent

_____ (b) 31.9 percent

_____ (c) 36.5 percent

An income between $40,000 and $79,999 can belong to one of these two groups:

$40,000–$59,999 or $60,000–$79,999. Add together the percent for each group: 17.3% + 14.6% = 31.9%. Therefore, the answer to question 3 is (b).

The chart on income shows one set of information, or group of statistics, namely, what percent of families in the United States was in each of six income groups in 2007. A chart can also show different groups of statistics at the same time. The following chart compares four sets of statistics for five countries in Southwest Asia/Africa.

COMPARING COUNTRIES OF SOUTHWEST ASIA/AFRICA

Country	Land Area (Square Miles)	Population (estimated 2008)	Literacy	Average Annual Income per Person (estimated 2007 in U.S. dollars)
Egypt	386,662	81,713,517	71%	$ 5,500
Iraq	167,556	28,221,181	74%	$ 3,600
Israel	8,019	7,112,359	97%	$28,500
Saudi Arabia	829,995	28,146,657	79%	$23,200
Syria	71,498	19,747,586	80%	$ 4,500

The four sets of statistics are

Land Area: the land size of the country, in square miles.

Population: how many people live in the country.

Literacy: the percent of people in the country who can read and write.

Average Annual Income per Person: the total of all the annual, or yearly, incomes in the country divided by the total number of people in the country. Example:

Total of annual incomes
People
$$\frac{\$30,000,000}{30,000} = \$1,000 \left\{ \begin{array}{l} \text{Average} \\ \text{annual} \\ \text{income} \\ \text{per} \\ \text{person} \end{array} \right.$$

(Note: The term "per capita," meaning per head, is often used in place of "per person.")

1. Which one of these Southwest Asian/ African countries on the chart has the largest population?

_____ (a) Egypt

_____ (b) Saudi Arabia

_____ (c) Syria

Which answer did you choose? Looking at the column marked Population, you can see that the largest number (81,713,517) is on the same line as Egypt. Therefore, the answer to question 1 is (a).

2. Using the chart, make a list of the five countries in the order of their land area, placing the largest country first.

1. _____

2. _____

3. _____

4. _____

5. _____

Looking at the column marked Land Area, you can see that the countries should be placed in the following order: Saudi Arabia (829,995 square miles); Egypt (386,662 square miles); Iraq (167,556 square miles); Syria (71,498 square miles); Israel (8,019 square miles).

3. How does the chart show that Israel has the highest percentage of people who can read and write? (Answer in two or three sentences.)

_____

_____

_____

_____

_____

What did you write? Here is an example of a possible answer to question 3.

In the column marked Literacy, you can see that Israel's literacy rate of 97% is much higher than the literacy rates in the other countries. Therefore, Israel has the highest percentage of people who can read and write.

The information you needed to answer questions 1 to 3 was shown on the chart. But what if a question asks for information that is not on the chart? Sometimes, of course, you won't be able to answer such a question. Other times you can find the answer by rearranging information on the chart or by combining two sets of statistics. For instance, by using the land area and population statistics on the chart, you can find the population density of each of the five countries. *Population density* means the average number of people living in a certain area, usually a square mile.

You can find the population density by dividing the population of a country by its land area. For example: To find the population density of the United States in 2008, you divide its population of 305,081,615 by its land area of 3,615,122 square miles, which comes out to more than 84 people per square mile.

With this information in mind, answer the following question.

4. Which of these countries has the highest population density?

_____ (a) Saudi Arabia

_____ (b) Syria

_____ (c) Iraq

Which answer did you choose? The country with the highest population density is the country that is the most crowded with people. To find out which one this is, divide the population of each of these countries by its land area. The one with the most people per square mile has the highest population density. Syria has a higher population density than Saudi Arabia or Iraq. Therefore, the answer to question 4 is (b).

5. At the time this chart was created, which word or phrase could have been eliminated if the population for 2008 and the average annual income per person for 2007 had been known?

_____ (a) estimated

_____ (b) square miles

_____ (c) in U.S. dollars

Which answer did you choose? Every ten years or so, most governments conduct a census, an official count of the population. The governments also collect statistics for each year between the last census and the present year. Though not as exact as a census, these statistics, known as estimated statistics, are based on the latest available information. This chart shows estimated statistics for population and average annual income per person and so it must use the word "estimated." If the chart showed "census" statistics, it would not need to use the word estimated. Therefore, the answer to question 5 is (a).

A. Study the following chart on immigration to the United States.

THE CHANGING FACE OF IMMIGRATION TO THE UNITED STATES
From Where Did the Immigrants Come?
Comparing 1905 and 2005

Area of the World	1905 Percent of Total Immigration	2005 Percent of Total Immigration
Europe	94.9%	13.7%
Asia	2.3%	26.7%
America (All countries of the Western Hemisphere except the United States)	2.5%	55.6%
Africa	0.1%	3.6%
Oceania (Australia, New Zealand, Pacific Islands)	0.1%	0.1%
All other areas of the world	0.1%	0.3%

Place a check mark next to the correct answers to questions 1 to 5.

1. The chart shows

   ___ (*a*) the number of immigrants who came to the United States in 1905 and 2005.

   ___ (*b*) what percentage of immigrants came to the United States from various countries between 1905 and 2005.

   ___ (*c*) that the percentage of immigrants coming to the United States from different areas of the world was not the same in 1905 as it was in 2005.

2. From which *one* of the following areas did the largest percentage of immigrants come in 1905?

   ___ (*a*) Europe

   ___ (*b*) Asia

   ___ (*c*) Africa

3. In 2005, the percentage of immigrants from Africa was

   ___ (*a*) 0.1 percent.

   ___ (*b*) 0.3 percent.

   ___ (*c*) 3.6 percent.

4. From which area did 55.6 percent of immigrants come in 2005?

   ___ (*a*) Asia

   ___ (*b*) America

   ___ (*c*) Europe

5. Which area had the least change in percentage from 1905 to 2005?

___ (*a*) Asia

___ (*b*) Oceania

___ (*c*) Africa

6. For both 1905 and 2005, choose the three areas listed on the chart from which the greatest percentage of immigrants came to the United States. Place the area with the largest percentage first, the area with the second largest percentage second, the area with the third largest percentage third.

1905	2005
1. _____	1. _____
2. _____	2. _____
3. _____	3. _____

7. What do you think is meant by the title of this chart, "The Changing Face of Immigration to the United States"? (Answer in three or four sentences.)

_____

_____

_____

_____

_____

_____

_____

_____

B. Study the following chart on telephone and Internet users in six countries.

TELEPHONE AND INTERNET USERS, BY COUNTRY, 1990 AND 2005
(rates per 1,000 People)

Country	Telephone (main lines)*		Cellular Phone		Internet	
	1990	2005	1990	2005	1990	2005
Australia	456	564	11	906	6	698
Canada	550	566	21	514	4	520
Israel	349	424	3	1,120	1	470
Japan	441	460	7	742	Not Known	668
Poland	86	309	0	764	0	262
United States	545	606	21	680	8	630

*Main line refers to a telephone that is connected to a phone line.

Place a check mark next to the correct answers to questions 1 to 8.

1. The chart

___ (a) shows how much time people in six countries spend on the telephone and the Internet.

___ (b) compares the numbers of telephone and Internet users in six countries in two different years.

___ (c) proves that people in some countries get their news from the Internet.

___ (d) gives the total number of telephones and computers bought in six countries in two different years.

2. The information given in the chart is for dates that are

___ (a) five years apart.

___ (b) 15 years apart.

___ (c) 20 years apart.

___ (d) 25 years apart.

3. Each figure on the chart represents the number of

___ (a) telephone users in a country.

___ (b) telephone and Internet users per 1,000 people in a particular country.

___ (c) telephone and Internet users per 10,000 people in a particular country.

___ (d) people in six countries who own a telephone and a computer.

4. Which one of these four countries had the smallest number of Internet users per 1,000 people in 2005?

___ (a) Australia

___ (b) Canada

___ (c) Japan

___ (d) Poland

5. In Israel in 1990, there were

___ (a) 3 cell phone users per 1,000 people.

___ (b) 21 cell phone users per 1,000 people.

___ (c) 460 cell phone users per 1,000 people.

___ (d) 1,120 cell phone users per 1,000 people.

6. Which one of these four countries had the smallest number of main line telephone users per 1,000 people in 2005?

___ (a) Canada

___ (b) Israel

___ (c) Japan

___ (d) United States

7. How many countries in the chart had more cellular phone users than the United States in 2005?

   ___ (a) one

   ___ (b) two

   ___ (c) three

   ___ (d) four

8. In 2005, how many more Internet users per 1,000 people did the United States have than Canada?

   ___ (a) 30

   ___ (b) 50

   ___ (c) 110

   ___ (d) 160

9. What information about cell-phone use in Japan might explain why the number of users of main line telephones in that country did not increase much between 1990 and 2005? (Answer in two or three sentences.)

   _____

   _____

   _____

   _____

   _____

10. "Some countries are surpassing the United States in cell-phone and Internet use." Use the information in the chart to agree or disagree with this statement. (Answer in two or three sentences.)

    _____

    _____

    _____

    _____

C. Study the following chart on the countries of Southeast Asia.

COMPARING SOUTHEAST ASIAN COUNTRIES

Country	Population (estimated 2008)	Population Density (people per square mile)	Land Area (square miles)	Average Annual Income per Capita (estimated in 2007 U.S. dollars, except as noted)
Cambodia	14,241,640	204	69,900	$1,800 (2006)
Indonesia	237,512,355	320	741,096	$3,400
Laos	6,677,534	73	91,428	$2,100
Malaysia	25,274,133	199	127,316	$13,300
Myanmar	47,758,181	182	261,969	$1,600 (2005)
Philippines	96,061,683	829	115,124	$3,400
Singapore	4,608,167	17,259	267	$49,700
Thailand	65,493,298	330	198,455	$7,900
Vietnam	86,116,559	677	127,243	$2,600
Totals	583,743,550	2,230	1,732,798	$9,533

Place a check mark next to the correct answers to questions 1 to 7.

1. Which country in Southeast Asia had the largest population?

___ (*a*) Indonesia

___ (*b*) Malaysia

___ (*c*) Vietnam

2. Which country in Southeast Asia has a land area of 198,455 square miles?

___ (*a*) Philippines

___ (*b*) Laos

___ (*c*) Thailand

3. Which country of Southeast Asia had the lowest population density?

___ (*a*) Laos

___ (*b*) Cambodia

___ (*c*) Malaysia

4. The three countries of Southeast Asia with the lowest annual income per capita were

___ (*a*) Philippines, Cambodia, Thailand.

___ (*b*) Cambodia, Laos, and Myanmar.

___ (*c*) Laos, Myanmar, and Indonesia.

5. What is the total population of all the countries of Southeast Asia that are listed?

___ (*a*) 318,743,550

___ (*b*) 413,743,550

___ (*c*) 583,743,550

6. How many countries had an annual income per capita above the average annual income per capita?

___ (a) two

___ (b) three

___ (c) four

7. How many countries have a land area of more than 100,000 square miles?

___ (a) two

___ (b) four

___ (c) six

8. Arrange the following five countries of Southeast Asia in the order of their population, placing the country with the largest population first, the next largest second, and so on: Indonesia, Myanmar, Philippines, Thailand, Vietnam.

1. _____

2. _____

3. _____

4. _____

5. _____

9. The Philippines had a larger population than Singapore. Yet Singapore had a greater population density than the Philippines. What information in the chart will give you the reason for this? (Answer in two or three sentences.)

_____

_____

_____

_____

_____

10. What information in the chart will most likely change when the countries listed conduct their next censuses? (Answer in two or three sentences.)

_____

_____

_____

_____

_____

Chapter 12
Picture and Circle Graphs

Charts are not the only way to make statistics easy to understand. Another way is to show statistics in drawings called *graphs*. In this chapter, you will learn about two kinds of graphs: picture graphs, or pictographs, and circle graphs.

Picture Graphs

The *picture graph* at the bottom of the page compares the population of five cities around the world.

Because it is a picture graph, the population statistics are given in pictures, or symbols, rather than in numbers. The note at the top of the graph states that each human figure symbol stands for 1 million people. By counting the number of symbols and multiplying by 1 million, you can find the population of each city.

1. Which city on the graph has the largest population?

_____ (a) Mumbai

_____ (b) Shanghai

_____ (c) Moscow

Which answer did you choose? Remember that each symbol on the graph stands for 1 million people. Because you are looking for the city with the largest population, you should be looking for the city with the greatest number of symbols. The city of Shanghai has the most symbols ($18\frac{1}{2}$). Therefore, the answer to question 1 is (b).

2. Which city on the graph has a population of $9\frac{1}{2}$ million?

_____ (a) Kinshasa

_____ (b) Rio de Janeiro

_____ (c) Moscow

Population of Five Cities

Cities	Population
(🧍 = 1 million people)	
Kinshasa, Democratic Republic of the Congo	🧍🧍🧍🧍🧍🧍🧍🧍🧍🧍
Shanghai, China	🧍🧍🧍🧍🧍🧍🧍🧍🧍🧍🧍🧍🧍🧍🧍🧍🧍🧍🧍
Moscow, Russia	🧍🧍🧍🧍🧍🧍🧍🧍🧍🧍🧍🧍
Rio de Janeiro, Brazil	🧍🧍🧍🧍🧍🧍🧍
Mumbai (Bombay), India	🧍🧍🧍🧍🧍🧍🧍🧍🧍🧍🧍🧍

Which answer did you choose? Because each symbol on the graph stands for 1 million people, a population of 9½ million has 9½ symbols. Kinshasa has 9½ symbols on the graph. Therefore, the answer to question 2 is (a).

3. Which two cities are closest in population?

_____ (a) Mumbai and Moscow

_____ (b) Kinshasa and Rio de Janeiro

_____ (c) Shanghai and Mumbai

Which answer did you choose? No two cities on the graph have the same population. But the two cities with the closest number of symbols are Moscow with 12½ symbols and Mumbai with 13½ symbols. Therefore, the answer to question 3 is (a).

4. Arrange the cities on the graph in order of their population. Place the city with the largest population first, the next largest second, and so on.

1. _____

2. _____

3. _____

4. _____

5. _____

How did you arrange these cities? Shanghai has the largest population with 18½ symbols. Mumbai is second with 13½ symbols. Moscow is third with 12½ symbols. Kinshasa is fourth with 9½ symbols. Rio de Janeiro is fifth with 7 symbols.

Picture graphs can show many other things besides differences in population. To show other subjects, different symbols are used. The meaning of the symbols is always explained on the graph.

Circle Graphs

Another important kind of graph is the *circle graph*, also called pie graph. This graph is divided into parts, or sections, that look like pieces of a pie. Each section stands for a certain percentage of the whole graph. All the sections of the graph add up to 100%.

Look at the following circle graph. It shows the percentage of land area that is contained in each continent. The graph lets

you see that all the sections or continents add up to 100%. It also lets you easily compare the sections with one another.

The Seven Continents' Land Area

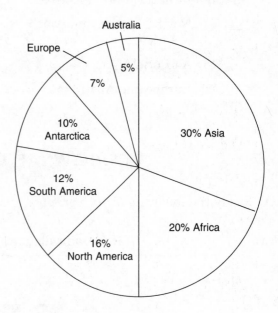

1. Which is the largest continent in land area?

_____ (a) Europe

_____ (b) Asia

_____ (c) Africa

Which answer did you choose? Remember that the largest continent has the highest percentage of the total land area. The highest percentage (30%) belongs to Asia. Therefore, the answer to question 1 is (b).

2. What percentage of the total land area is contained in South America?

_____ (a) 30 percent

_____ (b) 20 percent

_____ (c) 12 percent

Which answer did you choose? Look at the section of the graph labeled South America. You can see that South America contains 12% of the total land area. Therefore, the answer to question 2 is (c).

3. Which continent on the graph contains 16% of the total land area?

_____ (a) Africa

_____ (b) North America

_____ (c) Australia

What was your answer? The graph shows that North America contains 16% of the total land area. So the answer to question 3 is (b).

4. Which two continents added together contain 50% of the total land area?

_____ (a) North America and South America

_____ (b) Asia and Africa

_____ (c) Europe and Australia

What was your answer this time? The only two continents on the graph with land areas that add up to 50% are Asia with 30% and Africa with 20%. Together they contain one-half of the total land area. Therefore, the answer to question 4 is (b).

Being able to analyze picture graphs and circle graphs is another important Social Studies skill. The following exercises will give you more practice in using this skill.

USING WHAT YOU HAVE LEARNED

A. Study the following picture graph.

Railroad Mileage In Five African Countries

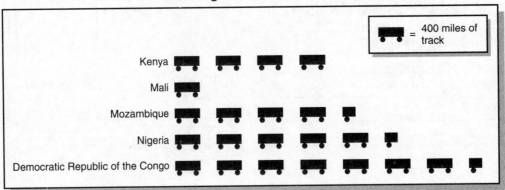

Place a check mark next to the correct answers to questions 1 to 8.

1. The picture graph shows

___ (a) the railroad mileage in five African countries.

___ (b) the number of railroad cars in five African countries.

___ (c) the five African countries with the longest railroad mileage.

2. The symbol used in this picture graph to represent miles of railroad is

___ (a) a railroad station.

___ (b) a railroad car.

___ (c) an automobile.

3. Each symbol on the graph stands for

___ (a) 100 miles of track.

___ (b) 250 miles of track.

___ (c) 400 miles of track.

4. Which country on the graph has just 1,600 miles of railroad track?

___ (a) Kenya

___ (b) Mali

___ (c) Democratic Republic of the Congo

5. Which country on the graph has the most miles of railroad track?

___ (a) Mozambique

___ (b) Democratic Republic of the Congo

___ (c) Kenya

6. How many miles of railroad track does Nigeria have?

___ (a) 2,000 miles

___ (b) 2,200 miles

___ (c) 2,400 miles

7. Which two countries on the graph have fewer miles of railroad track than Mozambique?

___ (a) Mali and Democratic Republic of the Congo

___ (b) Kenya and Mali

___ (c) Nigeria and Kenya

8. What does the graph tell you about the size of each country named on the graph?

___ (a) Mozambique is the largest.

___ (b) Mali is the smallest.

___ (c) There are no details or facts to give you the answer.

9. Arrange the five countries on the graph in the order of their railroad mileage. Place the country with the most miles of railroad track first, the next highest amount second, and so on.

1. _____

2. _____

3. _____

4. _____

5. _____

10. Use the information on the railroad mileage graph to make a chart that has numbers and words instead of symbols.

_____

B. Study the following circle graph on religions in India.

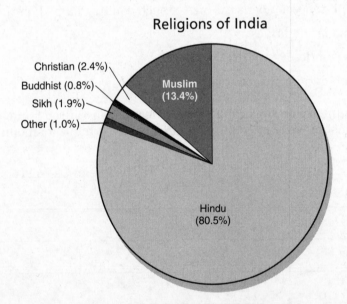

Religions of India

Christian (2.4%)
Buddhist (0.8%)
Sikh (1.9%)
Other (1.0%)
Muslim (13.4%)
Hindu (80.5%)

Place a check mark next to the correct answers to questions 1 to 4.

1. The circle graph shows

___ (a) how many people in India practice a religion.

___ (b) the growing importance of religion in India.

___ (c) what percentage of the Indian people practice each of the religions named on the graph.

2. What percentage of the Indian people practice the Muslim religion?

___ (a) 0.8 percent

___ (b) 2.4 percent

___ (c) 13.4 percent

3. Which religion in India is practiced by 2.4 percent of the people?

___ (a) Christian

___ (b) Buddhist

___ (c) Sikh

4. Which three religions are practiced by 95.8 percent of the Indian people?

___ (a) Christian, Sikh, and Hindu

___ (b) Muslim, Hindu, and Buddhist

___ (c) Hindu, Muslim, and Sikh

5. How does this circle graph show that the Hindu religion is the most widely practiced religion in India? (Answer in one or two sentences.)

_____

_____

_____

_____

C. Study the following circle graph on energy use in the United States.

United States Energy Use By Energy Source, 2007

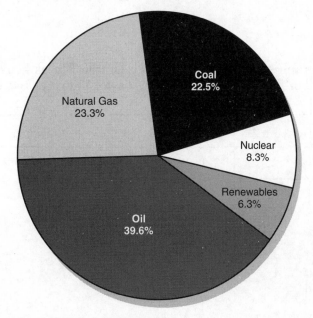

*Renewable energy sources can replenish or reproduce themselves. They include wood, waste, alcohol, hydropower, solar power, and wind power.

Place a check mark next to the correct answers to questions 1 to 5.

1. The graph shows

___ (*a*) the amount of energy used by the United States in 2007.

___ (*b*) the importance of using different energy sources.

___ (*c*) the percentage of different energy sources used in the United States in 2007.

2. Which one of the following was the leading source of energy used in the United States in 2007?

___ (*a*) coal

___ (*b*) oil

___ (*c*) natural gas

3. Which one of the following was the third-most-used energy source in the United States in 2007?

___ (*a*) coal

___ (*b*) natural gas

___ (*c*) nuclear

4. How much of the energy used in the United States in 2007 came from nuclear power?

___ (*a*) 7.0 percent

___ (*b*) 8.3 percent

___ (*c*) 22.5 percent

5. Hydropower, a renewable energy source, accounted for 2.4% of the energy used in the United States in 2007. How much of the energy used in the United States in 2007 came from renewable sources other than hydropower?

___ (*a*) 3.9 percent

___ (*b*) 7.0 percent

___ (*c*) 9.9 percent

6. How does the graph show that in 2007 the United States heavily depended on coal, natural gas, and oil for its energy needs? (Answer in one or two sentences.)

_____

_____

_____

Chapter 13

Bar Graphs

Another way to show information is by means of a *bar graph*. On such a graph, bars of different lengths are used to compare facts or statistics.

Simple Bar Graphs

The graph on this page uses bars to show the number of automobiles produced in 2007 by six countries. (These six countries were the leading producers of automobiles then.) At the top of each bar you can see the number of automobiles produced by each country. After the title of the graph is a note telling us that each number stands for millions of automobiles. For example, the number on top of Germany is 6.2. This means that Germany produced 6.2 million cars in 2007.

Be sure to check to see if a graph has a date or year. The information on this auto-mobile production graph is true only for 2007. Another graph with a different date or year would probably show different statistics.

Answer the following questions by referring to the automobile production graph.

1. The production of automobiles on the graph is shown in

_____ (*a*) tens of thousands of automobiles.

_____ (*b*) millions of automobiles.

_____ (*c*) tens of millions of automobiles.

Which answer did you choose? Look at the top of the graph. It shows the words "(in millions of automobiles)." This lets you know that the number on top of each bar stands for millions of automobiles. Therefore, the answer to question 1 is (*b*).

Leading Producers of Automobiles in 2007 (in millions of automobiles)

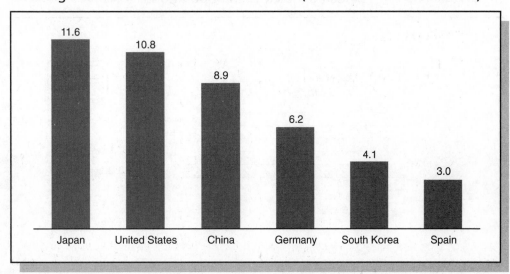

| Japan | United States | China | Germany | South Korea | Spain |
| 11.6 | 10.8 | 8.9 | 6.2 | 4.1 | 3.0 |

105

2. In 2007, China, Germany, South Korea, and Spain combined produced

____ (*a*) fewer automobiles than Japan and the United States combined.

____ (*b*) as many automobiles as Japan and the United States combined.

____ (*c*) more automobiles than Japan and the United States combined.

Which answer did you choose? The number of China, Germany, South Korea, and Spain add up to 22.2. The numbers for Japan and the United States added up to 22.4. Therefore, the answer to question 2 is (*a*).

Double Bar Graphs

Some bar graphs can show more than one kind of information at the same time.

The bar graph at the bottom of the page compares the population of four countries. Because it has two bars for each country, it is called a *double bar graph*. The first bar ☐ stands for the population in 2007 and the second bar ▨ for the expected population in the year 2050.

Answer the following questions using this double bar population graph.

1. Which country on the graph had the largest population in 2007?

____ (*a*) India

____ (*b*) Brazil

____ (*c*) China

Which answer did you choose? The white bars on the graph stand for the population in 2007. The longest white bar stands for the largest population. China has the longest white bar. Therefore, the answer to question 1 is (*c*).

2. By the year 2050, which country is expected to have a total population of 228.5 million?

____ (*a*) Brazil

____ (*b*) India

____ (*c*) United States

What was your answer? This crosshatched bar ▨ on the graph stands for the expected population in the year 2050. The crosshatched bar marked 228.5 million belongs to Brazil. Therefore, the answer to question 2 is (*a*).

3. Which country on the graph had a population nearest to that of the United States in 2007?

____ (*a*) India

____ (*b*) China

____ (*c*) Brazil

Which answer did you choose this time? Look at the length of the white bar belonging

Expected Increases in Population

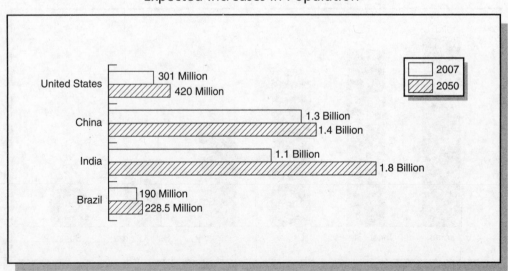

to the United States. Of the remaining three white bars, which one is nearest in length to the U.S. bar? You can see that Brazil's white bar is nearer in length than the white bars belonging to India and China. Therefore, the answer to question 3 is (c).

4. Which one of the following countries will probably have the largest increase (growth) in population by the year 2050?

_____ (a) China

_____ (b) India

_____ (c) Brazil

Which answer did you choose? Each country on the graph has two population bars. Of the three countries listed, find the one with the two population bars that are farthest in length from each other. It is the country that will probably have the largest increase in population. The bars that are farthest in length from each other belong to India. Therefore, the answer to question 4 is (b).

5. Why is this population graph called a double bar graph? (Answer in one or two sentences.)

_____

_____

_____

_____

_____

_____

What did you write? Here is an example of a possible answer to question 5.

This graph is called a double bar graph because two bars are used to show statistics for each country on the graph.

You have seen in this chapter how bar graphs show facts and information clearly and quickly. The following exercises will give you more practice in analyzing bar graphs.

USING WHAT YOU HAVE LEARNED

A. Study the bar graph on the next page.

Place a check mark next to the correct answers to questions 1 to 5.

1. The bar graph shows

___ (a) how many people worked in six South American countries in 2007.

___ (b) the per capita income of six South American countries in 2007.

___ (c) the per capita income of the poorest South American countries in 2007.

2. Which country on the graph had the highest per capita income?

___ (a) Argentina

___ (b) Brazil

___ (c) Chile

3. Which country on the graph had the lowest per capita income?

___ (a) Ecuador

___ (b) Argentina

___ (c) Chile

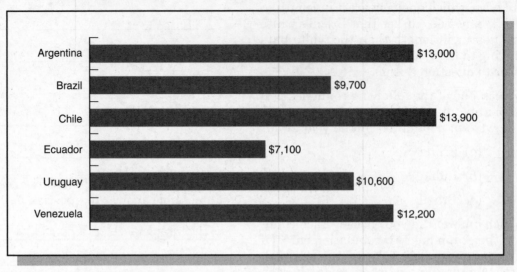

Per Capita Income in Six South American Countries in 2007

Country	Per Capita Income
Argentina	$13,000
Brazil	$9,700
Chile	$13,900
Ecuador	$7,100
Uruguay	$10,600
Venezuela	$12,200

4. Which country on the graph had a per capita income of $9,700?

___ (*a*) Brazil

___ (*b*) Uruguay

___ (*c*) Venezuela

5. Which two of the following countries had the closest per capita incomes?

___ (*a*) Ecuador and Chile

___ (*b*) Brazil and Uruguay

___ (*c*) Argentina and Venezuela

6. What do you think the following statement means?

"When you know the per capita income of a country, you know a lot more about a country than how much money its people make."

_____

_____

_____

_____

_____

_____

_____

B. Study the following bar graph on the immigration of people who came from other countries to live in the United States.

Immigration to the United States Since 1821

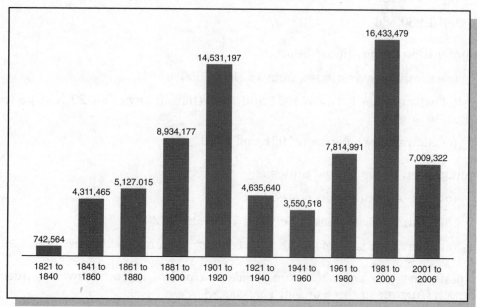

Place a check mark next to the correct answers to questions 1 to 8.

1. The bar graph shows how many people
   ___ (a) came to the United States between 1821 and 2006.
   ___ (b) were born in the United States between 1821 and 2006.
   ___ (c) left the United States between 1821 and 2006.

2. How many bars represent a 20-year period of time?
   ___ (a) none
   ___ (b) all except one
   ___ (c) all

3. The largest immigration to the United States took place between
   ___ (a) 1881 and 1900.
   ___ (b) 1901 and 1920.
   ___ (c) 1981 and 2000.

4. The smallest immigration to the United States took place between
   ___ (a) 1821 and 1840.
   ___ (b) 1921 and 1940.
   ___ (c) 1941 and 1960.

5. How many people immigrated to the United States between 1861 and 1900?
   ___ (a) 5,127,015
   ___ (b) 14,061,192
   ___ (c) 19,188,207

6. How many fewer people immigrated to the United States between 1961 and 1980 than between 1881 and 1900?

___ (a) 1,119,186

___ (b) 1,432,186

___ (c) 1,980,186

7. Immigration to the United States

___ (a) continually increased from 1821 to 2006.

___ (b) was greater between 1961 and 1980 than in any other 20-year period in U.S. history.

___ (c) slowed down between 1921 and 1960.

8. Immigration to the United States

___ (a) has continually decreased since 1921.

___ (b) continually increased between 1821 and 1920.

___ (c) was much greater in the 19th century than in the 20th century.

9. Explain how you know that the choice you picked as the answer to question 8 is correct. (Answer in three or four sentences.)

_____

_____

_____

_____

_____

_____

_____

10. Make a chart or pictograph to show the same information that appears on the immigration graph.

C. Study the following double bar graph on life expectancy in five countries.

Life Expectancy in Five Countries in 2007

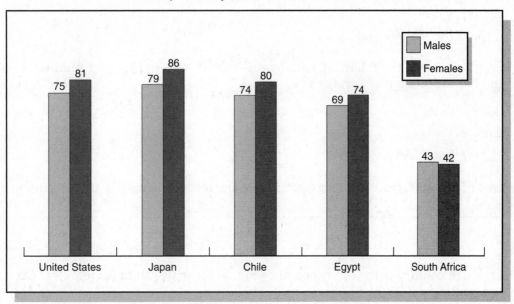

Place a check mark next to the correct answers to questions 1 to 6.

1. This double bar graph shows the life expectancy of

___ (*a*) males only.

___ (*b*) females only.

___ (*c*) males and females.

2. In which country can females expect to live the longest?

___ (*a*) Chile

___ (*b*) Egypt

___ (*c*) Japan

3. In which *two* countries is the number of years difference between the life expectancy of a man and a woman the same?

___ (*a*) United States and Chile

___ (*b*) United States and Japan

___ (*c*) Chile and Egypt

4. Which *one* of the following countries has the highest life expectancy for both females and males?

___ (*a*) United States

___ (*b*) Japan

___ (*c*) Egypt

5. Of the countries shown, the life expectancy of a man in Chile is closest to the life expectancy of a woman in

___ (a) South Africa.

___ (b) Egypt.

___ (c) the United States.

6. In which *one* of the following countries is the life expectancy of a man the closest to the life expectancy of a woman?

___ (a) Japan

___ (b) Chile

___ (c) South Africa

7. In which country can males expect to live the longest? (Answer in one sentence.)

_____

_____

8. In which country is the life expectancy higher for males than for females? (Answer in one sentence.)

_____

_____

9. How much longer can males in Japan expect to live than males in Egypt? (Answer in one sentence.)

_____

_____

10. Is the following statement true or false? Explain in one or two sentences.

"The double bar graph shows clearly why people in the United States live longer than people in Chile, Egypt, and South Africa."

_____

_____

_____

_____

_____

_____

Chapter 14
Line Graphs

Simple Line Graphs

A *line graph* uses one or more lines to show its information. When it uses only one line, it is often called a *simple line graph*.

The "simple" line graph below shows increases in world population from the year 1650 to the year 2100. It gives the world population for 1650, 1750, 1850, 1950, and 2000. It also shows the expected world population for 2050 and 2100. All these years are listed along the bottom of the graph.

Numbers in billions are listed on both sides of the graph. They stand for the number of people in the world.

Notice that there are six Xs on the graph. For each year, an X is drawn across from the population of that year. For example, look at the X above the year 1950. To find the world population in 1950, follow the X across to the population list on the right side of the graph. You can see that the world population in 1950 was just over 2 billion. In the same way, the other Xs can

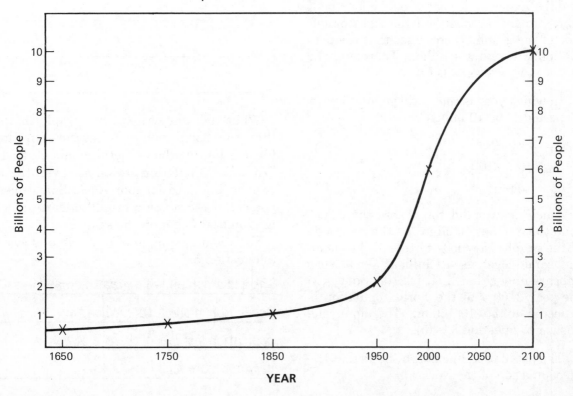

World Population Growth From 1650 to 2100

113

help you find the world population of the other years on the graph.

Most line graphs do not use Xs. They were put on this graph just to help you with this example. More important than the Xs is the line connecting them. Each X shows the world population for only one year. But the line lets you see how fast the world population has increased since 1650 and is expected to increase up to the year 2100.

Answer the following questions about the line graph.

1. The population figures can be found

_____ (a) along the bottom of the graph.

_____ (b) under each X.

_____ (c) along both sides of the graph.

What was your answer? On this graph the population figures can be found along both sides of the graph. Therefore, the answer to question 1 is (c).

2. What was the world's population in 1850?

_____ (a) about 1 billion

_____ (b) about 2 billion

_____ (c) about 3 billion

What was your answer? Find the year 1850 along the bottom of the graph. Next, find the X above the year 1850. Follow the X across to the numbers on the right or left side of the graph. You can see that the population was about 1 billion. Therefore, the answer to question 2 is (a).

3. In which year is the world population expected to be 10 billion?

_____ (a) 2050

_____ (b) 2100

_____ (c) 2200

Which answer did you choose this time? Find the number 10 billion on the right side of the graph. Now look for the X that is on the same level as 10 billion. What year appears under that X? It is 2100. So it is in the year 2100 that the world population is expected to be 10 billion. Therefore, the answer to question 3 is (b).

4. The population line graph shows that the population of the world

_____ (a) will stay the same over the next 20 years.

_____ (b) has been increasing since 1650.

_____ (c) never changes.

Which answer did you choose? If the line on the graph is straight across _____, it means that the population is staying the same. If the line is rising   , it means that the population is increasing. If the line is falling   , it means that the population is decreasing (becoming less). What kind of line do you find on this graph? One that is rising. This tells you that the population is increasing. Therefore, the answer to question 4 is (b).

5. How does the population line graph show that there will be a greater need to produce more food in the future? (Answer in one or two sentences.)

_____

_____

_____

_____

_____

_____

What did you write? This graph shows that the population will increase in the future, but it shows nothing about food. When the population grows, however, there is always a need for more food. Sometimes you can use facts on a graph to learn information that is not on the same graph.

Here is an example of a possible answer to question 5.

The line graph shows a great increase in

population in the future. When the

population increases, there is always a

need for more food.

Double Line Graphs

The line of the population graph shows one set of statistics: the changing population between 1650 and 2100. But you may want to put two sets of statistics on a line graph. To do this, you must use a separate line for each.

The graph on the foreign trade of Brazil at the bottom of the page uses two lines: a broken line and a solid line.

The value (cost or worth) of imports is shown by the broken line ----------. By looking at this line, we can tell how much money Brazil spent in five-year periods since 1980 to buy goods from other countries. To find out the value of Brazilian exports, we must look at the solid line ————. It shows how much money Brazil made in five-year periods since 1980 by selling goods to other countries. Because this graph uses two lines, it is called a *double line graph*.

1. The double line graph uses two lines to

_____ (a) show two different years.

_____ (b) make the graph easier to read.

_____ (c) show two different sets of statistics.

Which answer did you choose? This foreign trade graph uses two lines to show the imports and exports of Brazil: the broken one for the value of imports and the solid one for the value of exports. Therefore, the answer to question 1 is (c).

2. What was the value of exports in 1985?

_____ (a) slightly more than 15 billion U.S. dollars

_____ (b) slightly more than 25 billion U.S. dollars

_____ (c) slightly more than 35 billion U.S. dollars

Which answer did you choose? Find the year 1985 along the bottom of the graph and the solid line above the year 1985. (The solid line stands for the value of exports.) Place your finger on the solid line over 1985. If you move your finger directly across to the numbers on the left side of the graph, your finger will match up with 25, or more exactly just above 25. This means that the value of exports in 1985 was slightly more than 25 billion U.S. dollars. Therefore, the answer to question 2 is (b).

3. In which year was the value of Brazil's imports 20 billion U.S. dollars?

_____ (a) 1990

_____ (b) 1995

_____ (c) 2000

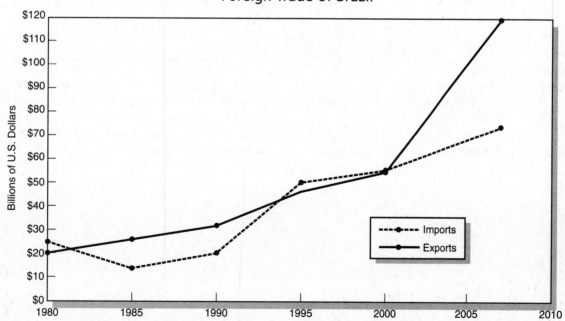

Foreign Trade of Brazil

What was your answer? Find the number 20 on the left side of the graph. The broken line stands for imports, so place your finger on the 20 and move it across the graph until it meets the broken line. Then look at the year below where your finger met the broken line. The year is 1990. This means that in 1990 the value of Brazilian imports was 20 billion U.S. dollars. Therefore, the answer to question 3 is (a).

4. What was the total value of all foreign trade in Brazil in 2000?

_____ (a) 25 billion U.S. dollars

_____ (b) 56 billion U.S. dollars

_____ (c) 111 billion U.S. dollars

What was your answer? To determine the total value of all foreign trade, you add the imports and the exports together. For 2000, the imports are valued at 56 billion U.S. dollars and the exports at 55 billion U.S. dollars. When you add these two numbers together, you get 111 billion U.S. dollars for the total value of all foreign trade in 2000. Therefore, the answer to question 4 is (c).

5. In which two years was the value of imports higher than the value of exports?

_____ (a) 1980 and 1990

_____ (b) 1980 and 1995

_____ (c) 1990 and 1995

What was your answer this time? You know that the broken line stands for imports and the solid line stands for exports. Does the broken line ever appear higher on the graph than the solid line? Yes, over the years 1980 and 1995. This means that the value of imports was higher than the value of exports in 1980 and 1995. Therefore, the answer to question 5 is (b).

6. How does the graph show that between 1980 and 2005, exports continually increased, but imports did not always increase? (Answer in three or four sentences.)

_____

_____

_____

_____

_____

_____

_____

_____

What did you write? Here is an example of a possible answer to question 6.

The export line went higher for each five-year period between 1980 and 2005. This means that between 1980 and 2005, exports continually increased. On the other hand, the import line dipped between 1980 and 1985. This means that imports did not always increase between 1980 and 2005.

Line graphs are used in many newspapers, books, and magazines. Being able to analyze them is an important Social Studies skill. The following exercises will give you more practice in developing this skill.

A. Study the following line graph on world production of crude oil.

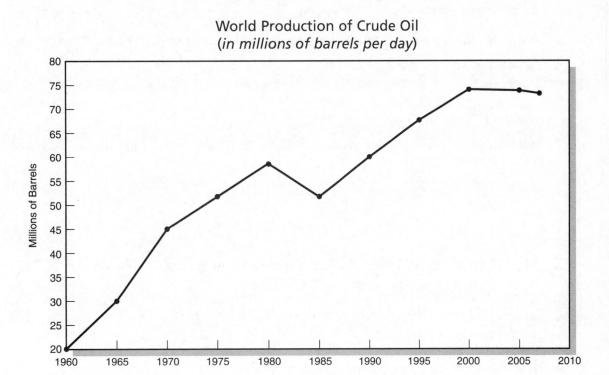

World Production of Crude Oil
(*in millions of barrels per day*)

Place a check mark next to the correct answers to questions 1 to 9.

1. The line graph shows how much crude oil

___ (*a*) was used throughout the world between 1960 and 2007.

___ (*b*) the United States exported to other countries between 1960 and 2007.

___ (*c*) was produced per day throughout the world between 1960 and 2007.

2. Oil production is shown on the graph in

___ (*a*) millions of barrels per day.

___ (*b*) millions of barrels per year.

___ (*c*) billions of barrels per day.

3. Most of the graph is divided into

___ (*a*) one-year time periods.

___ (*b*) five-year time periods.

___ (*c*) ten-year time periods.

4. The line of the graph shows that oil production

___ (*a*) increased for every year given.

___ (*b*) decreased for every year given.

___ (*c*) increased or decreased depending on the year given.

5. How much oil was produced in 1970?

    ___ (a) about 21 million barrels per day

    ___ (b) about 46 million barrels per day

    ___ (c) about 59 million barrels per day

6. In which year were about 30 million barrels of oil produced per day?

    ___ (a) 1965

    ___ (b) 1980

    ___ (c) 1995

7. In which one of the following years did oil production decrease from the year (or time period) before?

    ___ (a) 1965

    ___ (b) 1975

    ___ (c) 1985

8. Oil production for 2005 was almost the same as that for the combined years of

    ___ (a) 1960 and 1965.

    ___ (b) 1960 and 1970.

    ___ (c) 1960 and 1975.

9. How much more oil was produced in 2007 than in 1960?

    ___ (a) 42 million barrels per day

    ___ (b) 53 million barrels per day

    ___ (c) 64 million barrels per day

10. How does the graph show that oil production increased for most of the years between 1960 and 2007? (Answer in two or three sentences.)

    _____

    _____

    _____

    _____

    _____

B. Study the following double line graph on the foreign trade of Japan.

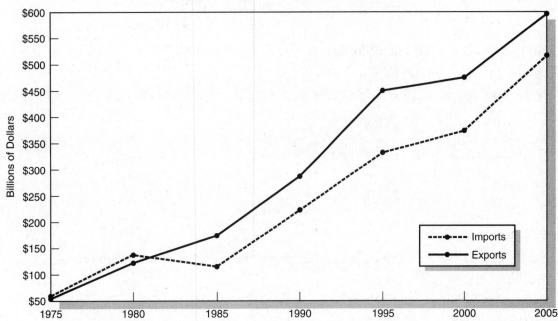

Foreign Trade of Japan, 1975–2005

Place a check mark next to the correct answers to questions 1 to 9.

1. The graph shows Japan's imports and exports for

____ (a) 5 years.

____ (b) 15 years.

____ (c) 30 years.

2. The solid line shows the value of Japan's

____ (a) imports.

____ (b) exports.

____ (c) total foreign trade.

3. In which year were Japan's imports greater than its exports?

____ (a) 1980

____ (b) 1990

____ (c) 2000

4. What was the value of Japan's exports in 1985?

____ (a) about $50 billion

____ (b) about $175 billion

____ (c) about $285 billion

5. In which year was the value of Japan's imports about $517 billion?

___ (a) 1995

___ (b) 2000

___ (c) 2005

6. What was the total of all foreign trade in Japan in 1995?

___ (a) nearly $800 billion

___ (b) nearly $444 billion

___ (c) nearly $107 billion

7. Japan's exports increased the most between

___ (a) 1975 and 1980.

___ (b) 1985 and 1990.

___ (c) 1990 and 1995.

8. In which year was the difference between the value of Japan's imports and exports about $53 billion?

___ (a) 1980

___ (b) 1990

___ (c) 1995

9. Between which two years did Japan's imports decrease in value while its exports continued to increase in value?

___ (a) 1980 and 1985

___ (b) 1985 and 1990

___ (c) 1995 and 2000

10. A *trend* is the general direction in which something moves. On occasion, the direction may change, but for the most part it remains the same. When the direction changes permanently, we say that a new trend has begun. Describe one trend that the graph shows involving Japanese imports and/or exports. (Answer in one or two sentences.)

_____

_____

_____

_____

_____

C. Study the following triple line graph. Use the same rules in studying this graph as you did in studying a double line graph.

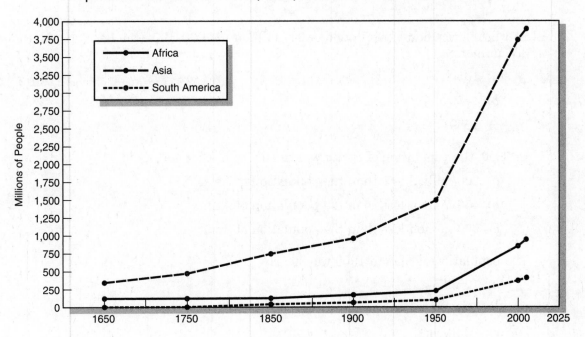

Population Growth In Africa, Asia, and South America Since 1650

Place a check mark next to the correct answers to questions 1 to 10.

1. South America is shown by which line?

___ (a) ----------

___ (b) ———

___ (c) —— —— ——

2. The population of Asia in 1850 was about

___ (a) 550 million.

___ (b) 750 million.

___ (c) 950 million.

3. The population of Africa in 2000 was slightly higher than

___ (a) 400 million.

___ (b) 800 million.

___ (c) 1.8 billion.

4. Which continent was the least populated in 1950?

___ (a) Africa

___ (b) Asia

___ (c) South America

5. The biggest increase in the population of Asia took place between

___ (a) 1650 and 1850.

___ (b) 1850 and 1950.

___ (c) 1950 and 2005.

6. South America had a population of 347 million in 2000. But Asia had a population of 335 million in

___ (a) 1650.

___ (b) 1750.

___ (c) 1850.

7. In 1650, the population of Africa was about

___ (a) 200 million less than the population of Asia.

___ (b) 450 million less than the population of Asia.

___ (c) 650 million less than the population of Asia.

8. The population of Asia in 1900 was nearly

___ (a) 1 million.

___ (b) 100 million.

___ (c) 1 billion.

9. Which statement is supported by the graph?

___ (a) The populations of Africa, Asia, and South America grew more between 1950 and 2005 than between 1650 and 1950.

___ (b) In 1750, the total population of Africa and South America was almost the same as the population of Asia.

___ (c) Since 1900, the population of South America has been greater than the population of Africa.

10. In 2005, the world population reached nearly 6.5 billion. From the graph, you can see that the majority of the world's population lived in

___ (a) Africa.

___ (b) Asia.

___ (c) Africa and South America.

Chapter 15
Photographs and Drawings

Pictures can tell a story or give information quickly and clearly. Many paragraphs may be needed to explain in writing what one picture shows. This is why pictures such as photographs and drawings are often used to teach Social Studies.

Photographs

Photographs show scenes and events as they look to the "eye" of the camera and to the person taking the picture. Look at the following photograph.

Picture A

© Toby Selander/Polaris Images

What does Picture A show? At first, the answer seems easy. Teenagers are doing what is called hip-hop dancing. You might know that hip-hop dancing began in the New York City borough of the Bronx. So you might think that this photograph was taken in the Bronx. But was it? The drawings on the wall behind the youngsters probably offer clues. But you would have to know what the images in the drawings represent.

This is why a photograph often comes with a caption next to or under it. In one or two sentences, the caption gives information to help you understand the full meaning of the photograph. Here is a caption for Picture A: "South African teenagers enjoy American hip-hop." With this caption, the photograph is no longer showing just young people dancing. More important, it shows the influence of American culture. South African youngsters, nearly 8,000 miles away from the Bronx, are performing a dance that began in that New York City borough.

Answer the following questions about Picture A.

1. Most likely, the five teenagers

    _____ (a) were paid to be in the photograph.

    _____ (b) have visited the Bronx.

    _____ (c) knew they were being photographed.

What answer did you choose? There is no way to know whether the teenagers were paid or ever visited the Bronx. But they are all looking into the camera. You could even say they are "showing off" for the camera. Therefore, the answer to question 1 has to be (c).

When you study a photograph, think about whether the people in the scene know they are having their picture taken. People often "perform" for the camera. People who do not know they are being photographed will probably reveal more of who they really are.

2. Why is the caption important to understanding the full meaning of this Picture A?

    _____

    _____

    _____

    _____

    _____

    _____

What did you write? Here is a possible answer to question 2.

The caption makes it clear that the teenagers are South African and hip-hop is American. With that information, a person is more likely to see that the photograph shows the influence of American culture on South African teenagers.

In looking at Picture A, did you ever think that it could be a fake? It used to be said that a photograph showed a scene as it really looked. But computer programs can now alter or change photographs. People can use the programs to add things to a photograph or take them out.

Picture A is real, but look at Pictures B and C.

Picture B

© Margaret Pelisson

Picture C

© Margaret Pelisson

You see two versions of the same photograph, which shows the lighthouse in Montauk, Long Island, in New York State. But the two versions do not show exactly the same scene. How are the scenes different?

Picture C is missing the tall structure to the left of the lighthouse. If you were to visit the lighthouse, you would see that structure. So Picture B shows the scene as it really is. Picture C was altered to remove the structure.

Photographs can be a valuable learning tool, but remember that computers can alter them in ways that are almost impossible to detect.

Drawings

You know that photographs are pictures taken with a camera. But the camera was invented in the mid-1800s, so it is impossible to have photographs of events that happened hundreds or thousands of years ago. Even since the invention of the camera, it has not always been possible to photograph every important event, person, or place.

Pictures made by an artist, or *drawings*, can take the place of photographs. Artists may be present at an event while it is happening. But if not, the artist has to read and study about the event before making a drawing of it. Remember that drawings, even though they may look like photographs, show only what the artist decided to put into the picture.

Look at the following drawing and its caption.

Ebony Magazine

Timbuktu in the 16th century. This great African city was destroyed by wars in the 1500s and was since rebuilt.

1. The drawing shows

_____ (*a*) a city, but it is impossible to know the name of the city.

_____ (*b*) the city of Timbuktu as it looked in the 16th century.

_____ (*c*) the city of Timbuktu as it looks today.

Which answer did you choose? The drawing shows a city. But you need a caption to find out the name of the city and to give you information about the city. Captions are just as important to drawings as they are to photographs. The caption of this drawing tells you that the city is Timbuktu as it looked in the 16th century. Therefore, the answer to question 1 is (*b*).

2. When you look at this drawing of Timbuktu,

_____ (*a*) you can be sure that this is how Timbuktu really looked.

_____ (*b*) you can compare this drawing with a photograph of Timbuktu.

_____ (*c*) you are seeing only what the artist wanted people to see.

Which answer did you choose this time? No one alive today has seen the city of Timbuktu as it was in the 1500s. No photographs exist of the city as it looked then because the camera had not yet been invented. Only through drawings do we know what the city may have been like. Some of these drawings were done centuries ago by people who saw Timbuktu with their own eyes. But proving that their drawings show Timbuktu as it really was would be difficult. You can be sure, however, that the artists drew Timbuktu as they wanted others to see it. Therefore, the best answer to question 2 is (c).

To get more information from pictures, ask yourself questions such as these when you look at a drawing or photograph:

- Does the picture show a present-day scene or something that happened in the past?
- Is it a country scene or a city scene?
- What kinds of buildings are shown? What are they probably used for?
- What kinds of people are shown? What are they doing? How are they dressed?
- What time of year is shown?

USING WHAT YOU HAVE LEARNED

A. Look at the following photograph and read the caption under it.

United Nations

A marketplace in Abidjan, the largest city of Côte d'Ivoire.

1. Describe what you can learn from this photograph without reading the caption. (Answer in two or three sentences.)

_____

_____

_____

_____

_____

_____

_____

2. What information in the caption could you *not* get just by looking at the photograph? (Answer in two or three sentences.)

_____

_____

_____

_____

_____

_____

_____

3. How does this photograph show that "traditional" Africa lives side by side with "modern" Africa? (Answer in two or three sentences.)

_____

_____

_____

_____

_____

_____

_____

The first atomic bomb was dropped on Hiroshima, Japan, on August 6, 1945. The United States dropped the bomb, hoping to bring an end to World War II. A week later, the Japanese surrendered and World War II was over.

B. Look at the photograph above and read the caption under it.

Place a check mark next to the correct answers to questions 1 to 3.

1. The destruction (damage, ruin) in the photograph was caused by

___ (*a*) an earthquake.

___ (*b*) a hurricane.

___ (*c*) an atomic bomb.

2. The photograph shows part of the city of

___ (*a*) Beijing.

___ (*b*) Hiroshima.

___ (*c*) Nagasaki.

3. The atomic bomb was dropped because

___ (*a*) the United States wanted to start a war with Japan.

___ (*b*) Japan had dropped an atomic bomb on the United States.

___ (*c*) the United States thought it would end World War II more quickly.

4. What details in the photograph indicate that the area shown was part of a city? (Answer in two or three sentences.)

_____

_____

_____

_____

_____

5. How does this photograph show that war is terrible? (Answer in two or three sentences.)

_____

_____

_____

_____

_____

C. Study the following drawing and read the caption under it.

Northwind Pictures

Napoleon's army retreating from Russia in 1812. Nearly one-half million French soldiers died trying to conquer Russia.

Place a check mark next to the correct answers to questions 1 to 5.

1. This drawing shows

___ (a) Napoleon's army on its way to Moscow.

___ (b) Napoleon's army retreating from Russia.

___ (c) the Russian army invading France.

2. The scene in the drawing took place in the

___ (a) winter.

___ (b) spring.

___ (c) summer.

3. You know that nearly one-half million French soldiers died in Russia because

___ (a) all the dead soldiers are shown in the drawing.

___ (b) the caption tells you.

___ (c) Napoleon is telling his generals the sad news.

4. There is no photograph of the event shown in the drawing because

___ (a) no one remembered to bring a camera.

___ (b) drawings are more interesting than photographs.

___ (c) the camera had not yet been invented.

5. Which one of the following statements is true?

___ (a) We know for sure that the artist was with Napoleon in Russia.

___ (b) The drawing shows only what the artist wanted us to see.

___ (c) Drawings never show events as they really happened.

6. History books tell us that Napoleon and his army suffered greatly during their invasion of Russia. How does the drawing on the previous page show some of the suffering experienced by Napoleon and his army? (Answer in two or three sentences.)

_____

_____

_____

_____

_____

Picture A

Commodore Matthew C. Perry of the United States sailed to Japan in 1853. This visit marked the first time an American was allowed to enter Japan.

Picture B

In 2008, Ryozo Kato, Ambassador of Japan to the United States, visited the New York Stock Exchange. Shown in the center, he rang the opening bell to begin the day's trading of stocks. The Stock Exchange often invites important visitors to New York City to ring the opening bell.

D. Look at the pictures on page 131 and read the captions under them.

Place a check mark next to the correct answers to questions 1 to 5.

1. Which statement is true?

   ___ (*a*) Pictures A and B are both drawings.

   ___ (*b*) Picture A is a drawing, and Picture B is a photograph.

   ___ (*c*) Picture A is a photograph, and Picture B is a drawing.

2. Picture A shows

   ___ (*a*) the arrival of Commodore Matthew Perry in Japan in 1853.

   ___ (*b*) the end of World War II.

   ___ (*c*) a scene in Japan today.

3. The caption to Picture A states that

   ___ (*a*) Japan was a poor country in 1853.

   ___ (*b*) the United States has copied many Japanese customs.

   ___ (*c*) Perry's visit was the first time an American was allowed to enter Japan.

4. Picture B shows

   ___ (*a*) the arrival of the Japanese ambassador to United States at the United Nations in 2008.

   ___ (*b*) a member of the New York Stock Exchange visiting Japan in 2008.

   ___ (*c*) the Japanese ambassador to United States on a visit to the New York Stock Exchange in 2008.

5. The people in Picture B are wearing

   ___ (*a*) traditional Japanese clothing.

   ___ (*b*) Western-style clothing.

   ___ (*c*) New York Stock Exchange uniforms.

6. Describe in your own words what you see in Picture A. (Answer in two or three sentences.)

   _____

   _____

   _____

   _____

   _____

   _____

   _____

7. Did Picture A have to be made while the scene it shows was taking place? (Answer in two or three sentences.)

_____

_____

_____

_____

_____

_____

_____

8. In what way are Pictures A and B telling a similar story? (Answer in two or three sentences.)

_____

_____

_____

_____

_____

_____

_____

_____

E. Study the following photographs.

Picture A

Picture B

Picture C

© Margaret Pelisson (all)

The ruins of the ancient city of Pompeii (Italy), with Mount Vesuvius in the background.

1. How might the three photos affect the way you look at the truthfulness of photographs from now on? (Answer in three or four sentences.)

_____

_____

_____

_____

_____

_____

_____

_____

2. Describe a reason why a person or a government would want to alter an image in a photograph. (Answer in three or four sentences.)

_____

_____

_____

_____

_____

_____

_____

_____

_____

Chapter 16
Political Cartoons

Most of us are familiar with drawings known as *cartoons*. They exaggerate (overstate) ideas and present them in a simplified form. They are usually funny, but they can also be serious.

When cartoons express a feeling or opinion about a current event, they are called political or editorial cartoons. You will find them in newspapers, in textbooks, and on the Internet. They are used in classroom lessons and appear on tests. Knowing how to interpret them is an important skill.

The drawing below may not look like a cartoon at first. It was drawn during World War I (1917–1918) to encourage young men to become soldiers. (Women did not serve in the armed services at that time.)

The man in the drawing is Uncle Sam. He is a made-up character who has represented the United States in art and writing for nearly 200 years.

Today, this drawing is often used as a cartoon with a personal or humorous caption, such as:

UNCLE SAM WANTS YOU

TO CLEAN YOUR ROOM

— or —

I WANT YOU

TO PAY HIGHER TAXES

Write a humorous caption of your own.

_____

_____

_____

_____

_____

_____

_____

_____

_____

_____

Library of Congress

Look at the following cartoon about Uncle Sam and answer the questions after it.

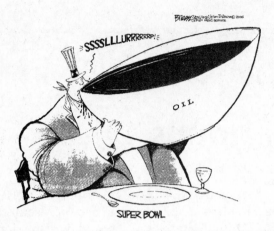

SSSSLLLURRRRRRP!

OIL

SUPER BOWL

Steve Breen, San Diego Union-Tribune © 2006

1. Which statement is most likely true?

_____ (a) The cartoon does not express an opinion.

_____ (b) The cartoon exaggerates the size of Uncle Sam and the bowl to express an opinion.

_____ (c) The cartoon shows the oil in the bowl in solid black to express an opinion.

Which answer did you choose? The artist (cartoonist) who drew the cartoon decided how the images would look. Uncle Sam and the bowl are much larger than the plate, spoon, and glass. More than likely, the cartoonist exaggerated Uncle Sam and the bowl to express an opinion. Therefore, the answer to question 1 is (b).

2. The bowl in the cartoon contains

_____ (a) olive oil.

_____ (b) peanut oil.

_____ (c) fuel oil.

Which answer did you choose? You might say that it is impossible to know from the cartoon what kind of oil is in the bowl. This brings up an important point. The cartoonist expects the viewer to have some knowledge of current events. Most people know that the United States needs more and more fuel oil to keep up its current style of living. Fuel oil powers most motor vehicles and heats many homes and businesses. If you know that, then you also know that the answer to question 2 is (c).

3. Do you think this cartoon is favorable to the way the people of the United States use oil? (Answer in two or three sentences.)

_____

_____

_____

_____

_____

_____

_____

What did you write? The exaggerated size of Uncle Sam and the bowl appear to be a criticism of the United States and its use of fuel oil. The United States has consumed (used up) too much of it. That is why Uncle Sam looks so heavy. The cartoonist is saying that the United States would be in better shape if it consumed less oil. If your answer contained these ideas, you wrote a good response.

4. Do you agree with the cartoon's message? Explain. (Answer in two or three sentences.)

_____

_____

_____

_____

_____

_____

_____

What did you write? A cartoon may be clever, but that does not mean it is stating the truth. Many people would say that the cartoon correctly gives the cause of the oil crisis in the United States. Other people would say that it gives only part of the story. In writing your answer, what mattered was that your opinion was reasonable and carefully thought out.

Just as there are cartoons about the United States, there are cartoons about almost every place on Earth. Here is even a cartoon about the whole Earth.

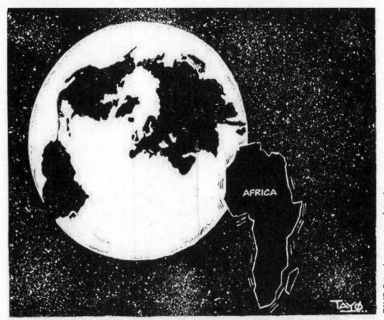

AFRICA

TAYO Fatunla www.tayofatunla.com

DRIFTING AWAY FROM THE MAP OF WORLD'S CONCERN

1. The above cartoon is

   _____ (*a*) about space travel.

   _____ (*b*) only about Africa.

   _____ (*c*) about the world's concern for Africa.

Which answer did you choose? If you looked just at the drawing, you might think that the cartoon is only about Africa. It is the only continent that is labeled and it is shown drifting away from Earth. But why is it drifting away? The caption gives us the answer. The purpose of the cartoon is to show that Africa is drifting away from the world's concern. In other words, the other continents have less and less interest in Africa and its needs. Therefore, the answer to question 1 is (*c*).

2. Which statement is most likely true?

   _____ (*a*) The cartoon proves that Africa has more serious problems than any other continent.

   _____ (*b*) The problems of Africa are of concern to the cartoonist.

   _____ (*c*) The cartoonist is not concerned with the problems of the other continents.

Which answer did you choose? Many people think that Africa has more serious problems than any other continent. But that is not what the cartoonist is trying to prove. We also have no way of knowing what the cartoonist thinks about problems in other parts of the world. But we can learn something from the caption. The cartoonist wants to point out that the rest of the world is ignoring Africa. This would matter only if Africa had problems and needed help from the rest of the world. Therefore, the cartoonist is showing concern for the problems of Africa, and the answer to question 2 is (*b*).

Political cartoons use a few images and perhaps a few words to bring your attention to a current event. You will know a good social studies cartoon when you see one. It will probably give you a chuckle or get you to say something like "That's for sure!" If you keep up with current events, you are more likely to understand and, therefore, enjoy Social Studies cartoons.

The following exercises will give you more practice in studying and interpreting Social Studies cartoons.

A. Look at the following cartoon about the Asian country of Myanmar, which was once called Burma. In 2008, a *typhoon* (severe storm) hit Myanmar, bringing strong winds, heavy rains, and severe floods.

Robert Ariail, The State Dist. by Newspaper Enterprise Association, Inc.

Place a check mark next to the correct answers to questions 1 to 5.

1. The military leader in the water represents the

   ___ (*a*) people of Myanmar.

   ___ (*b*) government of Myanmar.

   ___ (*c*) enemies of Myanmar.

2. What country is shown offering help to Myanmar?

   ___ (*a*) the United States

   ___ (*b*) South Africa

   ___ (*c*) Burma

3. The person completely underwater represents

   ___ (*a*) Burmese people who live in the United States.

   ___ (*b*) American businesses in Myanmar.

   ___ (*c*) the people of Myanmar.

4. The military leader claims that the people of Myanmar

   ___ (*a*) can shoulder (handle) the problems caused by the rains and floods.

   ___ (*b*) fear they will slip through the lifesaver and drown.

   ___ (*c*) will accept help only from countries in Southeast Asia.

5. The word "resilient," as used in the cartoon, means

___ (a) quiet.

___ (b) tough.

___ (c) poor.

6. In your opinion, why does the cartoon show the military leader standing on a person's shoulders? (Answer in two or three sentences.)

_____

_____

_____

_____

_____

_____

7. What would be a good caption for this cartoon?

_____

_____

_____

B. Look at the following cartoon.

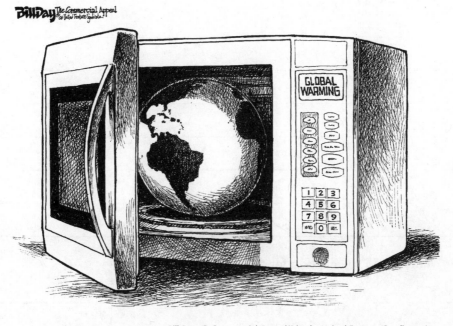

Bill Day: © Commercial Appeal/*Dist. by United Features Syndicate, Inc.*

Place a check mark next to the correct answers to questions 1 and 2.

1. The main purpose of this cartoon is to get people to think about the

___ (a) dangers of global warming.

___ (b) shrinking size of the Earth.

___ (c) effect of microwaves on global warming.

2. The control panel on the front of the microwave suggests that

___ (a) people can choose ways to ease global warming or to make it worse.

___ (b) no one can do anything about global warming.

___ (c) modern machines are totally responsible for global warming.

3. Is the cartoonist saying that it is too late to solve the problem raised in the cartoon? (Answer in two or three sentences.)

_____

_____

_____

_____

_____

4. In your opinion, is the problem raised in the cartoon real or imagined? (Answer in two or three sentences.)

_____

_____

_____

_____

_____

5. What would be a good caption for this cartoon?

_____

_____

C. The following cartoon deals with presidential elections in the United States. The president of the United States is often referred to as the most powerful leader in the Free World.

1. What do you think is meant by the term "Free World" as used in the cartoon? (Answer in one or two sentences.)

   _____

   _____

   _____

   _____

2. Why do you think the cartoonist calls the voter the most powerful person in the Free World? (Answer in two or three sentences.)

   _____

   _____

   _____

   _____

3. What might the cartoonist be saying to people who don't vote? (Answer in two or three sentences.)

   _____

   _____

   _____

   _____

D. Relying on your knowledge of Social Studies issues to understand a cartoon

1. What issue is the cartoonist bringing to the attention of the viewer? (Answer in two or three sentences.)

   _____

   _____

   _____

   _____

2. To what extent does the cartoonist express a point of view? (Answer in two or three sentences.)

   _____

   _____

   _____

   _____

3. Has the cartoon changed the way you feel about the issue? (Answer in two or three sentences.)

   _____

   _____

   _____

   _____

Globe and Map Skills

Chapter 17

Landforms

Our planet Earth is one of a group of planets that travel around the sun. For hundreds of years, people have been drawing maps to show what the Earth looks like. The following maps come in different sizes and shapes, but they all show the land and water that make up the Earth.

Globe

Good Point: It is the only type of map that shows the correct size, shape, and location of land and water areas.

Bad Point: Unless a globe is very large, it cannot show close-up views of areas on the earth.

Mercator Flat Map

Good Point: The straight lines going north to south and east to west make it easier to chart a course and, thus, sail in the right direction.

Bad Point: The land and water areas at the top and bottom of the map appear much larger than they actually are.

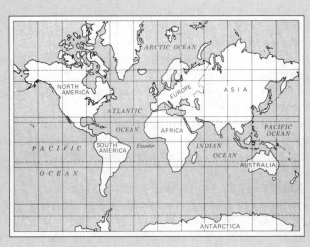

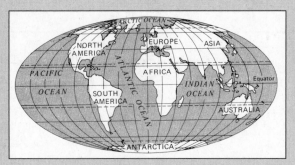

Mollweide Flat Map

Good Point: This map shows the true size of land and water areas and the lines running north and south as curved.

Bad Point: The land shapes are slightly distorted and untrue.

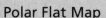

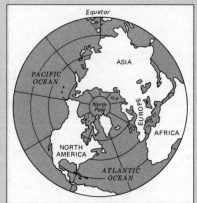

Polar Flat Map

Good Point: This map shows the shortest routes between places over the North Pole or the South Pole.

Bad Point: The land and water areas at the outer sections of the map are too large and have inaccurate shapes.

In this chapter, you will learn about the Earth's *landforms* and of their importance to human beings, animals, and plants. On the landforms, food is grown, cities are built, and products are manufactured.

Continents

The largest landforms on Earth are called *continents*, or mainlands. They are Asia, Africa, North America, South America, Antarctica, Europe, and Australia. Asia is the largest continent, and Australia is the smallest. The chart on page 146 shows the shape and land area of each continent. Inside the continents are countries. The countries are separated on some maps by boundary lines, which are decided by governments.

On the map of the world on page 145, you can see that there are many countries on most continents. The boundary lines on this map are shown by broken lines.

Notice on the map the countries on the continent of North America. The three largest are Canada, the United States, and Mexico. In the lower part of North America, you can see the countries that make up Central America. They are Panama, Costa Rica, Honduras, Guatemala, Nicaragua, Belize, and El Salvador. The continent of South America contains 13 countries. The continent of Africa is made up of about 50 countries. More than 40 countries are in Asia, and more than 50 are in Europe.

The boundary lines of many countries have changed over the years because of wars, invasions, or agreements made by countries. Remember that continents are large landforms made by nature, but most countries are parts of continents and are created by governments.

The continents of Europe and Asia share some countries. Both Turkey and Russia are countries partly in Europe and partly in Asia. The word Eurasia is sometimes applied to both Europe and Asia because they look like one large continent.

Notice on the map on page 145 that the continent of Australia is made up of only one country, with the same name—Australia. The continent of Antarctica is not always shown on maps. Because the climate is very cold in Antarctica, almost no one lives there. Also, the location of Antarctica makes it difficult to include on a map of other continents.

The World

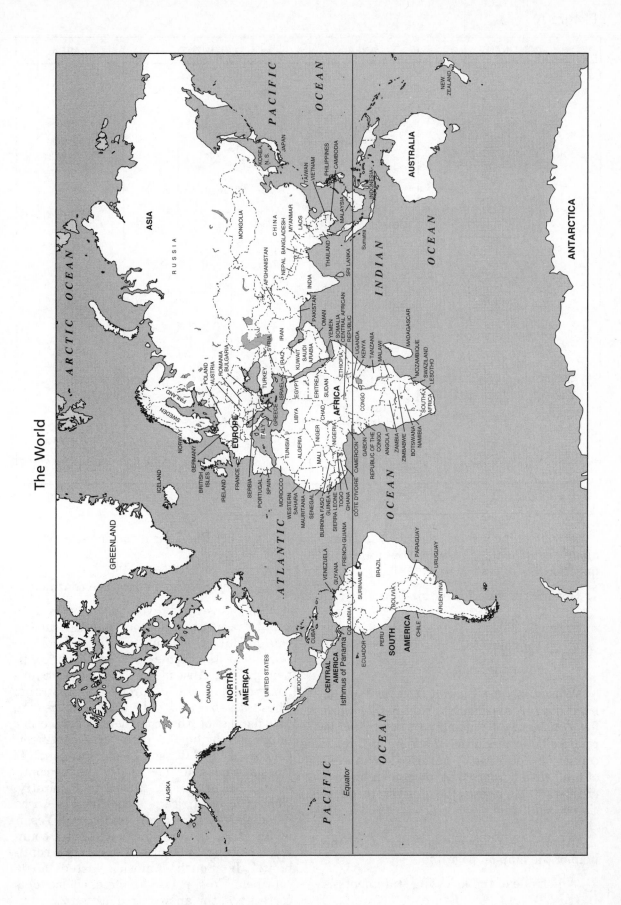

Picture A

CONTINENT	AREA	CONTINENT	AREA
Asia	16,988,000 Square Miles	South America	6,795,000 Square Miles
Africa	11,506,000 Square Miles	Antarctica	5,500,000 Square Miles
North America	9,390,000 Square Miles	Europe	3,745,000 Square Miles
		Australia	2,968,000 Square Miles

Let us see how much you have learned about continents. Answer the following question.

1. Governments decide the size and shape of

_____ (a) continents.

_____ (b) countries.

_____ (c) mainlands.

What was your answer? You read at the beginning of this chapter that another word for continent is "mainland." Both words refer to large landforms made by nature. A country is not made by nature. It is an area of land with borders that are drawn by governments. Therefore, the answer to question 1 is (b).

Answer the following question with the help of the map on page 145.

2. Which one of the following statements is true?

_____ (a) Russia is a continent.

_____ (b) Africa is a country.

_____ (c) South America is a continent.

Which answer did you choose? It is difficult to remember all the countries in the world. But it should not be difficult to remember the names of the seven continents: Asia, Africa, North America, South America, Antarctica, Europe, and Australia. These seven—and only these seven—are the names of the continents. Any other name cannot be the name of a continent. Choice (a) is "Russia is a continent." Is Russia named as one of the seven continents? No, it is not. Russia is a country. Choice (b) is "Africa is a country." Is Africa listed above as one of the continents? Yes, it is. So Africa is a continent and not a country. Choice (c) is "South America is a continent." Is South America listed as a continent? Yes, it is. Therefore, choice (c) is correct and the answer to question 2.

Answer again these two important questions. What is the difference between a continent and a country? What are the names of the seven continents?

Other Landforms

You now know that the Earth contains seven very large landforms called continents. It also contains other important landforms called *islands*. An island is a body of land completely surrounded by water. Most islands belong to a particular continent. For example, the island of Greenland is part of North America and the islands of Japan are part of Asia.

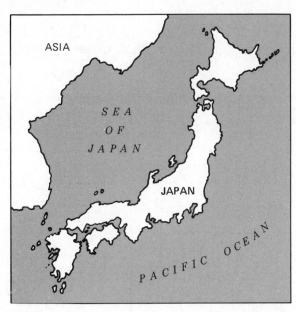

Locate the following islands on the map on page 145. Then, in the space provided, write the continent to which each island belongs.

Island—Continent

1. Sri Lanka_____

2. Madagascar_____

3. Sumatra (Indonesia) _____

The map on page 145 shows that Sri Lanka and Sumatra are part of Asia and that Madagascar is part of Africa.

Some islands are not part of a continent. For example, the islands of New Zealand are located near Australia. But they are not part of Australia.

There are two other important land shapes:

1. A *peninsula* is a body of land sticking out into the sea. It is almost completely surrounded by water. For example, Florida is a peninsula. Locate Florida on the world map on page 145. Then try to locate three more peninsulas on the map.

2. An *isthmus* is a narrow strip of land connecting two large landforms. For example, the Isthmus of Panama connects North America and South America. Find the Isthmus of Panama on the map below.

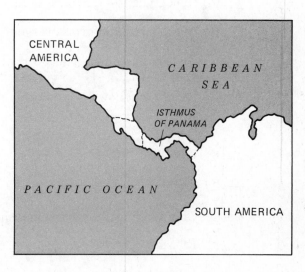

The following exercises will help you learn more about landforms and land shapes.

USING WHAT YOU HAVE LEARNED

A. Place a check mark next to the correct answers to questions 1 to 10.

1. Which of the following is the only map that shows the correct size and shape of land and water areas on the Earth?

    ___ (*a*) globe

    ___ (*b*) Mollweide

    ___ (*c*) polar

2. Which kind of map shows only straight lines going north to south and east to west?

    ___ (*a*) Mercator

    ___ (*b*) Mollweide

    ___ (*c*) globe

3. A map of the entire Earth will show

    ___ (*a*) five continents.

    ___ (*b*) six continents.

    ___ (*c*) seven continents.

4. Continents are

    ___ (*a*) the only landforms on Earth.

    ___ (*b*) the largest landforms on Earth.

    ___ (*c*) the smallest landforms on Earth.

5. Which one of the following landforms is completely surrounded by water?

    ___ (*a*) island

    ___ (*b*) isthmus

    ___ (*c*) peninsula

6. Europe and Asia together are sometimes called

    ___ (*a*) Russia.

    ___ (*b*) Eurasia.

    ___ (*c*) Greater Asia.

7. Which one of the following statements is true?

___ (a) Continents and countries are made by governments.

___ (b) Continents and countries are made by nature.

___ (c) Continents are made by nature, but countries are made by governments.

8. The three largest countries in North America are

___ (a) Canada, the United States, and Mexico.

___ (b) Canada, the United States, and Nicaragua.

___ (c) the United States, Mexico, and Panama.

9. Which one of the following statements is true?

___ (a) The islands of Japan are part of the continent of Asia.

___ (b) The islands of New Zealand are part of the continent of Australia.

___ (c) The island of Greenland is part of the continent of Europe.

10. Which one of the following statements is false?

___ (a) Florida is a peninsula.

___ (b) The Isthmus of Panama connects North America and South America.

___ (c) The Isthmus of Suez connects Europe and Asia.

B. Essay: "Why is it unfair to compare the United States and the continent of Africa?" (Answer in two or three sentences.)

_____

_____

_____

_____

_____

_____

_____

_____

_____

_____

_____

_____

C. Match the names of the continents in the list with their shapes below.

a. North America   e. Australia
b. Africa   f. Europe
c. South America   g. Antarctica
d. Asia

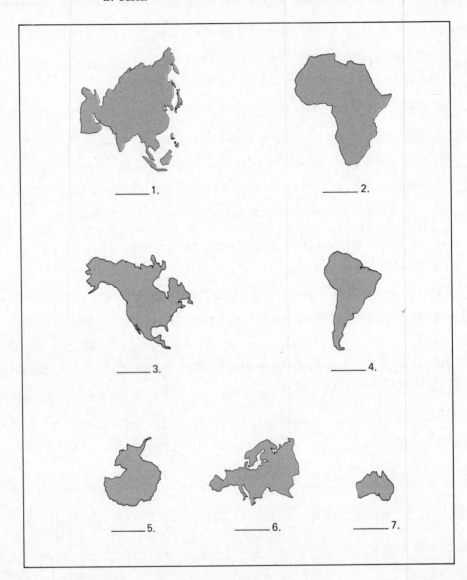

_____ 1.

_____ 2.

_____ 3.

_____ 4.

_____ 5.

_____ 6.

_____ 7.

D. Next to the name of each country in South America, write the number that matches its location on the map. If you need help, look at South America on the map on page 145.

Countries of South America

_____ Argentina

_____ Bolivia

_____ Brazil

_____ Chile

_____ Colombia

_____ Ecuador

_____ French Guiana

_____ Guyana

_____ Paraguay

_____ Peru

_____ Suriname

_____ Uruguay

_____ Venezuela

Chapter 18
Water Forms

Although the main landforms on the Earth, the continents, are huge, they do not cover even half of the Earth's surface. Only 30 percent of the Earth is covered with land. The remaining 70 percent is water.

The largest and most important bodies of water, or *water forms*, on the Earth are called *oceans*. There are four: the Pacific (the largest), the Atlantic, the Indian, and the Arctic.

Map A

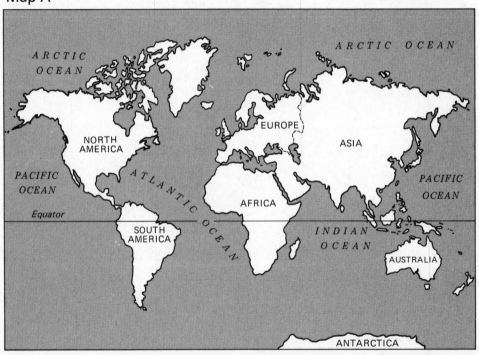

The location of the Earth's oceans is shown on Map A.

Three other types of large bodies of water are *seas*, *gulfs*, and *bays*. Gulfs and bays are parts of larger bodies of water that extend into land. Some seas, such as the Caspian Sea, are completely surrounded by landforms. Most seas, like all gulfs and bays, are only partly surrounded by landforms or extend deep into landforms. On Map B, you can see the Bering Sea, the Gulf of Alaska, and Bristol Bay. They are all parts of the Pacific Ocean.

Another type of body of water is a *strait*. Made by nature, it is a narrow stretch of

Map B

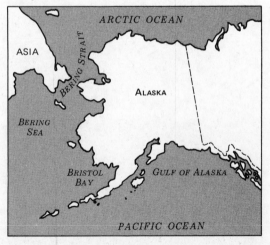

Map C

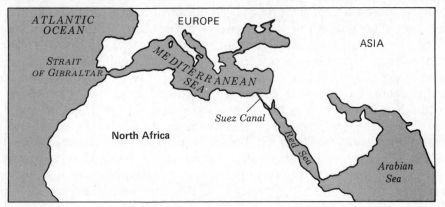

water connecting two larger bodies of water. The Bering Strait, on Map B, connects the Arctic Ocean and the Bering Sea. The Strait of Gibraltar, shown on Map C, connects the Atlantic Ocean and the Mediterranean Sea.

A second type of narrow body of water connecting two larger bodies of water is a *canal*. It is different from a strait because it is made by humans. You can see on Map C that the Suez Canal allows ships to sail from the Mediterranean Sea to the Red Sea. Can you think of any other famous canals or straits?

Many bodies of water lie within landforms. A body of water completely surrounded by land is called a *lake*. Map D shows Lake Nyanza in East Africa. Map D also shows another important body of water inside land: the Nile River. On a map, a *river* is usually shown by a blue or black line. The place where a river begins is called the *source* of the river. This might be water running down from the mountains or a lake. The main source of the Nile River is Lake Nyanza.

Map D

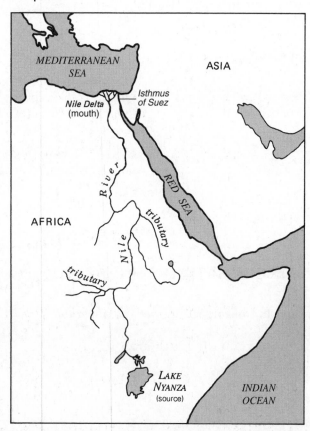

The Nile River flows into the Mediterranean Sea. The place where a river ends, or flows into a larger body of water, is called the *mouth* of the river. At the mouth of a river may be a large area of fertile soil that is good for growing plants. This area of fertile soil at the mouth of a river is called a *delta*. Find the Nile Delta on Map D.

Along the Nile River you can see other smaller rivers flowing into it. These smaller rivers that flow into a larger river are called *tributaries*. Some tributaries of the Nile are shown on Map D.

Answer the following questions to find out how much you have learned about water forms on the Earth.

1. The largest water forms on the Earth are

_____ (a) lakes.

_____ (b) oceans.

_____ (c) seas.

Which answer did you choose? On most maps, water is shown by the color blue or by a light shade of gray. Look at the large gray areas on Map A at the beginning of this chapter. These large gray areas have the following words written on them: *PACIFIC OCEAN, ATLANTIC OCEAN, INDIAN OCEAN, ARCTIC OCEAN.* These oceans are the largest water forms on the Earth. Therefore, the answer to question 1 is (b).

2. A part of a large body of water that extends into the land is called a

_____ (a) strait or canal.

_____ (b) lake or river.

_____ (c) bay or gulf.

Which answer did you choose? Do you know the meaning of each water form listed in the choices? You can find the meanings in this chapter. Choice (a) is "strait or canal." Because straits and canals are narrow bodies of water connecting two larger bodies of water, choice (a) cannot be the answer. Choice (b) is "lake or river." Lakes and rivers start inside land, and a river flows out to the sea. So choice (b) cannot be the answer. Choice (c) is "bay or gulf." Both bays and gulfs are bodies of water that extend into the land. Therefore, the answer to question 2 is (c).

3. Match the terms related to rivers in Column B with their meanings in Column A.

Column A

_____ 1. a fertile area of land at the mouth of a river

_____ 2. a place where a river begins

_____ 3. a smaller river flowing into a larger river

_____ 4. a place where a river ends

Column B

a. mouth

b. source

c. delta

d. tributary

An explanation of each of these terms is given in this chapter. Read over the chapter if you have forgotten their meanings. The correct answers are 1. *c*, 2. *b*, 3. *d*, 4. *a*.

The following exercises will help you learn more about the important water forms on the Earth.

USING WHAT YOU HAVE LEARNED

A. Place a check mark next to the correct answers to questions 1 to 5.

1. The largest bodies of water on the Earth are

___ (a) bays.

___ (b) lakes.

___ (c) oceans.

2. The largest ocean is the

___ (*a*) Atlantic Ocean.

___ (*b*) Pacific Ocean.

___ (*c*) Indian Ocean.

3. The percentage of the Earth covered by water is about

___ (*a*) 20 percent.

___ (*b*) 50 percent.

___ (*c*) 70 percent.

4. Which one of the following is NOT a water form?

___ (*a*) a strait

___ (*b*) a bay

___ (*c*) an isthmus

5. Which one of the following is made by humans?

___ (*a*) a gulf

___ (*b*) a strait

___ (*c*) a canal

B. Terms Related to Rivers

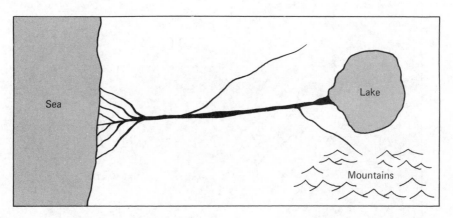

Write the following terms in the correct place on this map of a river. Then write what each word means.

Source _____

_____

Mouth _____

_____

Delta _____

_____

Tributary _____

_____

C. Types of Water Forms

Southeast Asia

Find an example of each of the following water forms on the map. Write the name of each example you find on the line to the left of the water form. Then write the definition of each water form on the line to the right of it. The first one is done for you.

Name	Water Form	Definition
Bengal	Bay	a large body of water
		extending into the land
	Strait	
	River	
	Ocean	
	Gulf	
	Sea	

Chapter 19
Using Directions

Directions

Being able to use *directions* correctly will help you locate places more easily. This is true whether you are trying to find your way around a city or looking for a city on a map. But how do you know what directions to use?

Look at Picture A, which shows a line, called an *axis*, running through the center of the Earth. This is an imaginary line because it does not really exist in the Earth. At the top end of the axis is the North Pole, and at the bottom is the South Pole.

All directions heading toward the North Pole are north (N). All directions heading toward the South Pole are south (S). If you face the North Pole, the direction on your left is west (W), and the one on your right is east (E). The directions north, south, west, and east are called *cardinal directions* (the most important ones). They can be seen in Picture B. If you are facing south, which direction is on your right? If you are facing west, which direction is on your left?

Picture A

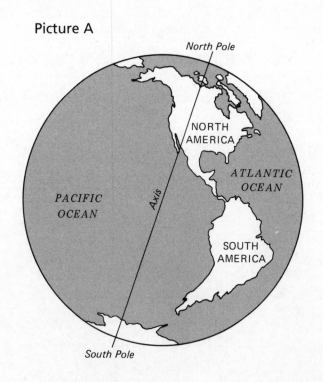

Picture B

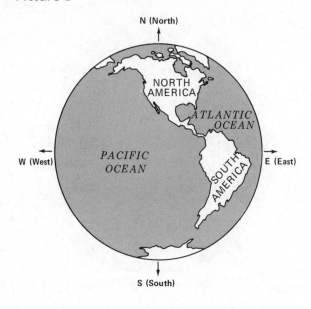

Picture C

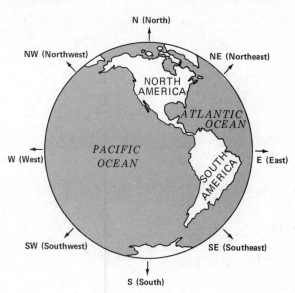

The direction between north and west is called northwest (NW). The direction between north and east is called northeast (NE). What is the direction between south and west called? What direction uses the letters SE? The directions northwest, northeast, southwest, and southeast are shown in Picture C. They are called *intermediate directions* because they are found between the cardinal directions.

Most maps have a directional compass or arrow on them to let you know where north is. On the maps you generally use, north is at the top. As you have learned, if you know where north is, you can easily determine where the other directions are.

Two other important directions are up and down. They are not the same as north and south. If you leave or go away from the Earth, the direction is up. If you then go toward the Earth, the direction is down. Picture D can help you understand what the directions up and down mean.

Hemispheres

Halfway between the North Pole and the South Pole is an imaginary line called the *equator*. In Picture E, you can see that the equator goes around the center of the Earth. It divides the Earth into two equal parts, called *hemispheres*. Hemisphere means half of a sphere or half of the Earth.

Picture D

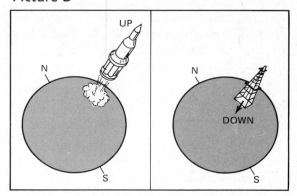

Picture E

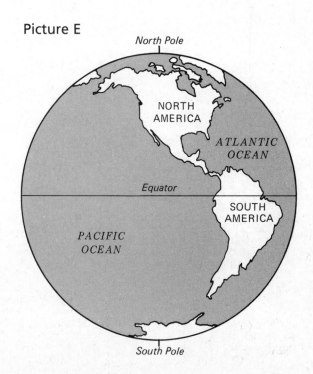

PICTURE F

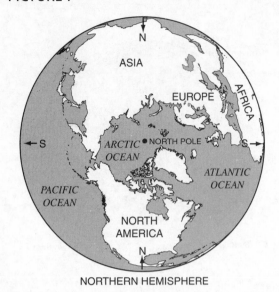

NORTHERN HEMISPHERE

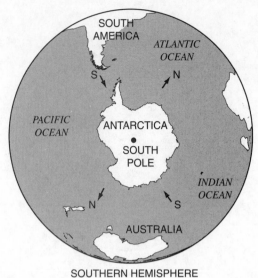

SOUTHERN HEMISPHERE

The Northern Hemisphere and the Southern Hemisphere can each be shown in another way. Picture F shows the Northern Hemisphere with the North Pole in the center and the Southern Hemisphere with the South Pole in the middle.

Picture G shows that the Earth can also be divided into the Western Hemisphere and the Eastern Hemisphere.

Picture H turns the Western Hemisphere and the Eastern Hemisphere around to show all of each hemisphere.

PICTURE G

WESTERN HEMISPHERE

EASTERN HEMISPHERE

PICTURE H

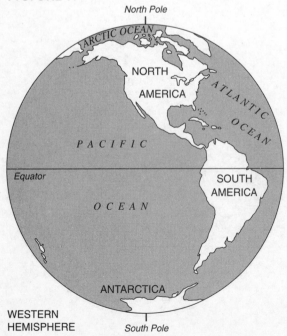

WESTERN HEMISPHERE

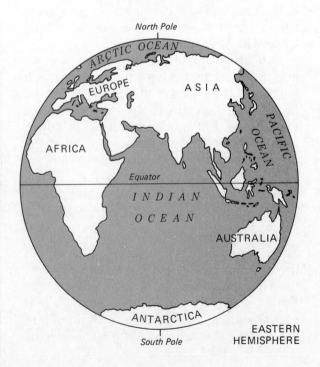

EASTERN HEMISPHERE

Answer the following questions to see how much you have learned about directions.

1. When you are facing north, the direction to your right is

_____ (*a*) north.

_____ (*b*) west.

_____ (*c*) east.

Which answer did you choose? Look at Picture B in this chapter. It shows the direction north at the top of the Earth. The direction on the right side of the Earth is east. Therefore, the answer to question 1 is (*c*).

2. If a country is located below, or south of, the equator, it is in

_____ (*a*) the Northern Hemisphere.

_____ (*b*) the Southern Hemisphere.

_____ (*c*) both the Northern Hemisphere and the Southern Hemisphere.

Which answer did you choose? Picture E shows how the equator divides the Earth into the Northern Hemisphere and the Southern Hemisphere. Any part of the Earth above, or north of, the equator is in the Northern Hemisphere. Any part of the Earth below, or south of, the equator is in the Southern Hemisphere. Therefore, the answer to question 2 is (*b*).

Answer questions 3 and 4 by using the following map.

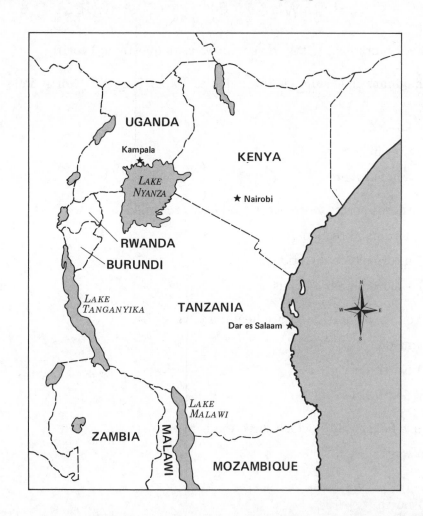

3. Fill in the blank with the correct cardinal direction: north, south, west, east.

Kenya is _____ of Tanzania.

Which direction did you choose? Is Kenya above (north of) Tanzania? Or is it below (south of) Tanzania? Or is Kenya left (west) or right (east) of Tanzania? You can see on the map that Kenya is above Tanzania. Therefore, Kenya is north of Tanzania.

4. Fill in the blank with the correct intermediate direction: northwest, northeast, southwest, southeast.

Dar es Salaam is _____ of Nairobi.

Which direction did you choose? Remember that intermediate directions are found between the cardinal directions. You can see on the map that Dar es Salaam is below Nairobi. Therefore, Dar es Salaam is south of Nairobi. But this is only part of the answer. Now you must find out if Dar es Salaam is southwest or southeast of Nairobi. The direction west is to the left on the map. The direction east is to the right. The map shows that Dar es Salaam is to the south and to the right of Nairobi. Therefore, the correct answer is that Dar es Salaam is southeast of Nairobi.

Using directions correctly is an important Social Studies skill because directions help you locate places on the Earth. The following exercises will give you more practice in learning this important skill.

USING WHAT YOU HAVE LEARNED

A. Place a check mark next to the correct answers to questions 1 to 10.

1. The imaginary line running through the Earth from the North Pole to the South Pole is

___ (a) an axis.

___ (b) the equator.

___ (c) a hemisphere.

2. The directions north, south, west, and east are called

___ (a) cardinal directions.

___ (b) intermediate directions.

___ (c) subordinate directions.

3. When you travel north, you are heading toward the

___ (a) moon.

___ (b) North Pole.

___ (c) South Pole.

4. If you are facing south, which direction is to your right?

___ (a) west

___ (b) east

___ (c) north

5. If you are traveling to the moon, you are going

___ (a) east.

___ (b) up.

___ (c) north.

6. The directions northwest, northeast, southwest, and southeast are called intermediate directions because they are

___ (a) located at the North Pole and the South Pole.

___ (b) found in the middle of the Earth.

___ (c) found between the cardinal directions.

7. The letters that stand for the direction northeast are

___ (a) NW.

___ (b) EN.

___ (c) NE.

8. The imaginary line called the equator divides the Earth into the

___ (a) Northern Hemisphere and the Southern Hemisphere.

___ (b) Eastern Hemisphere and the Western Hemisphere.

___ (c) Northern Hemisphere and the Eastern Hemisphere.

9. The center of the Southern Hemisphere is the

___ (a) equator.

___ (b) North Pole.

___ (c) South Pole.

10. If a country is located above, or north of, the equator, it is in

___ (a) the Northern Hemisphere.

___ (b) the Southern Hemisphere.

___ (c) both the Northern Hemisphere and the Southern Hemisphere.

B. Cardinal and Intermediate Directions

B-1. Using the map of Asia on page 164, fill in the correct cardinal directions. The first one is done for you.

north   south   west   east

1. Russia is _____ north _____ of China.

2. India is _____ of Russia.

3. Saudi Arabia is _____ of India.

4. Afghanistan is _____ of Iran.

5. Mongolia is _____ of Russia and _____ _____ of China.

6. The Philippines are _____ of Indonesia and _____ _____ of Japan.

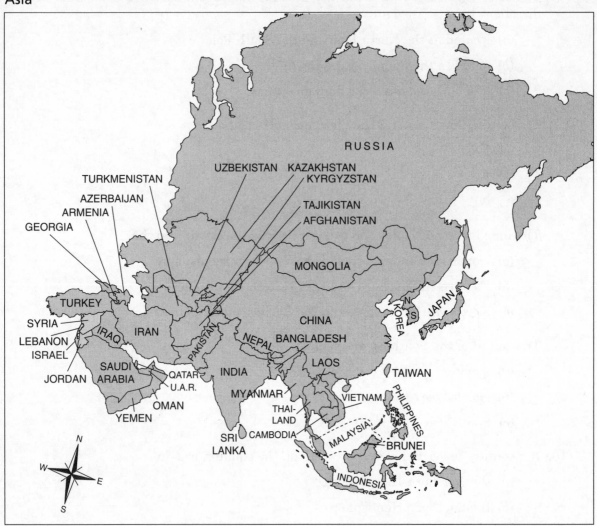

B-2. Using the map of Asia above, fill in the correct intermediate directions. The first one is done for you.

northwest   northeast   southwest   southeast

1. India is _____*southwest*_____ of Mongolia.

2. Pakistan is _____ of Sri Lanka.

3. Saudi Arabia is _____ of Russia.

4. North Korea is _____ of Pakistan.

5. Iran is _____ of Japan and _____ of Turkey.

6. Malaysia is _____ of India and _____ of the Philippines.

C. Cardinal and Intermediate Directions

Southwest Asia/Africa

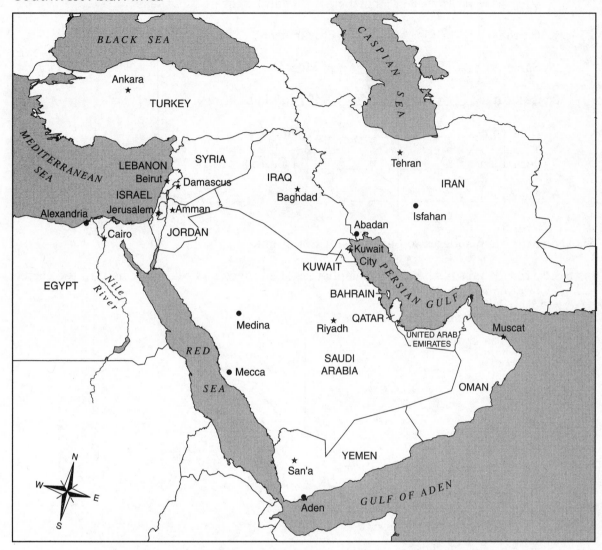

C-1. Using this map of Southwest Asia/Africa, fill in the correct cardinal direction. The first one is done for you. (Two directions may seem to fit each answer. Pick the one that is more correct than the other.)

north   south   west   east

1. Cairo is _____*south*_____ of Ankara.

2. Damascus is _____ of Baghdad.

3. Tehran is _____ of Abadan.

4. San'a is _____ of Riyadh.

5. Jerusalem is _____ of Baghdad.

6. Muscat is _____ of Mecca.

C-2. Using the map of Southwest Asia/Africa, fill in the correct intermediate directions. The first one is done for you.

northwest northeast southwest southeast

1. Cairo is _____southwest_____ of Damascus.

2. San'a is _____ of Muscat.

3. Ankara is _____ of Baghdad.

4. Abadan is _____ of Baghdad.

5. Jerusalem is _____ of Cairo.

6. Mecca is _____ of Cairo.

D. Using the Hemispheres to Learn About Continents

Study these maps of the four hemispheres. Then place a check mark next to the correct answers to questions 1 to 10.

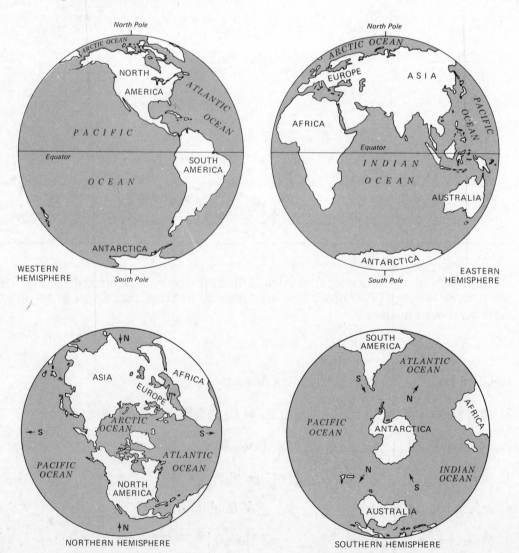

1. North America is in the

   ___ (a) Western Hemisphere.

   ___ (b) Southern Hemisphere.

   ___ (c) Eastern Hemisphere.

2. Asia is mostly in the

   ___ (a) Western Hemisphere.

   ___ (b) Southern Hemisphere.

   ___ (c) Eastern Hemisphere.

3. Australia is in the

   ___ (a) Northern Hemisphere.

   ___ (b) Western Hemisphere.

   ___ (c) Southern Hemisphere.

4. Most of South America is in the

   ___ (a) Northern Hemisphere.

   ___ (b) Southern Hemisphere.

   ___ (c) Eastern Hemisphere.

5. Europe is in both the

   ___ (a) Northern Hemisphere and the Southern Hemisphere.

   ___ (b) Eastern Hemisphere and the Western Hemisphere.

   ___ (c) Northern Hemisphere and the Eastern Hemisphere.

6. Which continent is found in the Northern Hemisphere, the Southern Hemisphere, and the Eastern Hemisphere?

   ___ (a) Africa

   ___ (b) North America

   ___ (c) Australia

7. The equator does NOT pass through

   ___ (a) South America.

   ___ (b) Africa.

   ___ (c) Australia.

8. Traveling east from Asia, you would first come to

___ (*a*) North America.

___ (*b*) Africa.

___ (*c*) Europe.

9. Africa is located

___ (*a*) northeast of Asia.

___ (*b*) southeast of Asia.

___ (*c*) southwest of Asia.

10. The hemisphere with the most land area is the

___ (*a*) Western Hemisphere.

___ (*b*) Northern Hemisphere.

___ (*c*) Southern Hemisphere.

Chapter 20
Map Keys and Scales

As you know, a map is a drawing that shows part or all of the surface of the Earth. It can be very simple and show only a small part of a country, city, or town, or it can give a lot of details about all the countries of the world.

Map Keys

Let us first look at a simple map of a part of Egypt. (See page 170.)

What does this map of northern Egypt show? On it are many symbols. Some of them are:

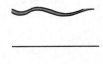

Without knowing the meaning of the symbols, it is impossible to understand what the map is supposed to show.

A very important part of the map is missing: the *key*, or legend, to explain the meaning of each symbol on the map. By looking at the key, you would know what the map shows.

Here is the key that belongs to the map of northern Egypt.

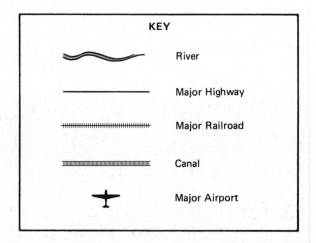

Use this key to help you answer the following questions about the map of Egypt.

1. The symbols used on the map of Egypt show

   _____ (a) how many people live in Egypt.

   _____ (b) how much food is grown in Egypt.

   _____ (c) many of the ways people travel in Egypt.

   Which answer did you choose? The key shows different symbols that clearly stand for ways of traveling. These symbols represent rivers, highways, railroads, canals, and airports. Therefore, the answer to question 1 is (c).

2. The symbol for a canal on the map is

   _____ (a) ——————————

   _____ (b) +++++++++++++++++++

   _____ (c) ▦▦▦▦▦▦▦▦▦▦▦

   Which answer did you choose? To find the meaning of a symbol on the map, you have to look at the key. The key shows that the symbol for a canal is ▦▦▦▦▦▦▦▦▦ . Therefore, the answer to question 2 is (c).

3. Which one of the following cities on the map has a major airport?

   _____ (a) Cairo

   _____ (b) Tanta

   _____ (c) El Mansura

   What was your answer? The key tells you that ✈ is the symbol for an airport. Now check to see if any of the cities in question 3 has this symbol next to it on the map. You can see that, of the cities named, only Cairo has the airport symbol next to it. Therefore, the answer to question 3 is (a).

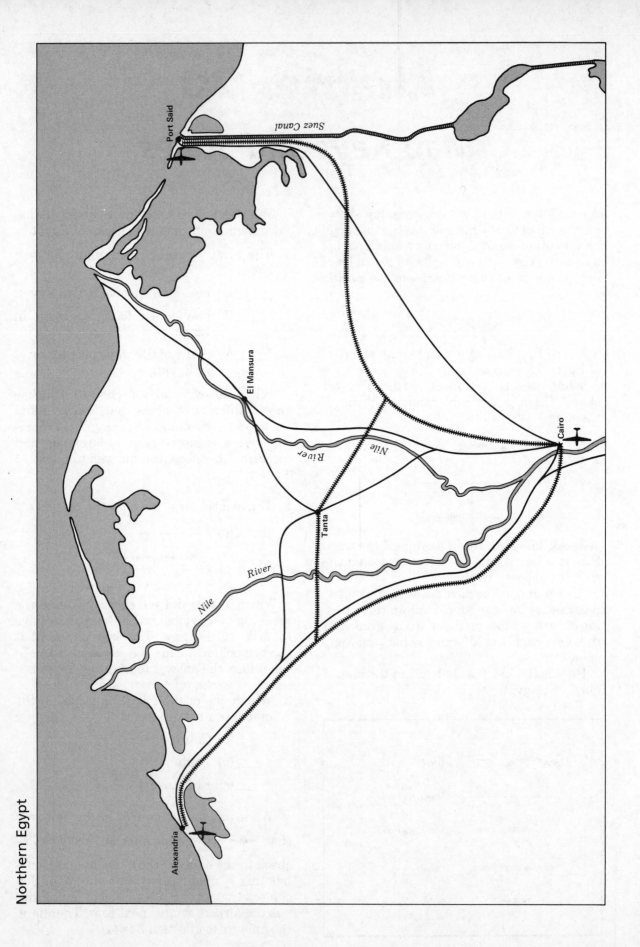

Northern Egypt

4. According to the map, which city does NOT seem to be as important as the other three?

_____ (a) Alexandria

_____ (b) Tanta

_____ (c) Cairo

_____ (d) Port Said

Which answer did you choose this time? Important cities tend to have many means of traveling. According to the map, Alexandria, Cairo, and Port Said have more means of traveling than Tanta. All four cities have major highways and railroads, but only Alexandria, Cairo, and Port Said have major airports. Therefore, the answer to question 4 is (b).

These four questions have shown you how important keys are in understanding maps. Fortunately, most maps have keys to help us interpret the symbols and special markings on them.

Map Scales

Suppose that you want to use the map on page 170 to plan a trip around northern Egypt. Before you visit all the cities, you might want to know how far apart they are. How can you use this map to answer your question? The key for it on page 169 does not help because it does not show the distances between the cities on the map. Something else is needed to find this information.

Before we find out what this item is, we need to know how distance is measured. In the United States, long distances are usually measured in miles. But in almost every other country in the world, long distances are measured in kilometers. (This is a unit of measurement in the metric system.) One mile is equal to 1.6 kilometers.

To measure distance on a map, you need a *scale* of miles and kilometers. A scale tells you how many miles or kilometers on the Earth a certain area on a map represents. The scale for the map of Egypt on page 172 looks like this:

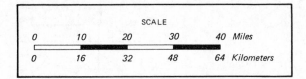

Each black or white section on the scale stands for 10 miles, or 16 kilometers, on the Earth. By finding out how many sections there are between cities on the map, you can find out how many miles or kilometers apart the cities are.

On the scale for the map of northern Egypt, each black or white section is a half inch long. So you can also say that each half inch on the map stands for 10 miles, or 16 kilometers. An inch (one black section and one white section together) stands for 20 miles, or 32 kilometers.

The map on page 172 shows the five important cities that appear on the map of northern Egypt on page 170. A scale is shown at the bottom of the map. Sections of the scale are drawn between some of the cities. Answer the questions that follow by using the scale.

1. How many miles apart are Tanta and El Mansura?

_____ (a) 10 miles

_____ (b) 30 miles

_____ (c) 50 miles

Which answer did you choose? The scale shows that each black and each white section stands for 10 miles. There are three sections between Tanta and El Mansura on the map. Three sections times 10 miles equals 30 miles. Therefore, the answer to question 1 is (b).

2. How many kilometers apart are Tanta and Cairo?

_____ (a) 88 kilometers

_____ (b) 108 kilometers

_____ (c) 168 kilometers

Which answer did you choose? You can count five and one-half black and white sections between Tanta and Cairo on the map. Each section stands for 16 kilometers. Five and one-half sections times 16 kilometers equals 88 kilometers. Therefore, the answer to question 2 is (a).

3. About how many miles apart are El Mansura and Port Said?

_____ (a) 35 miles

_____ (b) 55 miles

_____ (c) 110 miles

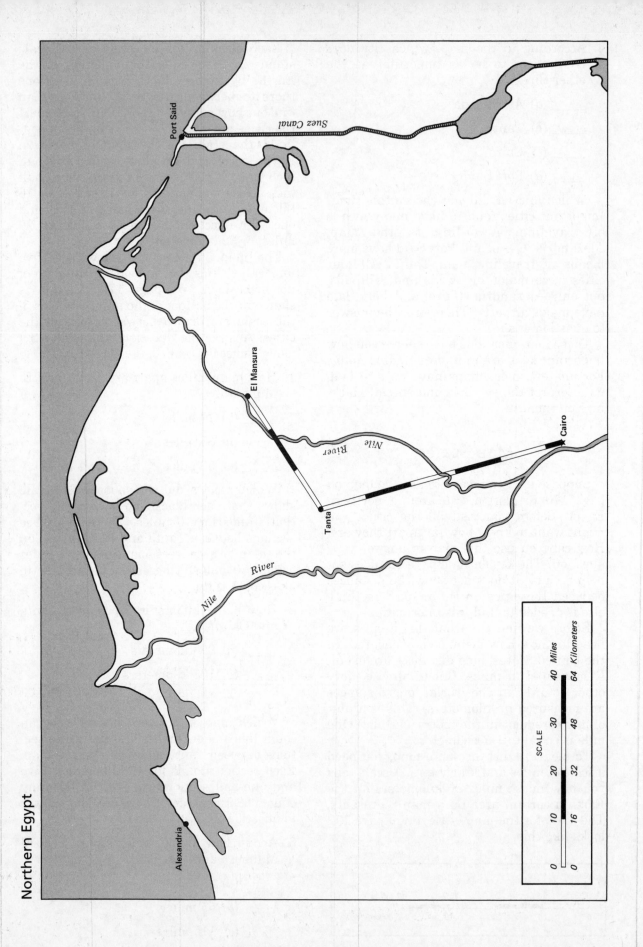

Northern Egypt

Which was your answer? This time there are no sections of a scale connecting the two cities. You have to use the scale below the cities and a ruler, a piece of paper, or maybe your finger to measure the distance between the cities. (Remember to measure from dot to dot.) If you measure carefully, you will see that it will take five and one-half sections (2¾ inches) to connect El Mansura and Port Said on the map. Five and one-half sections times 10 miles equals 55 miles. You can also find the answer using inches. Two and three-fourths inches times 20 miles for each inch equals 55 miles. Therefore, the answer to question 3 is (b).

Not all maps have the same scale. The scales on two maps may stand for different distances depending on what is to be shown on the maps. The following two maps of Egypt have different scales.

The scale on Map A shows that each inch stands for 300 miles, or 480 kilometers.

The scale on Map B shows that each inch stands for 600 miles, or 960 kilometers.

Look at the map on page 172. On its scale, each black or white section stands for 10 miles, or 16 kilometers. How is it different from the maps of Egypt on pages 173 and 174? While they show all of Egypt, the map on page 172 shows only a part of Egypt. To show the whole country at this scale would take up much more room than is available on these pages.

Map A

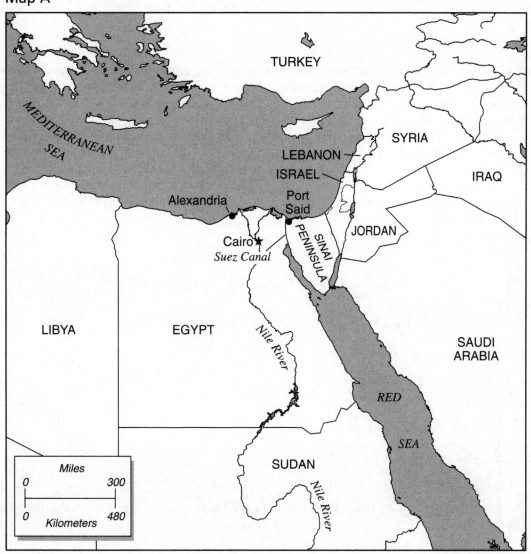

Map B

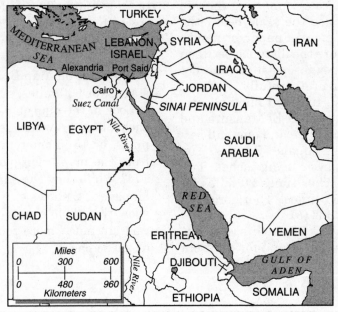

How is Map A on page 173 different from Map B on page 174? More countries can be seen on Map B than on Map A. Each inch on the scale for Map B stands for 600 miles, or 960 kilometers. This is a longer distance than an inch on the scale for Map A stands for. Fewer details can be shown on a map picturing a large area than on a map the same size that pictures a smaller area. For example, Ethiopia does not even appear on Map A. But the countries that do appear, such as Egypt and Jordan, are larger on Map A than on Map B.

Map keys help you to understand the symbols used on maps. Scales help you find the distances between places on the maps. Before you answer the following questions, study the keys and scales on the maps.

USING WHAT YOU HAVE LEARNED

A. Place a check mark next to the correct answers to questions 1 to 5.

1. Symbols used on a map are

___ (a) explained in the glossary.

___ (b) explained in the key.

___ (c) not explained at all.

2. A scale on a map is used to

___ (a) explain symbols on the map.

___ (b) tell how many miles or kilometers on Earth a certain space on the map represents.

___ (c) tell what kind of map it is.

3. Which one of the following statements is true?

___ (a) All maps use the same scale.

___ (b) Two maps of different countries can never use the same scale.

___ (c) The scales on maps may stand for different distances depending on what is to be shown on the maps.

4. On a certain map, 1 inch is equal to 150 miles on Earth. If there are 2 inches between cities on that map, then the cities are

___ (a) 150 miles apart.

___ (b) 300 miles apart.

___ (c) 450 miles apart.

5. On a certain map, 1 inch is equal to 250 kilometers on Earth. If there are 3 inches between cities on that map, then the cities are

___ (a) 250 kilometers apart.

___ (b) 500 kilometers apart.

___ (c) 750 kilometers apart.

B. Study the following map of Russia, Ukraine, and Belarus.

Major Cities of Russia, Ukraine, and Belarus

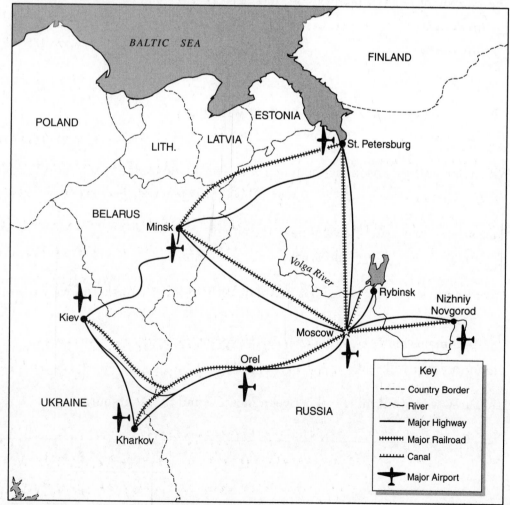

Place a check mark next to the correct answers to questions 1 to 8.

1. The map of parts of Russia, Ukraine, and Belarus shows

___ (a) ways of traveling between major cities.

___ (b) how many railroads link the major cities.

___ (c) how many highways link the major cities.

2. All the symbols on the map are

___ (a) explained in a dictionary.

___ (b) explained in the key.

___ (c) not explained at all.

3. The symbol for a major airport is

___ (a) ▐▐▐▐▐▐▐▐▐▐▐▐▐▐▐▐

___ (b) 〜〜

___ (c) ✈

4. The symbol for a major highway is

___ (a) ▬▬▬

___ (b) ▰▰▰▰▰▰▰

___ (c) ▬ ▬ ▬ ▬

5. Which city on the map does NOT have a major airport?

___ (a) Moscow   ___ (b) Kiev   ___ (c) Rybinsk

6. Which one of the following is the name of a river found on the map?

___ (a) Nizhniy Novgorod   ___ (b) Minsk   ___ (c) Volga

7. The canal on the map is located near the city of

___ (a) Moscow.   ___ (b) Minsk.   ___ (c) Kiev.

8. According to the map, you cannot travel directly between Minsk and Kiev by

___ (a) airplane.

___ (b) a major highway.

___ (c) a major railroad.

9. List three ways you can travel between Moscow and St. Petersburg.

_____

_____

_____

10. How does the map show that Moscow must be the most important city in the area shown?

_____

_____

_____

_____

C. Look at the cities on this map of Russia, Ukraine, and Belarus. Study the scale at the bottom of the map.

Major Cities of Russia, Ukraine, and Belarus

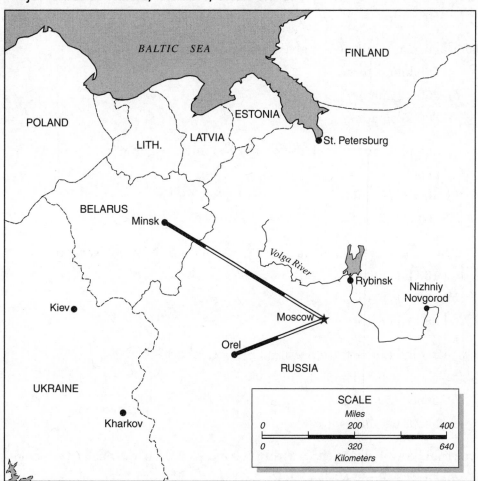

Place a check mark next to the correct answers to questions 1 to 10.

1. The scale shows how

___ (*a*) big each country is.

___ (*b*) many miles or kilometers each inch on the map represents.

___ (*c*) people travel from Moscow to Minsk.

2. Each inch on the scale stands for

___ (a) 100 miles, or 160 kilometers.

___ (b) 200 miles, or 320 kilometers.

___ (c) 300 miles, or 480 kilometers.

3. On the map, how many inches are there between Moscow and Minsk?

___ (a) 1 inch

___ (b) 2 inches

___ (c) 3 inches

4. About how many miles apart are Moscow and Minsk?

___ (a) 100 miles

___ (b) 200 miles

___ (c) 400 miles

5. About how many kilometers apart are Minsk and Orel?

___ (a) 160 kilometers

___ (b) 560 kilometers

___ (c) 800 kilometers

6. How many miles apart are Moscow and Nizhniy Novgorod?

___ (a) about 250 miles

___ (b) about 350 miles

___ (c) about 400 miles

7. How many kilometers apart are St. Petersburg and Nizhniy Novgorod?

___ (a) 160 kilometers

___ (b) 660 kilometers

___ (c) 880 kilometers

8. How many miles apart are Kiev and St. Petersburg?

___ (a) about 250 miles

___ (b) about 450 miles

___ (c) about 650 miles

9. If you could travel only to cities within 300 miles of Moscow, which cities could you visit?

___ (a) Orel, Nizhniy Novgorod, Rybinsk

___ (b) Kiev, Minsk, Rybinsk

___ (c) St. Petersburg, Orel, Kiev

10. If you traveled from Kiev to Minsk to St. Petersburg, how many miles would you travel?

___ (a) 300 miles

___ (b) 700 miles

___ (c) 960 miles

D. Study the following map of Africa.

Transportation in Africa

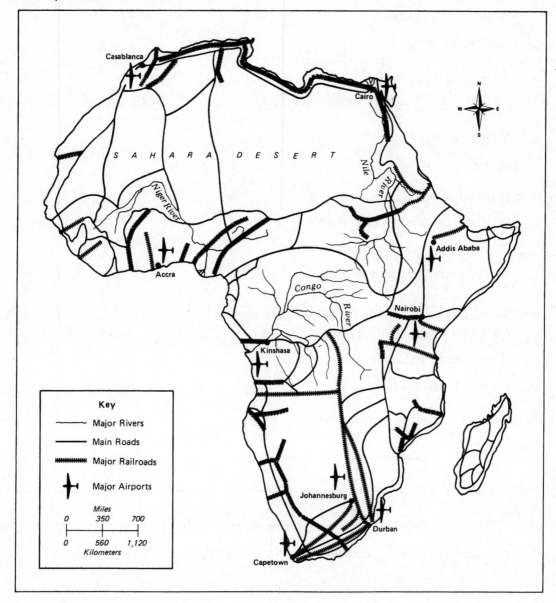

Place a check mark next to the correct answers to questions 1 to 6.

1. The map shows

   ___ (a) how many railroads there are in Africa.

   ___ (b) how many people live in Africa.

   ___ (c) the major ways of traveling in Africa.

2. The symbols on the map are

   ___ (a) explained in the text.

   ___ (b) explained in the key.

   ___ (c) not explained at all.

3. The symbol ——————— on the map stands for

___ (*a*) main roads.

___ (*b*) major railroads.

___ (*c*) major rivers.

4. The symbol ✈ stands for

___ (a) major cities.

___ (*b*) major airports.

___ (*c*) major canals.

5. The scale tells you

___ (*a*) distance in miles or kilometers.

___ (*b*) the weight of an area of a country.

___ (*c*) the population of a country.

6. Which two cities are on major rivers?

___ (*a*) Addis Ababa and Accra

___ (*b*) Durban and Capetown

___ (*c*) Kinshasa and Cairo

7. List the three major rivers shown on the map.

_____

_____

_____

8. List three different ways you could travel between Cairo and Casablanca.

_____

_____

_____

9. Why do you think there are few symbols on the area of the map marked Sahara Desert? (Answer in one or two sentences.)

_____

_____

_____

_____

10. Why is having an airport important to many cities in Africa? (Answer in two or three sentences.)

_____

_____

_____

_____

_____

Answer questions 11 to 15 with the help of the scale in the key on page 179. (Clue: See how many times the scale will fit between each of the cities named in the questions.) Place a check mark next to the correct answers.

11. About how many miles apart are Addis Ababa and Nairobi?
___ (a) 100 miles
___ (b) 300 miles
___ (c) 500 miles
___ (d) 700 miles

12. About how many kilometers apart are Durban and Capetown?
___ (a) 560 kilometers
___ (b) 1,260 kilometers
___ (c) 1,600 kilometers
___ (d) 2,200 kilometers

13. How many miles apart are Cairo and Casablanca?
___ (a) about 350
___ (b) about 700
___ (c) about 2,300
___ (d) about 3,360

14. About how many kilometers apart are Kinshasa and Nairobi?
___ (a) 1,120 kilometers
___ (b) 2,520 kilometers
___ (c) 3,360 kilometers
___ (d) 4,000 kilometers

15. The distance between Accra and Johannesburg can be expressed as
___ (a) 2,975 miles or 4,760 kilometers.
___ (b) 3,500 miles or 5,600 kilometers.
___ (c) 4,000 miles or 6,400 kilometers.
___ (d) 7,000 miles or 11,200 kilometers.

Chapter 21
Political Maps

Most people use maps to find cities and countries. A map that shows mainly cities and countries is a *political map*. (The word "political" means having to do with government.) A political map uses symbols to show where cities are located and lines to show the size and shape of each country. These symbols and lines are explained in a key on the map.

On most political maps, the key looks like the one on the map on page 183.

The symbol used in the key to show a city is a dot •. A star ★ indicates the capital city of a country. This is where the national government is located. Lines show the boundaries of countries, that is, where a country begins and ends. These dividing lines may look like any one of the following: ——— ———— —··— .

The names of countries are usually written in capital letters, such as VIETNAM. Sometimes colors are used on a map to help you see the size and shape of countries. (Of course, these lines and colors do not really exist on the Earth.)

The following political map shows mainland Southeast Asia as it is today. ("Mainland" means the part connected to the continent. It does not include any of the island nations of Southeast Asia.) In the bottom right corner of the map is a key that explains the symbols and lines used on the map. Study the map and its key.

1. The political map on page 183 shows

_____ (a) how many people live in mainland Southeast Asia.

_____ (b) the important rivers of mainland Southeast Asia.

_____ (c) the countries and major cities of mainland Southeast Asia.

Which answer did you choose? Look at the key on the map. It shows the symbols for boundary lines and cities in mainland Southeast Asia. Therefore, the answer to question 1 is (c).

2. Which two countries share the same boundary line?

_____ (a) Myanmar and Vietnam

_____ (b) Laos and Cambodia

_____ (c) Thailand and Vietnam

What was your answer? First, you have to locate the countries listed in choices (a), (b), and (c). They are written on the map in capital letters. Then you have to study the boundary lines of each country. The boundary line on the map looks like this ——— . You should be able to see that only Laos and Cambodia share the same boundary. The southern part of Laos borders on the northern part of Cambodia. Therefore, the answer to question 2 is (b).

_____ 3. True or False: Ho Chi Minh City is the capital of Vietnam.

What was your answer this time? The key uses a dot to show a city and a star to show the capital city of a country. Ho Chi Minh City has a dot, and Hanoi has a star. Therefore, Hanoi is the capital of Vietnam, and the answer to question 3 is False.

The political map on page 183 shows the countries of mainland Southeast Asia as they are today. A political map showing Southeast Asia in the 1920s would look very different. Because boundaries of many countries have changed over the years, it is

Mainland Southeast Asia Today

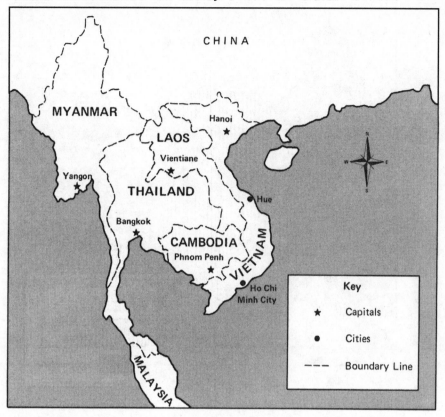

always important to know what time period a map is dealing with.

Look at the map on page 184 of mainland Southeast Asia as it was in 1925. Notice how it is different from the map of Southeast Asia today. The key is also different. It shows which areas of mainland Southeast Asia were controlled by European countries in 1925.

1. The map shows mainland Southeast Asia

_____ (a) today.

_____ (b) in 1925.

_____ (c) in 1700.

What was your answer? Perhaps the most important fact on a political map is the date. The date tells you what year or century the information on the map reflects. If a political map has no date, it usually means that the map is showing cities and countries as they appear today. In the map title, the year 1925 appears. This tells you that the map shows the countries of Southeast Asia as they were in 1925. Therefore, the answer to question 1 is (b).

2. The key on this map shows

_____ (a) the boundary lines of the countries.

_____ (b) the capital cities of the countries.

_____ (c) which European countries controlled parts of Southeast Asia in 1925.

What was your answer? The key shows that parts of Southeast Asia were controlled by European countries in 1925. Therefore, the answer to question 2 is (c).

3. Which one of the following areas on the map was *not* controlled by a European country in 1925?

_____ (a) Burma

_____ (b) Indochina

_____ (c) Siam

Which answer did you choose? Here again the key helps you to answer the question. The key shows that the area colored dark gray on the map was independent, or free from European control, in 1925. Only

Mainland Southeast Asia, 1925

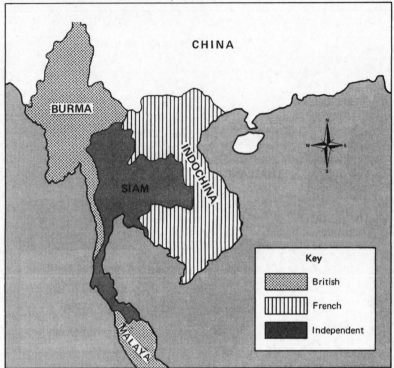

Siam is colored dark gray on the map. Therefore, the answer to question 3 is (c).

Notice that the country named Siam on the 1925 map is named Thailand on today's map and Burma is now named Myanmar. Over the years, some countries have changed their names.

4. The area named Indochina on the 1925 map is now the three countries of

_____ (a) Vietnam, Thailand, and Myanmar.

_____ (b) Vietnam, Laos, and Cambodia.

_____ (c) Myanmar, Thailand, and Cambodia.

What was your answer? You have to look at both maps of mainland Southeast Asia to answer this question. First, look at the area named Indochina on the 1925 map. Notice the size and shape of Indochina. Now look at the same area on the map of Southeast Asia today. You can see that the same area has been divided into three countries: Vietnam, Laos, and Cambodia. Therefore, the answer to question 4 is (b).

When you study a political map, be sure to look closely at the key. Also, be sure that you know the year or the time period the map is showing.

You will study political maps more than any other kind of map in your Social Studies classes. The following exercises will give you practice in using political maps.

USING WHAT YOU HAVE LEARNED

A. True or False: If every part of the statement is true, write **T**.

If any part of the statement is false, write **F**.

_____ 1. A political map shows only how many people live in a city or country.

_____ 2. Boundary lines between countries never change.

3. On the map of mainland Southeast Asia at the beginning of this chapter, you know that Myanmar is a country because its name is written in capital letters across its land area.

____ 4. On the map of mainland Southeast Asia at the beginning of this chapter, the symbol used to show a capital city is a dot.

____ 5. A political map can be drawn to show cities and boundaries at different times in history.

B. Study the following political map of Southwest Asia/Africa.

Southwest Asia/Africa

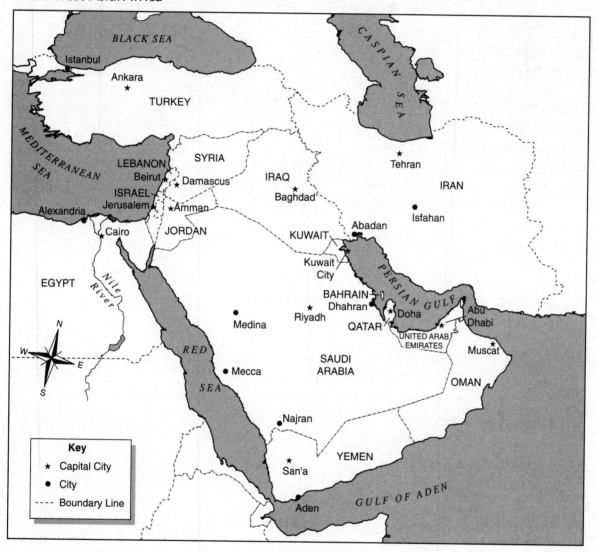

Place a check mark next to the correct answers to questions 1 to 9.

1. The map shows

____ (*a*) all the cities of Southwest Asia/Africa.

____ (*b*) the countries and important cities of Southwest Asia/Africa.

____ (*c*) oil production in Southwest Asia/Africa.

2. The symbol on the map used to show a capital city is a

___ (a) •

___ (b) ★

___ (c) ---- |

3. The boundary line between countries on this map looks most like

___ (a) ———

___ (b) ----------

___ (c) —··—

4. Which one of the following cities is the capital of Iraq?

___ (a) Cairo

___ (b) Riyadh

___ (c) Baghdad

5. Which one of the following cities is the capital of Saudi Arabia?

___ (a) San'a

___ (b) Riyadh

___ (c) Damascus

6. Which one of the following cities is NOT a capital city?

___ (a) Ankara

___ (b) Tehran

___ (c) Mecca

7. How many countries are shown and labeled on this map?

___ (a) 10

___ (b) 15

___ (c) 20

8. Which two of these countries on the map share the same boundary line?

___ (a) Egypt and Iran

___ (b) Turkey and Saudi Arabia

___ (c) Saudi Arabia and Jordan

9. Which country is north of Syria?

___ (a) Turkey

___ (b) Oman

___ (c) Iran

10. List the six countries on the map that share a boundary line with Iraq.

_____

_____

_____

C. Study the political maps of Africa on pages 187 and 188.

Map A—Africa in 1914

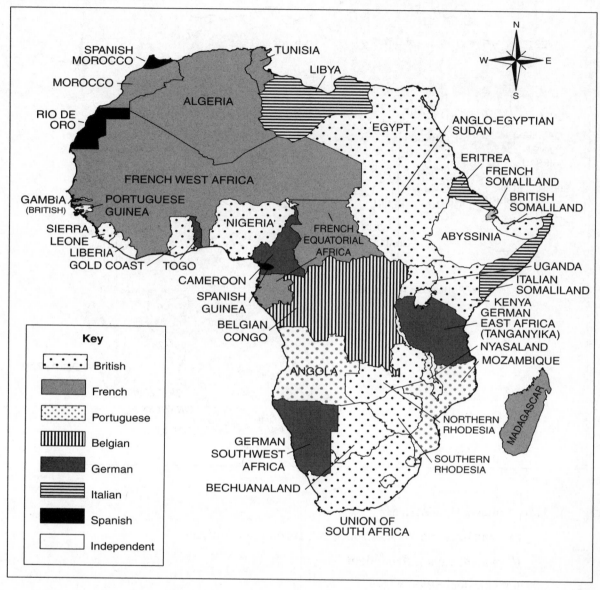

Place a check mark next to the correct answers to questions 1 to 8.

1. The two maps of Africa show that

   ____ (*a*) the boundaries of countries in Africa have not changed at all between 1914 and today.

   ____ (*b*) most of Africa is still controlled by Europeans today.

   ____ (*c*) there have been many political changes in Africa between 1914 and today.

2. Map A shows Africa in 1914, and Map B shows Africa

   ____ (*a*) in 1924.

   ____ (*b*) in 1950.

   ____ (*c*) today.

Map B—Africa Today

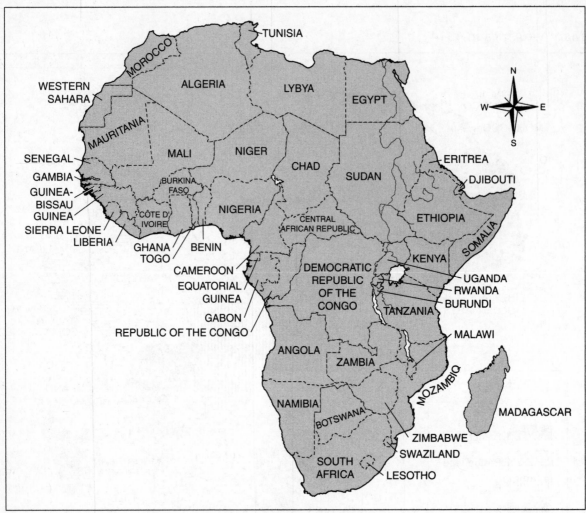

3. Map A shows that Africa

___ (a) was once mostly controlled by European countries.

___ (b) was always independent.

___ (c) is independent today.

4. According to Map A, which European country controlled the areas of Africa with the pattern [   ] ?

___ (a) Britain

___ (b) France

___ (c) Italy

5. According to Map A, which of these countries was independent in 1914?

___ (a) Liberia

___ (b) Kenya

___ (c) Angola

6. Map B shows that Africa is

   ___ (a) one large country.

   ___ (b) a continent containing many countries.

   ___ (c) a continent containing few countries.

7. The country Mali in Map B was once part of the area in Map A named

   ___ (a) German East Africa.

   ___ (b) French Equatorial Africa.

   ___ (c) French West Africa.

8. Which country did Northern Rhodesia become?

   ___ (a) Zimbabwe

   ___ (b) Zambia

   ___ (c) Tanzania

9. List five countries, now independent, that were controlled by Britain in 1914.

10. Why are there more boundary lines on today's map of Africa than there are on the 1914 map? (Answer in one or two sentences.)

D. Study the political maps of South America on pages 190 and 192.

D-1. Study Map A and its key. Then place a check mark next to the correct answers to questions 1 to 5.

   1. Map A shows the political boundaries of South America

      ___ (a) in 1800.

      ___ (b) in 1900.

      ___ (c) today.

   2. The patterns in the key show

      ___ (a) the crops produced in South America in 1800.

      ___ (b) the size of countries in South America today.

      ___ (c) the areas in South America controlled by European countries in 1800.

Map A—South America in 1800

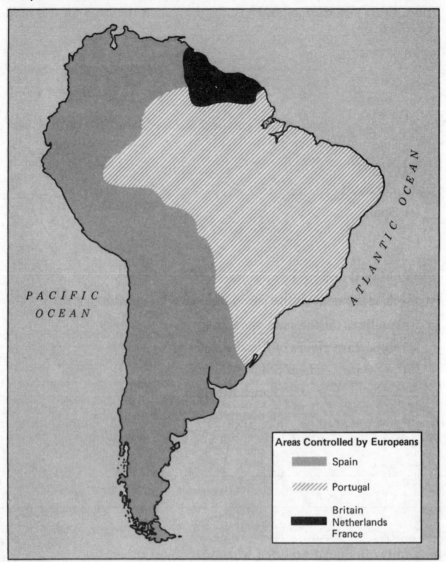

PACIFIC
OCEAN

ATLANTIC OCEAN

Areas Controlled by Europeans

Spain

Portugal

Britain
Netherlands
France

3. The land area colored gray on Map A was under the control of

___ (a) Spain.

___ (b) Portugal.

___ (c) Britain.

4. Britain, the Netherlands, and France controlled the area on the map that looks like this:

___ (a) ▬▬

___ (b) ▨▨▨

___ (c) ■■■

5. Which country controlled the smallest area of land in South America in 1800?

___ (a) France

___ (b) Portugal

___ (c) Spain

D-2. Study Map B and its key on page 192.

Place a check mark next to the correct answers to questions 1 to 5.

1. The broken lines on the map show the

  ___ (a) important rivers of South America.

  ___ (b) main railroads of South America.

  ___ (c) main highways of South America.

  ___ (d) boundaries between countries of South America.

2. The capital of Brazil is

  ___ (a) Rio de Janeiro.

  ___ (b) São Paulo.

  ___ (c) Brasília.

  ___ (d) Montevideo.

3. The country in South America with two capital cities is

  ___ (a) Brazil.

  ___ (b) Ecuador.

  ___ (c) Argentina.

  ___ (d) Bolivia.

4. Ecuador shares a boundary line with

  ___ (a) Peru.

  ___ (b) Argentina.

  ___ (c) Paraguay.

  ___ (d) Venezuela.

5. Bogotá is the capital city of

  ___ (a) Venezuela.

  ___ (b) Colombia.

  ___ (c) Chile.

  ___ (d) Peru.

D-3. Use the directional compass on Map B to help you answer questions 1 to 10. Write the correct cardinal and intermediate directions in the blanks.

north   south   west   east

1. Brazil is _____ of Paraguay.

2. Guyana is _____ of Venezuela.

3. Peru is _____ of Colombia.

4. Chile is _____ of Argentina.

5. Suriname is _____ of Uruguay.

Map B—South America Today

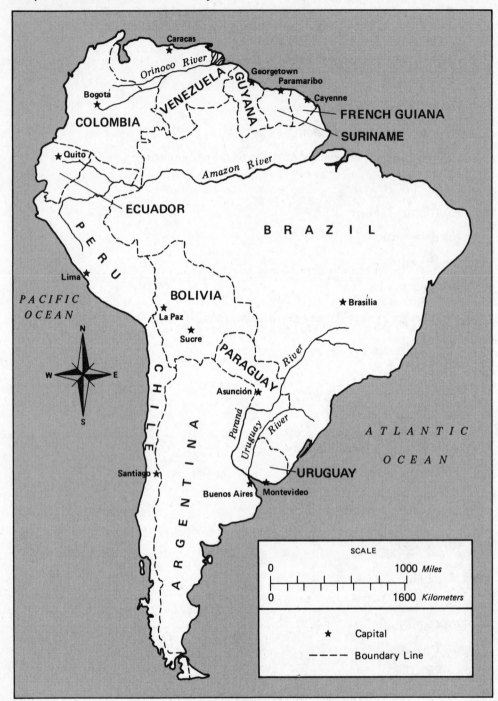

northwest   northeast   southwest   southeast

6. Sucre is _____ of Asunción.

7. Bogotá is _____ of Quito.

8. Bogotá is _____ of Caracas.

9. Buenos Aires is _____ of Lima.

10. Brasília is _____ of Santiago.

D-4. Study the scale on Map B. Then answer each of the following questions in a sentence.

1. How many miles are there between Buenos Aires and Montevideo?

_____

_____

2. How many miles are there between Bogotá and Cayenne?

_____

_____

3. How many miles are there between Asunción and Montevideo?

_____

_____

4. How many kilometers are there between Quito and Lima?

_____

_____

5. How many miles are there between La Paz and Brasília?

_____

_____

Using Latitude and Longitude

Chapter 22
Latitude on Globes and Maps

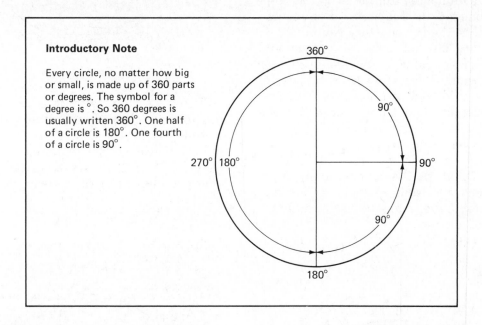

Introductory Note

Every circle, no matter how big or small, is made up of 360 parts or degrees. The symbol for a degree is °. So 360 degrees is usually written 360°. One half of a circle is 180°. One fourth of a circle is 90°.

The Earth is such a large place that directions alone will not help you find exact locations of places. Other guides are also needed. They are supplied by a system of imaginary lines that are drawn on many maps and globes.

You already know of the imaginary line called the equator, which divides the Earth into the Northern Hemisphere and the Southern Hemisphere. Picture A on page 196 shows the location of the equator on the Earth. All other imaginary lines in Picture

A are used to show distances north or south of the equator. The distance north or south of the equator is called *latitude*. That is why these imaginary lines are called *lines of latitude*. They are also called *parallels of latitude* because they never meet. They remain the same distance from each other all the way around the Earth.

Latitude, or distance from the equator, is measured in degrees. Each parallel of latitude is one degree from the parallel above or below it. One degree of latitude equals about

Picture A

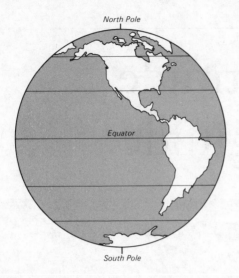

A degree of latitude north of the equator may have an N after it. For example, 60°N means 60° north of the equator.

Picture C shows that there are also 90° from the equator to the South Pole. A degree of latitude south of the equator may have an S after it. For example, 60°S means 60° south of the equator.

Picture C

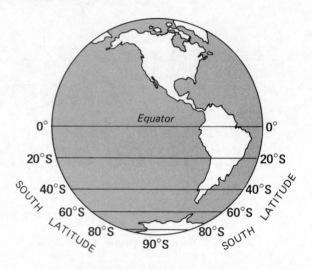

69 miles on the Earth's surface. Since latitude measurement starts at the equator, the equator is marked 0°. Every other line of latitude is numbered from 1° to 90°. 90° represents one-fourth of a circle, or one-fourth of 360°. (See the Introductory Note.)

There are 90° between the equator and the North Pole and 90° between the equator and the South Pole. As a result, 90 lines of latitude would be drawn north of the equator or south of the equator on a map of the Earth. But this could make the map too crowded. So maps and globes generally show only some of the lines of latitude. Picture B, of the Western Hemisphere, shows lines of latitude for every 20° north of the equator. Other maps may show different degrees of latitude.

Picture D shows why it is important to look for the letter N or S after a degree of latitude. Both the Northern Hemisphere and the Southern Hemisphere contain 0° to 90°. The N or S tells you in which hemisphere a degree of latitude is located.

Picture D

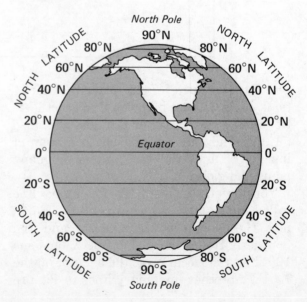

Picture B

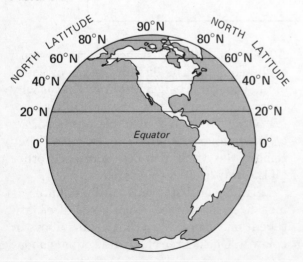

Use the information you have learned in this chapter to answer the following questions.

1. Lines of latitude are used on a map

_____ (a) to show that maps are better than globes.

_____ (b) to find distances north or south of the equator.

_____ (c) to find distances west or east of the equator.

Which answer did you choose? A line of latitude alone means nothing. It has meaning only when it is used along with the equator. This is because a line of latitude tells you only one thing—how far a place is north or south of the equator. Therefore, the answer to question 1 is (b).

2. Lines of latitude are also called parallel lines because they

_____ (a) cross one another halfway around the Earth.

_____ (b) meet at the North Pole.

_____ (c) remain the same distance from each other all the way around the Earth.

Which answer did you choose? Lines of latitude never meet. They remain the same distance from each other all around the Earth, which is why they are called parallel lines. Therefore, the answer to question 2 is (c).

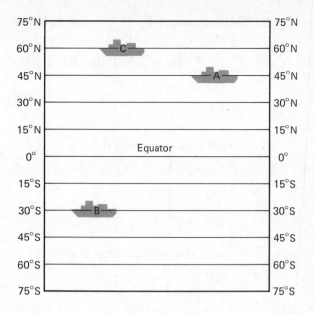

3. Look at the diagram. Then decide which ship is in trouble at 45°N.

_____ (a) Ship A

_____ (b) Ship B

_____ (c) Ship C

Which answer did you choose this time? You are looking for the ship that is in trouble at 45°N. The N after 45°N tells you that you must look north of the equator. Starting at the equator, move your finger north. Stop when you come to the line marked 45°N. You will see that it is Ship A that is on the 45°N line of latitude. Therefore, the answer to question 3 is (a).

The following exercises will give you practice in finding distances and locations with the help of latitude.

USING WHAT YOU HAVE LEARNED

A. Place a check mark next to the correct answers to questions 1 to 10.

1. The imaginary line that goes around the center of the Earth is

___ (a) an axis.

___ (b) a pole.

___ (c) the equator.

2. The imaginary lines used on a map to show distance north or south of the equator are called

___ (a) lines, or parallels, of latitude.

___ (b) degrees.

___ (c) circles.

3. Latitude is measured in

___ (a) miles.

___ (b) inches.

___ (c) degrees.

4. What is the symbol for a degree?

___ (a) +

___ (b) °

___ (c) '

5. How many degrees are in a circle?

___ (a) 90°

___ (b) 180°

___ (c) 360°

6. How many degrees are in a large circle?

___ (a) 360°

___ (b) 400°

___ (c) 460°

7. From the equator to the North Pole, there are

___ (a) 90°.

___ (b) 180°.

___ (c) 360°.

8. From the equator to the South Pole, there are

___ (a) 90°.

___ (b) 180°.

___ (c) 360°.

9. From the North Pole to the South Pole, there are

___ (a) 90°.

___ (b) 180°.

___ (c) 360°.

10. A degree of latitude north or south of the equator

___ (*a*) touches the North Pole or the South Pole.

___ (*b*) runs from the North Pole to the South Pole.

___ (*c*) is often followed by an N or an S.

B. Latitude and Location

B-1. Write the degrees of latitude at which ships 1 to 10 are located. The first one is done for you.

Ship 1 _____15°N_____   Ship 6 _____

Ship 2 _____   Ship 7 _____

Ship 3 _____   Ship 8 _____

Ship 4 _____   Ship 9 _____

Ship 5 _____   Ship 10 _____

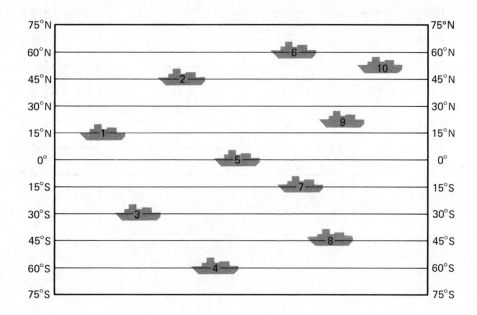

B-2. Locate the following degrees of latitude on the chart below by placing the number before each degree on the correct line of latitude. The first one is done for you.

1. 40°S
2. 60°N
3. 30°N
4. 20°N
5. 70°N

6. 0°
7. 25°S
8. 48°N
9. 5°N
10. 60°S

11. 30°S
12. 55°S
13. 18°N
14. 62°S
15. 27°N

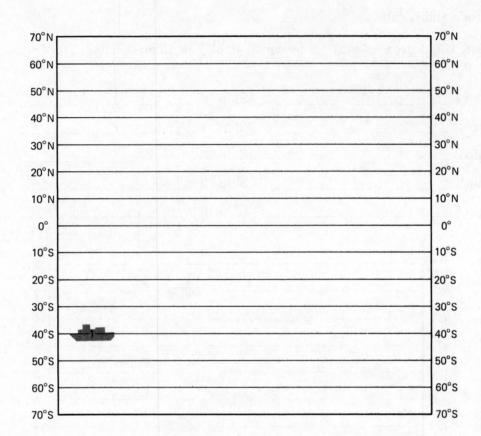

C. In this chapter, you learned that every degree of latitude on a map equals 69 miles on the Earth. If two cities are one degree apart on a map, then they are 69 miles apart on the Earth. If two cities are two degrees apart on a map, then they are 138 miles apart on the Earth. Here is how it is done: 69 miles × 2 = 138 miles. Look at the map of Chile, in South America. Use this map to answer the following questions on finding distances.

Chile

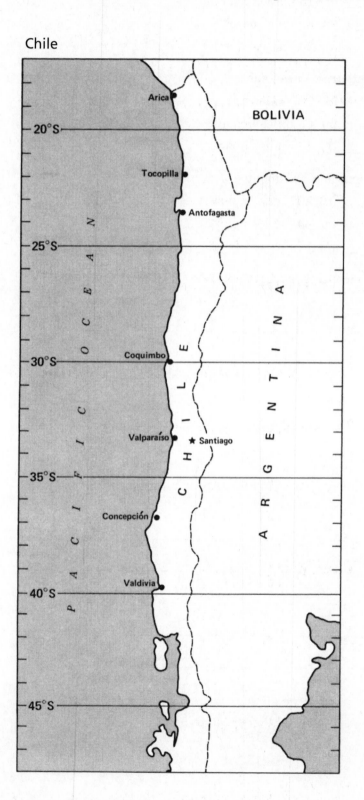

1. Each degree on a map is equal to

   _____ (a) 52 miles on the Earth.

   _____ (b) 69 miles on the Earth.

   _____ (c) 100 miles on the Earth.

2. If two cities are three degrees apart on a map, they are

   _____ (a) 69 miles apart on the Earth.

   _____ (b) 138 miles apart on the Earth.

   _____ (c) 207 miles apart on the Earth.

3. If two cities are five degrees apart on a map, they are

   _____ (a) 69 miles apart on the Earth.

   _____ (b) 345 miles apart on the Earth.

   _____ (c) 690 miles apart on the Earth.

4. The city of Santiago can be found at about

   _____ (a) 23°S.

   _____ (b) 33°S.

   _____ (c) 37°S.

5. The city of Arica is located about

   _____ (a) 690 miles south of the equator.

   _____ (b) 1,276 miles south of the equator.

   _____ (c) 1,380 miles south of the equator.

For questions 6–8, you should mark two answers. One is to show how many degrees apart the cities are. The second is to show how many miles apart the cities are.

6. The city of Tocopilla and the city of Antofagasta are about

    ___ (a) one degree apart.   ___ (d) 138 miles apart.

    ___ (b) two degrees apart.   ___ (e) 69 miles apart.

    ___ (c) three degrees apart.   ___ (f) 207 miles apart.

7. The city of Coquimbo and the city of Valparaíso are about

    ___ (a) one degree apart.   ___ (d) 207 miles apart.

    ___ (b) two degrees apart.   ___ (e) 69 miles apart.

    ___ (c) three degrees apart.   ___ (f) 138 miles apart.

8. The city of Valdivia and the city of Concepción are about

    ___ (a) three degrees apart.   ___ (d) 207 miles apart.

    ___ (b) four degrees apart.   ___ (e) 345 miles apart.

    ___ (c) five degrees apart.   ___ (f) 276 miles apart.

9. What do we mean when we say that Concepción is located at 37°S? (Answer in one or two sentences.)

_____

_____

_____

_____

10. Imagine that the degrees on the map had been written without the letter S. For example, the map showed 30° instead of 30°S. How would you still be able to tell by the degrees that Chile is in the Southern Hemisphere? (Answer in two or three sentences.)

_____

_____

_____

_____

_____

Chapter 23
Latitude and Climate

Is there one line of latitude that is more important than any other line of latitude? By now you should be able to answer that the equator is the most important line of latitude. All other lines of latitude are drawn parallel to the equator.

In addition to the equator, there are several other important parallels of latitude. (See Picture A.) They are the *Tropic of Cancer*, the *Tropic of Capricorn*, the *Arctic Circle*, and the *Antarctic Circle*. These imaginary lines are used to show different climate areas on the Earth. (*Climate* is the weather in an area over a long period of time.)

Let us look first at the Tropic of Cancer and the Tropic of Capricorn. The Tropic of Cancer is a line of latitude 23½°N of the equator. The Tropic of Capricorn is a line of latitude 23½°S of the equator. As shown in Picture B, the area of the Earth between these two parallel lines is called the *low*

latitudes. The climate in this area is almost always warm or hot.

Two other important parallels are the Arctic Circle and the Antarctic Circle. The Arctic Circle is a line of latitude 66½°N of the equator. Between 66½°N and the North Pole is the area called the Arctic. The North Pole is the center of the Arctic, as shown in Picture C on page 204.

The Antarctic Circle is a line of latitude 66½°S of the equator. The area between 66½°S and the South Pole is called the Antarctic. At the center of the Antarctic is the South Pole, as shown in Picture C.

The areas of the Arctic and the Antarctic are called the *high latitudes*, or the *polar zones*. Few people live in the high latitudes because of the extremely cold climate that exists for most of the year. Picture C shows where the high latitudes are located on the Earth.

Picture A

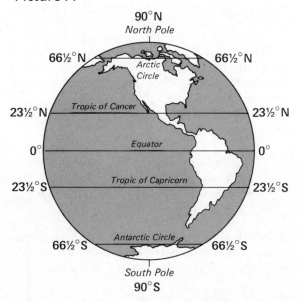

Picture B

Picture C

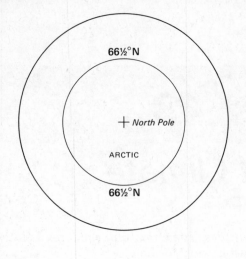

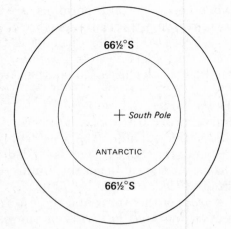

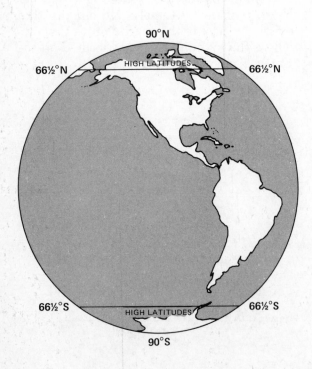

The areas between 23½° and 66½° in both the Northern Hemisphere and the Southern Hemisphere are called the *middle latitudes*. (See Picture D.) They have this name because they are between the high latitudes and the low latitudes. The middle latitudes have four seasons—spring, summer, fall, and winter. Most of the people in the world live in the middle latitudes because of the favorable (good, pleasing) climate.

Picture D

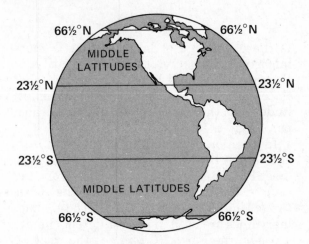

Using the information you learned in this chapter, answer the following questions.

1. In this chapter, you have seen that certain lines of latitude are used

   _____ (a) to show the time.

   _____ (b) to locate sinking ships.

   _____ (c) to show different climate areas on the Earth.

Which answer did you choose? Different areas of the Earth have different climates. You have read in this chapter that lines of latitude are used to show where these climate areas are located. Therefore, the answer to question 1 is (c).

_____ 2. True or False: Few people live in the high latitudes because the climate is extremely cold most of the year.

What was your answer? The high latitudes are found between the Arctic Circle and the North Pole and between the

Antarctic Circle and the South Pole. The areas of the Earth around the North Pole and the South Pole are extremely cold most of the year. This is why few people live in the high latitudes. Therefore, the answer to question 2 is True.

3. A city located between the Tropic of Cancer and the Arctic Circle is likely to have

_____ (a) only a hot climate.

_____ (b) only a cold climate.

_____ (c) a climate with four seasons.

Which answer did you choose this time? The area between the Tropic of Cancer and the Arctic Circle is called the middle latitudes. The middle latitudes do not have the extreme heat of the low latitudes or the extreme cold of the high latitudes. Instead, the middle latitudes have four seasons with changing temperatures. Therefore, the answer to question 3 is (c).

You have seen in this chapter how certain lines of latitude are used to show climate areas on the Earth. The following exercises will give you more practice in learning about latitude and climate.

USING WHAT YOU HAVE LEARNED

A. Place a check mark next to the correct answers to questions 1 to 5.

1. The name given to the line of latitude at 23½°N is the

___ (a) Arctic Circle.

___ (b) Tropic of Cancer.

___ (c) equator.

2. The name given to the line of latitude at 66½°S is the

___ (a) Tropic of Capricorn.

___ (b) Antarctic Circle.

___ (c) Arctic Circle.

3. The Tropic of Capricorn is located at

___ (a) 23½°.

___ (b) 23½°N.

___ (c) 23½°S.

4. The Arctic Circle is located at

___ (a) 66½°.

___ (b) 66½°N.

___ (c) 66½°S.

5. The term "middle latitudes" refers to the area of the Earth between

___ (a) 23½°N to 66½°N and 23½°S to 66½°S.

___ (b) 23½°N to 66½°N only.

___ (c) 23½°S to 66½°S only.

B. True or False: If every part of the statement is true, write **T**.
If any part of the statement is false, write **F**.

_____ 1. The area of the Earth between 23½°N and 23½°S is called the middle latitudes.

_____ 2. The climate of the low latitudes is generally extremely cold.

_____ 3. The area north of 66½°N is called both the Arctic and the high latitudes.

_____ 4. The area between 66½°S and the South Pole is likely to have only a hot season.

_____ 5. There are four seasons in the middle latitudes.

C. Important Lines of Latitude and Climate Areas

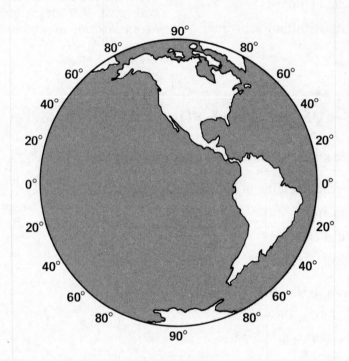

C-1. On the map above, draw and label the following important lines of latitude:

Equator   Arctic Circle
Tropic of Cancer   Antarctic Circle
Tropic of Capricorn

C-2. Label on the map the following climate areas:

low latitudes   middle latitudes   high latitudes

Chapter 24
Longitude on Globes and Maps

Lines of latitude show only distances north and south of the equator. To measure east and west distances, it is necessary to have another system of imaginary lines on the Earth. Distance east or west is called *longitude*, and the lines to measure this distance are called *meridians of longitude*. In Picture A, you see that lines of longitude run north and south between the North Pole and the South Pole.

Picture A

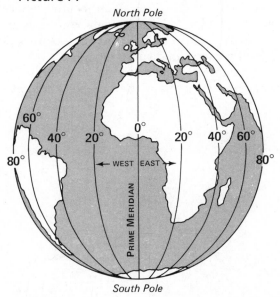

To measure longitude, you need a starting line. You learned that parallels of latitude are measured north or south from the equator. The equator is the starting line for measuring latitude. For measuring longitude, the starting line is the *Prime Meridian*, a line of longitude that runs through Greenwich, England. Picture A shows where the Prime Meridian is located.

All lines of longitude are measured in degrees east or west of the Prime Meridian. Each meridian is one degree from the meridian next to it. Starting from the Prime Meridian, which is marked 0°, meridians are marked going east from 1° to 180°E. Going west, the meridians are marked from 1° to 180°W.

It is important to use W (west) or E (east) after a degree of longitude. For example, if you were told to find 120° on Picture B (next page), you would have trouble because 120° appears twice on the map. The W or E tells you if you are looking for 120° west or 120° east of the Prime Meridian.

Meridians are not parallel lines; that is, they are not always the same distance from one another. Look again at Picture A, and you will see that the meridians are farthest apart at the equator and closest together at the poles. At the equator, one degree of longitude equals about 69 miles on the Earth. Near the poles, one degree of longitude equals only a few miles.

In Picture A you see nearly one half of the Earth and less than one half of 360°. You see 80° west of the Prime Meridian and 80° east of the Prime Meridian. Both parts add up to 160°. On a different kind of map of the Earth, a Mollweide map, for example, all 360° can be shown. In Picture B on page 208, you can see 180° west of the Prime Meridian and 180° east of the Prime Meridian.

Understanding how to use lines of longitude is an important Social Studies skill. But it would be impossible to find the exact location of a place on the Earth with only a line of longitude. To find the exact location of a place, it is necessary to use both a line of latitude and a line of longitude. Here is an example to show why you need the two lines.

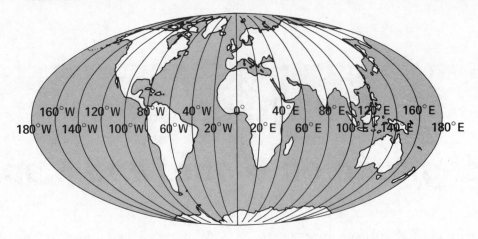

Suppose you live in a town that has the streets mapped in Picture C. You asked your friend to meet you on 10th Avenue. Would it be easy for your friend to find you? Probably not. Since 10th Avenue runs for at least five blocks, your friend would have to walk blocks to find you. But what if you told your friend to meet you where 10th Avenue meets Jay Street, or at the intersection of 10th and Jay? Your friend would walk along 10th Avenue until he got to Jay Street. Then he would stop and wait for you. By using the intersection of two streets or two lines in giving your location, your friend would be able to find you easily.

Picture D shows how latitude and longitude lines look when they are put together on the same map. They meet and cross like street intersections. Let us use the lines of latitude and longitude in Picture D to locate something on the Earth. Imagine that a ship is sinking. It sends out a radio message that it is at 20°N 40°W. This means that the ship is 20° north of the equator and 40° west of the Prime Meridian. It is located where the 20°N latitude line meets and crosses the 40°W longitude line. Latitude is always given first and longitude second.

The captain of the rescue ship finds the 20°N line on a map. (Remember that lati-

Picture C

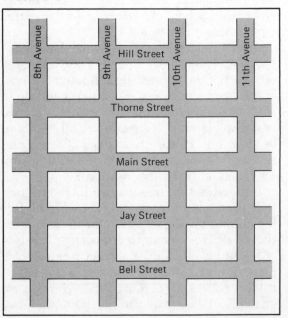

Picture D

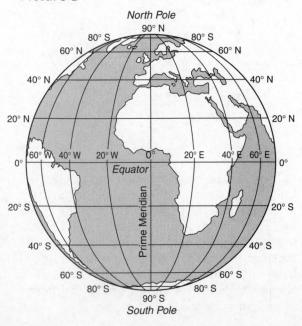

tude lines run east and west across a map, or from left to right.) The captain knows to look north of the equator because of the N after 20°. After the captain finds 20°N, he looks for the 40°W line of longitude. (Lines of longitude run north and south, or from the top to the bottom of the map.) The captain knows that there are two 40° lines on the map, but he wants the 40° line that is west of the Prime Meridian, or 40°W. He puts one finger on the 40°W line and another finger on the 20°N line and moves his fingers along the two lines until they meet. At the place where the two lines meet (20°N 40°W), the captain will find the sinking ship.

Let us see if you can use lines of latitude and longitude to locate a ship. A ship is in trouble at 40°S 60°E. Mark an X on the map in Picture D where you think this ship can be found.

Where did you place the X? The first degree (40°S) is a line of latitude. The S tells you that it is a line of latitude south of the equator. The second degree (60°E) is a line of longitude. The E tells you that it is a line of longitude east of the Prime Meridian.

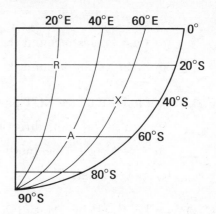

Picture E

You will find the ship where these two lines meet. If you put an X on the map in Picture D in the same place as the letter X in Picture E, then you have found the ship.

You have seen in this chapter that it is necessary to use two lines on a map to find the exact location of a thing or a place. These two lines are a parallel of latitude and a meridian of longitude. The following exercises will give you more practice in finding the exact location of places on the Earth.

USING WHAT YOU HAVE LEARNED

A. Place a check mark next to the correct answers to questions 1 to 8.

1. Lines of longitude are used to find distance

   ___ (*a*) east or west of the Prime Meridian.

   ___ (*b*) north or south of the equator.

   ___ (*c*) north or south of the Prime Meridian.

2. The most important line of longitude is the

   ___ (*a*) equator.

   ___ (*b*) axis.

   ___ (*c*) Prime Meridian.

3. Lines of longitude are also called

   ___ (*a*) parallels.

   ___ (*b*) meridians.

   ___ (*c*) latitudes.

4. Lines of longitude run

___ (a) north to south.

___ (b) east to west around the Earth.

___ (c) west to east around the Earth.

5. Lines of longitude are NOT parallel lines because they

___ (a) run in the same direction.

___ (b) get closer to one another as they near the poles.

___ (c) never meet.

6. On a map, the Prime Meridian is at

___ (a) 0°.

___ (b) 15°W.

___ (c) 30°E.

7. The Prime Meridian runs through

___ (a) Mumbai, India.

___ (b) Chicago, Illinois.

___ (c) Greenwich, England.

8. If an oil spill is located at 60°W, this means that the spill is

___ (a) 60° west of the equator.

___ (b) 60 miles west of the Prime Meridian.

___ (c) 60° west of the Prime Meridian.

9. Is the following statement true or false? "It is not necessary to write W (west) or E (east) after a degree showing longitude." (Explain in one or two sentences.)

_____

_____

_____

_____

10. Is the following statement true or false? "You need to know only the degree of longitude of a place to know its exact location." Explain your answer in one or two sentences.

_____

_____

_____

_____

B. Longitude and Location

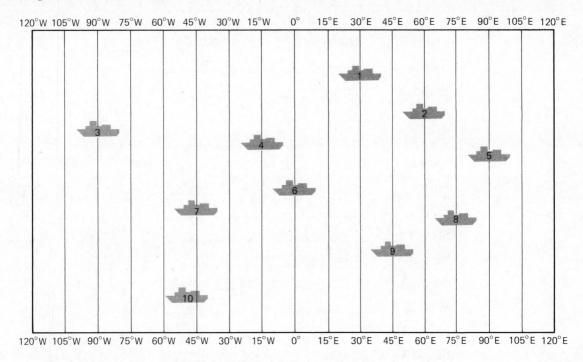

In the spaces provided, write the degrees of longitude where ships 1 to 10 are located. The first one is done for you.

Ship 1 _____30°E_____   Ship 5 _____   Ship 8 _____

Ship 2 _____   Ship 6 _____   Ship 9 _____

Ship 3 _____   Ship 7 _____   Ship 10 _____

Ship 4 _____

C. Latitude, Longitude, and Location

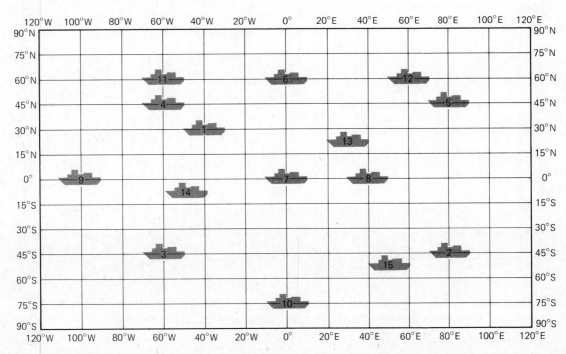

In the spaces provided, write the latitude and longitude of ships 1 to 15 shown on the diagram at the bottom of page 211. The first two are done for you.

	Latitude	Longitude
Ship 1	30°N	40°W
Ship 2	45°S	80°E
Ship 3		
Ship 4		
Ship 5		
Ship 6		
Ship 7		
Ship 8		
Ship 9		
Ship 10		
Ship 11		
Ship 12		
Ship 13		
Ship 14		
Ship 15		

D. Degrees of Latitude and Longitude

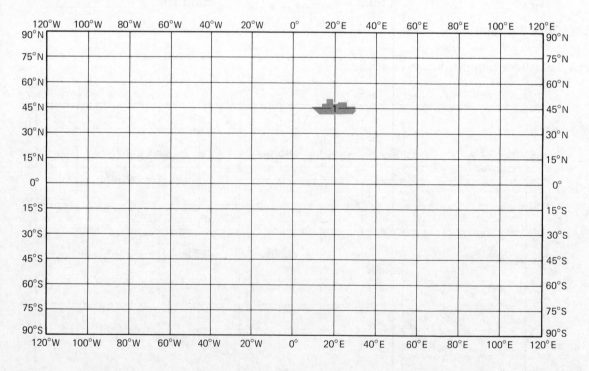

Locate the following degrees of latitude and longitude on the above diagram. Write the number before each degree of latitude and longitude in the correct place on the diagram. The first one is done for you.

1. 45°N 20°E	6. 30°N 80°E	11. 50°N 40°E
2. 60°N 60°E	7. 60°S 100°E	12. 50°S 50°E
3. 45°S 40°E	8. 75°N 0°	13. 70°N 110°W
4. 75°S 75°W	9. 0° 0°	14. 80°S 0°
5. 0° 20°W	10. 15°N 80°W	15. 25°N 75°E

E. Study the following map of Mexico and the Caribbean World.

Mexico and the Caribbean World

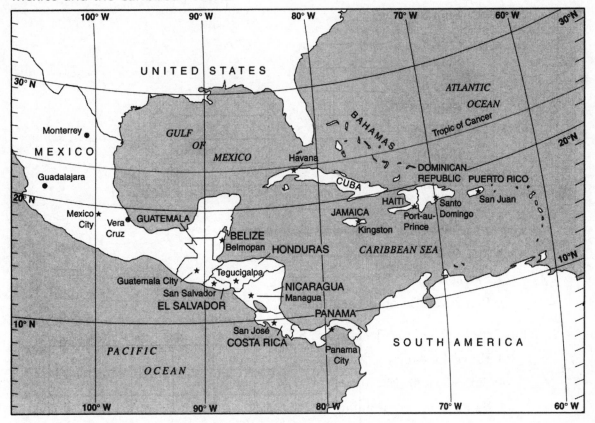

Place a check mark next to the correct answers to questions 1 to 10.

1. The equator (0°) divides the Earth into the Northern Hemisphere and the Southern Hemisphere. Therefore, the area on the map is in the

___ (a) Northern Hemisphere.

___ (b) Southern Hemisphere.

___ (c) Northern Hemisphere and the Southern Hemisphere.

2. The Tropic of Cancer runs through

___ (a) Cuba.

___ (b) Jamaica.

___ (c) Mexico.

3. Monterrey, Mexico, is located in the

___ (a) low latitudes.

___ (b) middle latitudes.

___ (c) high latitudes.

4. San Juan, Puerto Rico, is located in the

___ (a) low latitudes.

___ (b) middle latitudes.

___ (c) high latitudes.

5. Mexico City is located at

___ (a) 19°N 99°W.

___ (b) 99°N 19°W.

___ (c) 19°N 19°W.

6. Havana, Cuba, is located at

___ (a) 83°N 22°W.

___ (b) 23°N 83°W.

___ (c) 22°N 22°W.

7. Which city on the map is located at 10°N 84°W?

___ (a) Panama City, Panama

___ (b) San José, Costa Rica

___ (c) Belmopan, Belize

8. Which city on the map is located at 18°N 70°W?

___ (a) Kingston, Jamaica

___ (b) San Salvador, El Salvador

___ (c) Santo Domingo, Dominican Republic

9. Each degree of latitude on a map stands for 69 miles on the Earth. Therefore, the distance between Monterrey, Mexico, and Mexico City is about

___ (a) 210 miles.

___ (b) 414 miles.

___ (c) 690 miles.

10. Each degree of latitude stands for 69 miles on the Earth. The distance between Havana, Cuba, and San José, Costa Rica, is about

___ (a) 300 miles.

___ (b) 600 miles.

___ (c) 900 miles.

Chapter 25
Longitude and Time

If you were to visit a television news station, you might see clocks on the wall like the ones in the drawing. They show different times in different cities in the world. The clocks show that when it is 4 A.M. in San Francisco, it is 7 A.M. in New York, 1 P.M. in Rome, 2 P.M. in Cairo, and 8 P.M. in Beijing. These time differences can be shown on a map with the help of lines of longitude.

In the last chapter, you learned that lines of longitude are used to measure distance east or west of the Prime Meridian. Besides measuring distance, lines of longitude are used to help you find what time it is in different parts of the world. Map A, on the next page, shows how lines of longitude are used to show time.

The lines of longitude on Map A are 15° apart. They run 15°, 30°, 45°, and so on.

Each of these lines of longitude has a different time. For example, the line of longitude marked 0° is 12 noon. The line marked 30°W is 10 A.M. The line 45°E is 3 P.M.

You may wonder why there is a line every 15° on a map showing time. The Earth turns, or rotates, on its axis from west to east. Every 24 hours the Earth makes a complete 360° turn. By dividing 24 into 360, you get 15. This means that for every 15° of longitude, there is a difference in time of one hour.

Each 15° line of longitude is at the center of a *time zone*, which spreads 7½° west and 7½° east of the center line. For example, the center line of longitude, or standard meridian, for the Mountain Time Zone in the United States is 105°W. The area covered by the Mountain Time Zone is between 97½°W and 112½°W. All of the places in the

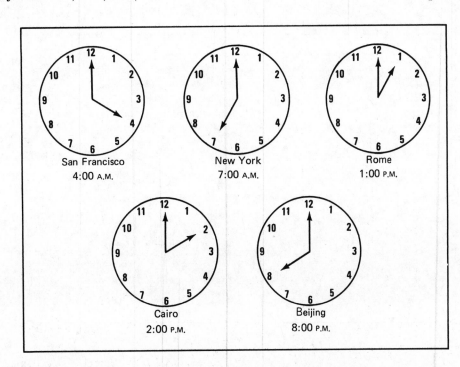

San Francisco
4:00 A.M.

New York
7:00 A.M.

Rome
1:00 P.M.

Cairo
2:00 P.M.

Beijing
8:00 P.M.

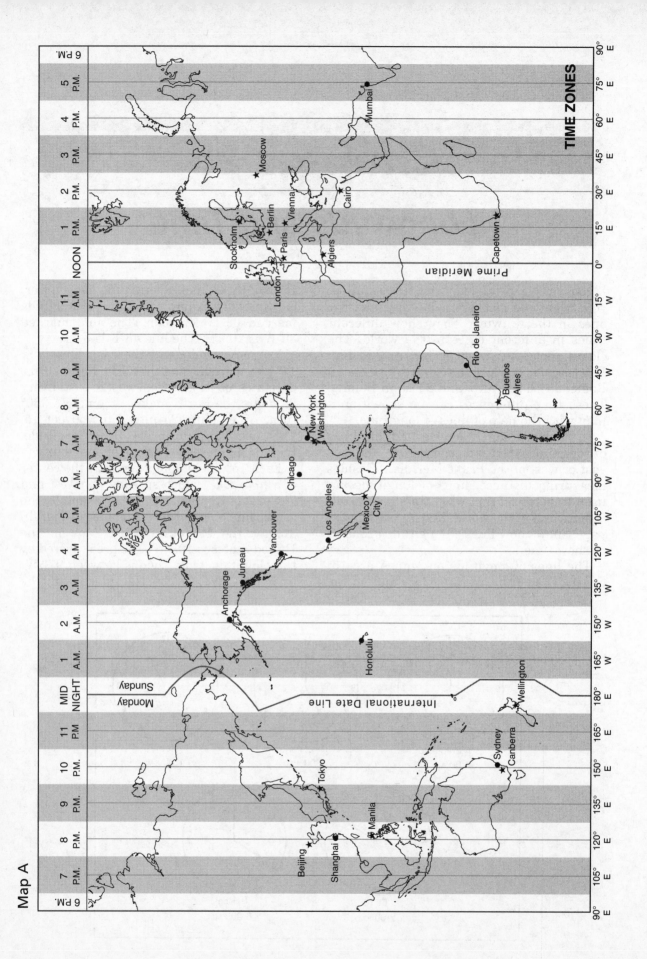

Map A

TIME ZONES

Mountain Time Zone have the same time. Actually, none of the 24 time zones has a straight north-south boundary. Zone lines zig-zag to meet the needs of the people living in the areas affected by the time changes.

When it is noon in a time zone, the 11½ time zones to the left (the west) of it are in *ante meridiem* time, or A.M. This is any time between midnight and noon. Times that are A.M. are said to be in the morning. The 11½ time zones to the right (the east) of the noon time zone are in *post meridiem* time, or P.M. This is any time between noon and midnight. Times that are P.M. are said to be in the afternoon, evening, or night.

You can see on Map A that when you travel east, or to the right, the time continues to become one hour later as you move into each time zone. For example, when it is 12 noon in London, it is 1:00 P.M. in Vienna. When you travel west, or to the left, the time continues to become one hour earlier as you move from zone to zone. For example, when it is 9:00 A.M. in Rio de Janeiro, it is 8:00 A.M. in Buenos Aires.

On Map A, look at the line of longitude marked 180°. This line is called the *International Date Line*. When you travel from east to west across the International Date Line, you jump ahead to the same time the next day. If it is 2 P.M. on Sunday east of the International Date Line, it is 2 P.M. on Monday west of the International Date Line. Likewise, if you travel west to east across the International Date Line, you go back a day. If it is 9 A.M. on Friday west of the International Date Line, it is 9 A.M. on Thursday east of the International Date Line.

Use Map A to answer the following questions on longitude and time.

_____ 1. True or False: There is a one-hour difference in time for every 30° of longitude.

What was your answer? If you divide 24 hours into 360°, you get 15° for each hour. You can also see on Map A that each one-hour time zone covers 15° and not 30°. Therefore, the answer to question 1 is False.

2. On Map A, it is 3:00 P.M. on the line of longitude marked

_____ (a) 15°E.

_____ (b) 45°E.

_____ (c) 135°E.

Which answer did you choose? Find the line of longitude marked 3:00 P.M. on Map A. Remember that you are looking for 3:00 P.M., not 3:00 A.M. The 3:00 P.M. line of longitude is east of the Prime Meridian. When you find the 3:00 P.M. line, follow the line all the way down with your finger. At the bottom of the line, you will see 45°E. Therefore, the answer to question 2 is (b).

3. What time is it in New York on the map?

_____ (a) 2:00 A.M.

_____ (b) 7:00 A.M.

_____ (c) 1:00 P.M.

Which answer did you choose? First find New York on the map. The standard meridian that determines the time for New York is 75°W. It is marked 7:00 A.M. Therefore, the answer to question 3 is (b).

Map A shows that it is 12 noon in London. But you know that it does not stay 12 noon in London all day long. As the Earth rotates on its axis, the time in a place changes. This is because the position of a place on Earth in relation to the sun changes. The rotation turns a place toward or away from the sun.

Study Pictures A and B on page 218 to see how time changes.

You see that Pictures A and B show the same degrees of longitude. All line of longitude are 15° apart. But the times are different in each picture. On Picture A, 0° (the Prime Meridian) shows 12 noon. This means that the sun is shining directly over the time zone of 0°. Each hour, the Earth rotates 15° to the east. This makes the sun appear to be moving to the west. Picture B shows you where it is 12 noon one hour later. The direct sun is now over 15°W. So it is 12 noon at 15°W in Picture B and 1:00 P.M. at 0°. One hour later, it will be 12 noon at 30°W, 1:00 P.M. at 15°W, and 2:00 P.M. at 0°. This hour-by-hour change happens 24 times a day as the Earth makes one complete rotation.

Answer the following questions using Pictures A and B on page 218.

1. When it is 10:00 A.M. at 30°W, it is _____ at 30°E.

What time did you fill in? Which picture shows 10:00 A.M. at 30°W? It is Picture A. Now on Picture A look for the 30°E line of longitude. Since 30°E has a time of 2:00 P.M., the answer to question 1 is 2:00 P.M.

Picture A

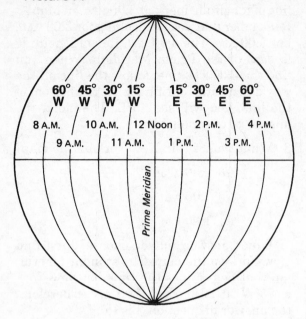

Picture B (One Hour Later)

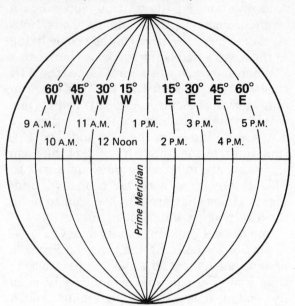

You could also find the answer to question 1 in another way. When you travel from 30°W to 30°E in Picture A, you pass through four lines of longitude. These four lines are 15°W, 0°, 15°E, and 30°E. Each of these lines represents one hour. By adding these four hours to the 10:00 A.M. at 30°W, you come to 2:00 P.M. at 30°E.

Suppose it is 2:00 P.M. at 30°E, and you are asked what time it is at 30°W. To find out, you subtract four hours from 2:00 P.M. You would then know it is 10:00 A.M. at 30°W.

2. When it is 2:00 P.M. at 45°W, it is _____ _____ at 45°E.

What time did you fill in? Neither Picture A nor Picture B shows 2:00 P.M. at 45°W. Picture B shows that it is 10:00 A.M. at

45°W and 4:00 P.M. at 45°E. How many hours' difference is there between 10:00 A.M. and 2:00 P.M.? There is a difference of four hours. So the time you want to find out is four hours after the time shown in Picture B. You must add four hours to the 4:00 P.M. found at 45°E. This gives you 8:00 P.M. Therefore, when it is 2:00 P.M. at 45°W, it is 8:00 P.M. at 45°E.

You could also have found the answer to question 2 in another way. You could have counted the time zones between 45°W and 45°E. There are six of them. Then you could have added that number to 2:00 P.M.

The following exercises will give you more practice in understanding longitude and time zones.

USING WHAT YOU HAVE LEARNED

A. True or False: If every part of the statement is true, write **T**.
If any part of the statement is false, write **F**.

_____ 1. The Earth makes one complete rotation every 24 hours.

_____ 2. For every 15° of longitude, there is a difference of one hour in time.

_____ 3. Time zones always have straight boundaries.

_____ 4. It is 12 noon everywhere on the Earth at the same time.

_____ 5. The letters A.M. stand for the 12 hours before 12 noon.

_____ 6. Post meridiem means the 12 hours after 12 noon.

_____ 7. The line of longitude at 180° is called the Prime Meridian.

_____ 8. When you travel across the International Date Line, you stay in the same day.

_____ 9. When you cross the Prime Meridian, you stay in the same day.

_____ 10. It takes one hour for the Earth to rotate 15°.

B. Longitude and Time Change

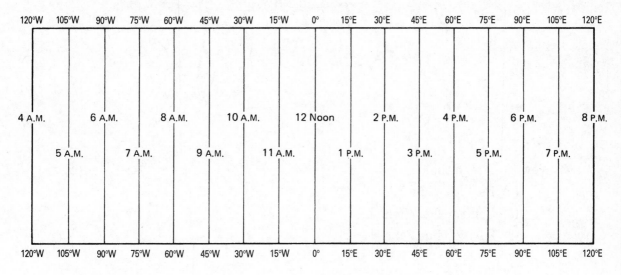

Use the diagram above to help you answer the following questions.

1. On the diagram, it is 12 noon at _____ degrees.

2. According to the diagram, the sun is directly overhead at _____ degrees.

3. When it is 9 A.M. at 45°W, it is _____ at 45°E.

4. When it is 10 A.M. at 30°W, it is _____ at 60°E.

5. When it is 5 P.M. at 75°E, it is _____ at 75°W.

6. When it is 10 A.M. at 45°W, it is _____ at 45°E.

7. When it is 10 A.M. at 60°W, it is _____ at 75°E.

8. When it is 7 P.M. at 45°E, it is _____ at 0°.

9. When it is 4 P.M. at 15°W, it is _____ at 15°E.

10. When it is 7 P.M. at 60°W, it is _____ at 60°E.

C. Time Zones in the United States

C-1. Place a check mark next to the correct answers to questions 1 to 10. Use the map on page 220 to help you answer the questions.

1. From the map, you can see that the 48 states of the United States that border each other have

____ (*a*) one time zone.

____ (*b*) four time zones.

____ (*c*) ten time zones.

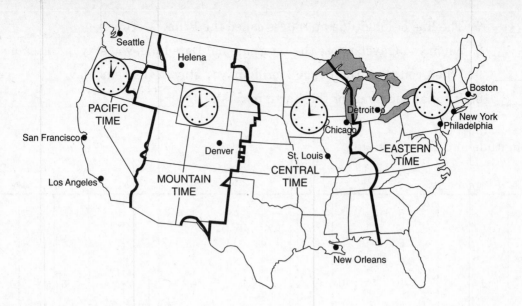

2. New York is in the

____ (a) Eastern Time Zone.

____ (b) Central Time Zone.

____ (c) Pacific Time Zone.

3. Chicago is in the

____ (a) Eastern Time Zone.

____ (b) Central Time Zone.

____ (c) Mountain Time Zone.

4. Denver is in the

____ (a) Eastern Time Zone.

____ (b) Mountain Time Zone.

____ (c) Pacific Time Zone.

5. San Francisco is in the

____ (a) Central Time Zone.

____ (b) Mountain Time Zone.

____ (c) Pacific Time Zone.

6. Which one of the following statements is true?

____ (a) It is the same time everywhere in the United States.

____ (b) Chicago and Denver always have the same time.

____ (c) There is a time difference of one hour between neighboring time zones on the map.

7. The map shows that it is

____ (a) 2 o'clock in Boston.

____ (b) 3 o'clock in Boston.

____ (c) 4 o'clock in Boston.

8. What is the time difference between New York and San Francisco?

___ (a) two hours

___ (b) three hours

___ (c) four hours

9. Mountain Time means the time it is

___ (a) at the top of a mountain.

___ (b) where there are mountains.

___ (c) in a particular time zone in the United States.

10. If it is 11 A.M. in Detroit, in New Orleans it is

___ (a) one hour earlier.

___ (b) one hour later.

___ (c) the same time.

C-2. Fill in the correct times based on the Time Zone map.

1. When it is 1 o'clock in Los Angeles, it is _____ o'clock in Chicago.

2. When it is 5 o'clock in Philadelphia, it is _____ o'clock in New Orleans.

3. When it is 2 o'clock in San Francisco, it is _____ o'clock in Denver.

4. When it is 5 o'clock in Denver, it is _____ o'clock in New York.

5. When it is 4 o'clock in St. Louis, it is _____ o'clock in Seattle.

D. In your own words, explain why different places in the United States show different hours on the clock at the same moment. In other words, why is it 9 A.M. in Seattle and 11 A.M. in St. Louis when it is noon in Philadelphia? (Answer in three or four sentences.)

_____

_____

_____

_____

_____

_____

_____

_____

UNIT SEVEN

Studying Special-Purpose Maps

Chapter 26

Population Maps

So far you have seen maps that were drawn to show the shapes of landforms and water forms, the boundaries of countries, and the location of cities. Another important type of information that can be shown on a map is population, or the total number of people living in a place. A map that shows the population of cities and countries is called a *population map*.

Symbols

The key on the following population map of China includes symbols commonly used to show population figures for cities. Note that each symbol stands for a different number of people.

Study the map on page 223 and then answer the following questions about it.

1. The map shows

_____ (a) the entire population of China.

_____ (b) how many people live in eastern China.

_____ (c) the population of eight cities in China.

Which answer did you choose? The map shows only eight cities in China. Each one has a symbol next to it. These symbols and the population that each represents are explained in the key. Because the map shows the population only of these eight cities, the answer to question 1 is (c).

2. The city of Beijing has a population

_____ (a) between 11 million and 20 million.

_____ (b) between 21 million and 30 million.

_____ (c) over 30 million.

Which answer did you choose? Look on the map for the city of Beijing and the symbol next to it. The key shows that this symbol ♦ stands for a population between 11 million and 20 million. Therefore, the answer to question 2 is (a).

China

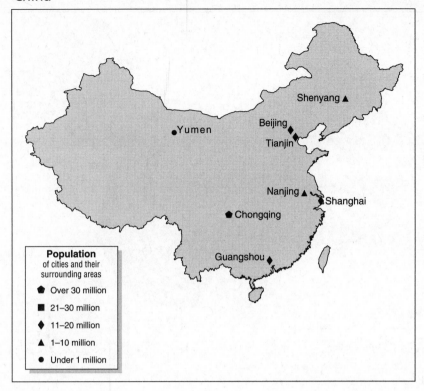

3. How many cities on the map have a population between 1 million and 10 million?

_____ (a) 0

_____ (b) 1

_____ (c) 2

What was your answer? A population between 1 million and 10 million would have the symbol ▲. This symbol appears next to Shenyang and Nanjing. Therefore, the answer to question 3 is (c).

Dots

The map you just studied shows the population of eight important cities in China. But people live not only in cities but throughout a country. Population maps can be drawn to show the average population of a small area or of an entire country. This kind of map is called a *population density map*. (Population density means the average number of people living in a certain area of land.) The map on page 224 is a population density map of China.

This map uses dots to show how many people live in certain areas of China. Each dot stands for a particular number of people. Areas on the map with few dots have few people living in them. Areas with many dots have many people living in them.

Use the dot population density map of China on page 224 to help you answer the following questions.

1. Each dot on the map stands for

_____ (a) 1 million people.

_____ (b) 2 million people.

_____ (c) 3 million people.

What was your answer? The key on the map shows that each dot stands for 3 million people. Therefore, the answer to question 1 is (c).

2. Most people in China live in

_____ (a) northern China.

_____ (b) western China.

_____ (c) eastern China.

Which answer did you choose? Remember that the area of the country with the most dots has the most people. Because the map shows that eastern China has the most dots, the answer to question 2 is (c).

China

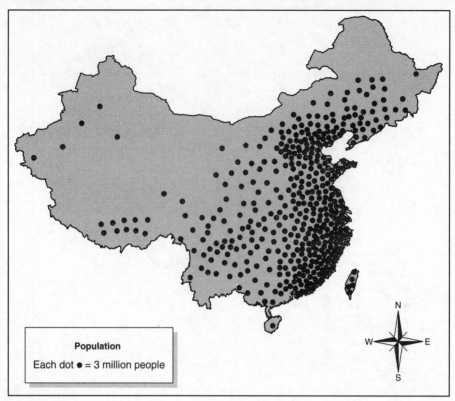

Population

Each dot ● = 3 million people

N
W   E
S

Patterns

Sometimes a population density map uses patterns (designs) or colors instead of dots. The patterns or colors show how many people live in a certain area of land. On this kind of population density map, the key may look something like the following:

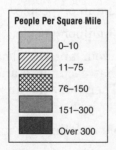

People Per Square Mile

	0–10
	11–75
	76–150
	151–300
	Over 300

The patterns and population statistics may be different on different maps. But the key will always explain what population statistics the patterns represent.

Let us look at an example to see how this key works. In the key, the pattern ▨ stands for 11 to 75 people per square mile.

This means that wherever this pattern appears on the map, between 11 and 75 people live on every square mile of land.

Study the population density map of China on page 225. The key on it is the same as the one to the left.

1. This population density map of China shows how many people live

_____ (*a*) in cities.

_____ (*b*) on farms.

_____ (*c*) in certain areas of the country.

Which answer did you choose? The key shows that patterns on the map stand for different populations in different areas of China. By using the key, you can see how many people live in a certain area of China. Therefore, the answer to question 1 is (*c*).

2. The pattern ▨ stands for

_____ (*a*) 11 to 75 people per square mile.

_____ (*b*) 76 to 150 people per square mile.

_____ (*c*) 151 to 300 people per square mile.

China

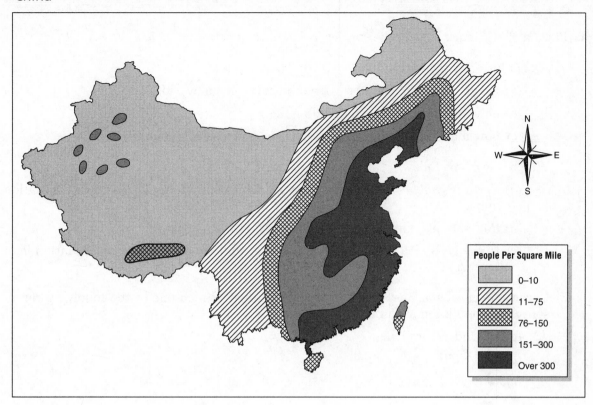

People Per Square Mile

	0–10
	11–75
	76–150
	151–300
	Over 300

Which answer did you choose? The key shows that the pattern ▨ stands for 76 to 150 people per square mile. This means that wherever this pattern appears on the map, there are between 76 and 150 people per square mile of land. Therefore, the answer to question 2 is (*b*).

3. Which area of China has the fewest people?

_____ (*a*) eastern China

_____ (*b*) western China

_____ (*c*) southern China

Which answer did you choose? According to the key, the area of China with the fewest people (0 to 10) is shown on the map by the pattern ▭ . This pattern is found mainly in western China. It can be assumed

then that the section of China with the fewest people is in the west. So the answer to question 3 is (*b*).

In question 3, you learned that the lowest population density in China is generally in the western part of the country. But you did not learn why western China has the fewest people. A population map shows where people live in a country, but it does not show why people live in certain areas. Before you can know why people live in an area, you need to know more about what the area is like. In general, people live where they can grow food or earn a living in some other way.

In this chapter, you have studied three different kinds of population maps. These maps use symbols, dots, or patterns to show population and population density. The following exercises will give you practice in using these three important kinds of population maps.

A. Place a check mark next to the correct answers to questions 1 to 5.

1. A population map shows

___ (*a*) which cities and countries are important in the world.

___ (*b*) how many people like to live in cities.

___ (*c*) how many people live in certain cities or areas of a country.

2. Which one of the following statements is true?

___ (*a*) Certain symbols always stand for the same population figures on all population maps.

___ (*b*) Population symbols are usually not explained.

___ (*c*) It is a good idea to check the key to see what the symbols on a population map represent.

3. Caracas, Venezuela, has a population of 3 million. Which one of the following represents the population of Caracas?

___ (*a*) ■ Under 1 million

___ (*b*) ▲ 1 million to 5 million

___ (*c*) ● Over 5 million

4. Which one of the following statements is *most likely* to be true?

___ (*a*) Most people do not care where they live.

___ (*b*) Most people like to live in areas with steep mountains.

___ (*c*) Most people like to live where they can earn a living.

5. If each dot on a population density map equals 200,000 people, what would be the population of a section that has four dots?

___ (*a*) 400,000

___ (*b*) 8,000,000

___ (*c*) 800,000

B. Study the following population map of Japan.

Place a check mark next to the correct answers to questions 1 to 10.

1. The map shows the population of

___ (*a*) the entire country of Japan.

___ (*b*) the major cities of Japan.

___ (*c*) each island of Japan.

2. Which symbol is used to show a city with a population between 4 million and 6 million?

___ (*a*) ●

___ (*b*) ♦

___ (*c*) ■

Japan

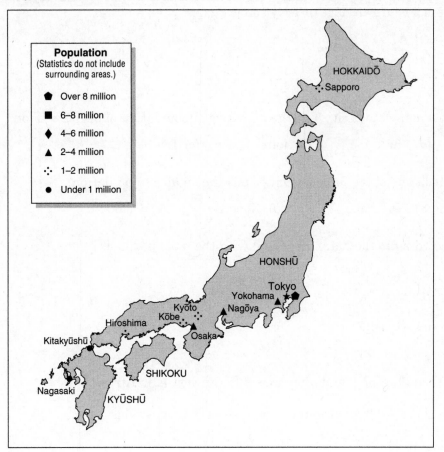

3. The symbol ● stands for a population of

___ (a) under 1 million.

___ (b) 1 million to 2 million.

___ (c) over 2 million.

4. The city of Kyōto has a population

___ (a) under 1 million.

___ (b) between 1 and 2 million.

___ (c) over 2 million.

5. One of the following cities has a population of 3,643,641. Which city is it?

___ (a) Yokohama

___ (b) Kitakyūshū

___ (c) Tokyo

6. Which city has a population over 2 million, but not over 4 million?

___ (a) Nagasaki

___ (b) Hiroshima

___ (c) Osaka

7. Tokyo, the capital city, has a population of more than 8 million. Which population symbol is drawn next to Tokyo on the map?

___ (a) ♠

___ (b) ♦

___ (c) ▲

8. How many other cities on the map have a population of over 2 million?

___ (a) three   ___ (b) four   ___ (c) five

9. Which one of the following cities has the smallest population?

___ (a) Nagasaki   ___ (b) Kōbe   ___ (c) Osaka

10. According to the map, the island with the most people is

___ (a) Hokkaidō.

___ (b) Kyūshū.

___ (c) Honshū.

C. Study the following population map of Southwest Asia/Africa.

Place a check mark next to the correct answer to questions 1 to 4.

1. The map shows

___ (a) the population of major cities of Southwest Asia/Africa.

___ (b) the population density of countries of Southwest Asia/Africa.

___ (c) important cities of Southwest Asia/Africa.

2. Each dot • on this map stands for

___ (a) 200,000 people.

___ (b) 300,000 people.

___ (c) 500,000 people.

3. Which one of the following countries shows the greatest density of people?

___ (a) Egypt

___ (b) Saudi Arabia

___ (c) Iran

4. In Saudi Arabia, most of the people live in the

___ (a) northern part of the country.

___ (b) central part of the country.

___ (c) southern part of the country.

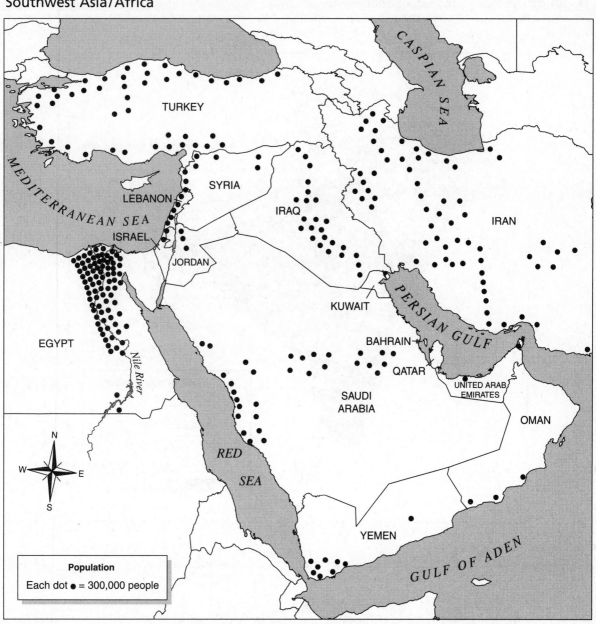

The following labels appear on the map:

CASPIAN SEA

TURKEY

MEDITERRANEAN SEA

SYRIA

LEBANON

ISRAEL

JORDAN

IRAQ

IRAN

EGYPT

Nile River

KUWAIT

PERSIAN GULF

BAHRAIN

QATAR

UNITED ARAB EMIRATES

SAUDI ARABIA

OMAN

RED SEA

YEMEN

GULF OF ADEN

N W E S

Population

Each dot ● = 300,000 people

5. Why do you think there are so many dots in Egypt along the Nile River? (Answer in one or two sentences.)

_____

_____

_____

_____

D. Study the following map of South Asia.

South Asia

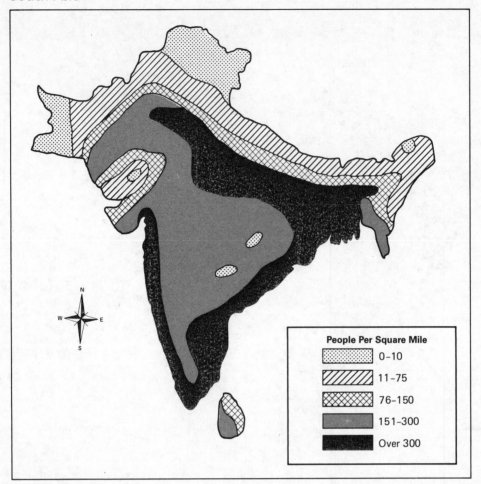

Place a check mark next to the correct answers to questions 1 to 5.

1. The map shows the

___ (*a*) boundary lines of different countries in South Asia.

___ (*b*) population of major cities in South Asia.

___ (*c*) population density of South Asia.

2. The population statistics on the map are shown by

___ (*a*) symbols.

___ (*b*) dots.

___ (*c*) patterns.

3. The pattern [pattern] stands for

___ (*a*) 11 to 75 people per square mile.

___ (*b*) 76 to 150 people per square mile.

___ (*c*) 151 to 300 people per square mile.

4. The pattern ▮▮▮ stands for

___ (a) 76 to 150 people per square mile.

___ (b) 151 to 300 people per square mile.

___ (c) over 300 people per square mile.

5. A population of 200 people per square mile is shown on the map by which pattern?

___ (a) ▨

___ (b) ▨

___ (c) ▨

E. Study the map of Africa on page 232.

Place a check mark next to the correct answers to questions 1 to 9.

1. The map shows the

___ (a) population density of Africa.

___ (b) population of the major cities of Africa.

___ (c) boundary lines of countries in Africa.

2. The population statistics on the map are shown by

___ (a) symbols.

___ (b) dots.

___ (c) patterns.

3. The meanings of the patterns on the map are

___ (a) explained in the index.

___ (b) explained in the key.

___ (c) not explained at all.

4. The pattern ▧ stands for

___ (a) 11 to 50 people per square mile.

___ (b) 51 to 100 people per square mile.

___ (c) 101 to 150 people per square mile.

5. The pattern ▮ stands for

___ (a) 51 to 100 people per square mile.

___ (b) 101 to 150 people per square mile.

___ (c) over 150 people per square mile.

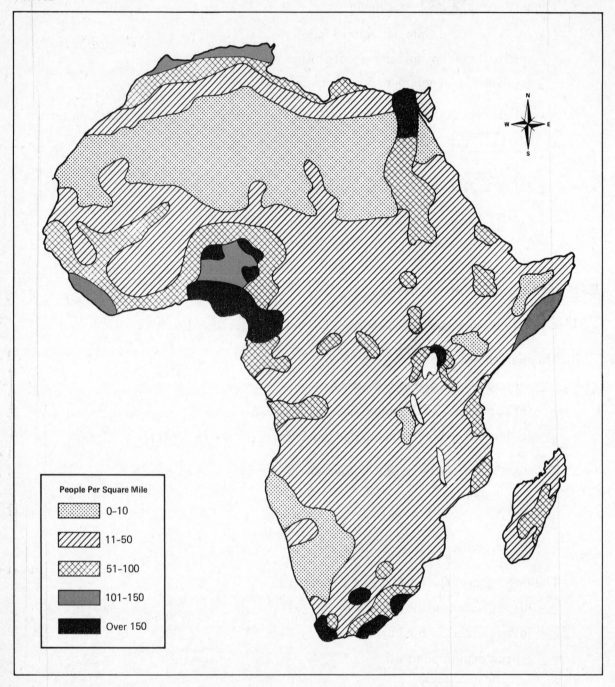

People Per Square Mile

	0–10
	11–50
	51–100
	101–150
	Over 150

6. A population of 200 people per square mile is shown on the map by the pattern

___ (a) [ ] .

___ (b) [ ] .

___ (c) [ ] .

7. Which pattern on the map covers an area of Africa that is probably desert?

_____ (a) [light dotted pattern]

_____ (b) [dark gray pattern]

_____ (c) [black pattern]

8. A large city is most likely to be located in an area with which pattern?

_____ (a) [light dotted pattern]

_____ (b) [black pattern]

_____ (c) [black pattern]

9. Most of Africa has a population density

_____ (a) of less than 51 people per square mile.

_____ (b) at about 51 people per square mile.

_____ (c) of more than 51 people per square mile.

10. In one or two sentences of your own words, answer the following question. "What does a population density map show?"

_____

_____

_____

_____

Chapter 27
Relief Maps

Most maps are printed on flat paper. But we know that the surface of the Earth is not completely flat. Various types of geographical features make the Earth's surface uneven. They include:

Mountains: landmasses much higher than nearby areas

Volcanoes: mountains with an opening in the top or side through which melted rock, steam, and ashes are forced out from inside the Earth

Plateaus: high, flat landforms

Hills: high, rounded landforms, usually not as tall as mountains

Where there are no high landforms, the Earth may be covered by *plains*—areas of low, flat land.

How can we show on paper what these landforms of different heights look like? One way is to show a side view, as in this drawing.

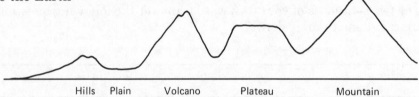

Hills   Plain   Volcano   Plateau   Mountain

Another way is to draw a map that shows the height, or altitude, of landforms. This type of map is called a *relief map.*

Where do we start measuring altitude? The height of land is very different in different parts of the world. Only the surface of the water of the oceans is the same height throughout most of the world. Therefore, the measurement of altitude starts on the surface of the oceans. This surface is called *sea level.*

A relief map uses different patterns or colors to show the altitude of landforms. The key on a relief map shows these patterns or colors and the altitudes they represent.

Below is a cross-section relief map. It shows the same drawing of landforms that you saw above. This time patterns have been added to show the altitudes of the landforms. The key next to the drawing gives the altitude of each of these patterns. By using the key, you can see how high the landforms are.

Answer the following questions using the drawing below.

1. The pattern ▨ stands for

_____ (a) 1,001 to 2,000 feet above sea level.

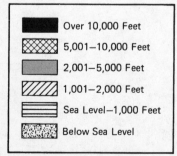

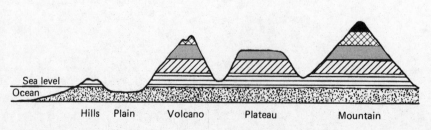

Hills   Plain   Volcano   Plateau   Mountain

_____ (b) 2,001 to 5,000 feet above sea level.

_____ (c) 5,001 to 10,000 feet above sea level.

Which answer did you choose? The key shows that the pattern ▨ stands for 1,001 to 2,000 feet above sea level. This means that every area on the drawing with this pattern has an altitude between 1,001 and 2,000 feet. Therefore, the answer to question 1 is (a).

2. The top of the mountain in the drawing has an altitude

_____ (a) between 2,001 and 5,000 feet.

_____ (b) between 5,001 and 10,000 feet.

_____ (c) over 10,000 feet.

What was your answer? The pattern at the top of the mountain is ▬ . The key shows that any area with this pattern has an altitude of over 10,000 feet. Therefore, the answer to question 2 is (c).

South America

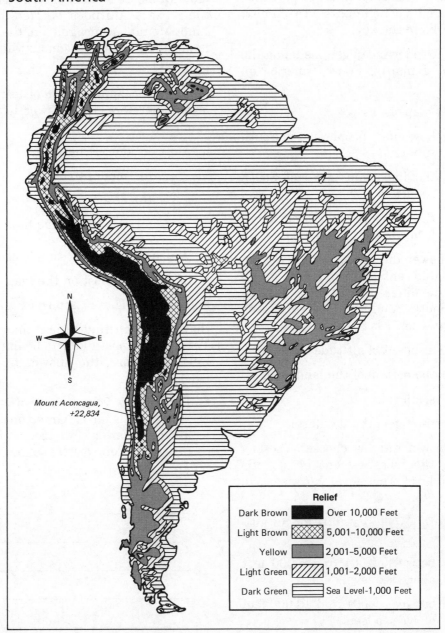

Mount Aconcagua, +22,834

Relief

Dark Brown	▬	Over 10,000 Feet
Light Brown	▧	5,001–10,000 Feet
Yellow	▨	2,001–5,000 Feet
Light Green	▨	1,001–2,000 Feet
Dark Green	☰	Sea Level–1,000 Feet

In some areas of the world, dry land is actually located below sea level. The plain in the drawing is below sea level and is shown with the pattern ▨ . Higher land around the plain keeps it from being flooded by ocean water.

Most relief maps use a top view rather than a side view of an area. The maps you have studied in earlier chapters all use top views, as if you were looking down at an area. The most common top-view relief map looks like the map of South America on page 235. Different patterns are used to show the altitudes of landforms. The key tells you what altitude each pattern represents. Some maps use colors in place of patterns. The colors used most often are written next to the patterns in the key.

Answer the following questions using the top-view relief map of South America on page 235.

1. The relief map shows

_____ (a) how many people live in South America.

_____ (b) the important cities of South America.

_____ (c) the altitudes of different land-forms in South America.

Which answer did you choose? The key shows that different patterns on the map stand for the different altitudes of land-forms in South America. Therefore, the answer to question 1 is (c).

2. The measurement of altitude starts at

_____ (a) the bottom of the landform.

_____ (b) sea level.

_____ (c) the top of the landform.

Which answer did you choose? The key shows that the measurement of altitude starts at sea level. Therefore, the answer to question 2 is (b).

3. The pattern ▨ stands for an altitude

_____ (a) between 2,001 and 5,000 feet above sea level.

_____ (b) between 5,001 and 10,000 feet above sea level.

_____ (c) over 10,000 feet above sea level.

Which answer did you choose? The pattern ▨ on the key stands for an altitude between 2,001 and 5,000 feet. Therefore, the answer to question 3 is (a).

4. Mount Aconcagua, shown on the map of South America, has an altitude of

_____ (a) 10,000 feet.

_____ (b) 16,880 feet.

_____ (c) 22,834 feet.

Which answer did you choose? Very high mountains are usually shown on a map with their exact altitudes written near them. Find Mount Aconcagua on the map. The name and height of the mountain are shown like this: Mount Aconcagua, +22,834. This means that Mount Aconcagua is 22,834 feet above sea level. Therefore, the answer to question 4 is (c).

5. Most of South America is

_____ (a) mountainous.

_____ (b) desert.

_____ (c) flat with some hills.

Which answer did you choose? The patterns used the most on the map are ▨ and ▤ . These patterns represent land that has an altitude of less than 2,000 feet. This land is most likely to be flat with some hills. Therefore, the answer to question 5 is (c).

6. Explain in your own words why this statement is false: "Green on a relief map always stands for trees and grass." (Answer in one or two sentences.)

_____

_____

_____

_____

_____

_____

What did you write? Most students believe that the green on a relief map stands for trees and grass. But this is not true. Green is the most commonly used color for land that is at a low altitude. The key on this map of South America tells you that light green and dark green stand for altitudes between sea level and 2,000 feet. So green usually stands for low altitude and *not* for trees and grass. If this idea was part of your answer, you wrote a good answer to question 6.

7. Why do you think few people live in areas shown on the map with the pattern ▆▆ ? (Answer in three or four sentences.)

_____

_____

_____

_____

_____

_____

_____

_____

_____

_____

_____

_____

What answer did you write? The key shows that the pattern ▆▆ stands for areas with an altitude of over 10,000 feet. These areas are almost certainly mountainous. High mountain areas generally have a cold climate and are not good for growing crops. So, few people want to live in mountainous areas. If your answer contains some of these ideas, you wrote a good answer to question 7.

The relief maps in the exercises that follow do not all look alike. The keys will help you to understand these maps.

USING WHAT YOU HAVE LEARNED

A. Place a check mark next to the correct answers to questions 1 to 9.

1. A relief map shows
   ___ (*a*) how many people live in a country.
   ___ (*b*) why people live on high landforms.
   ___ (*c*) the altitude of landforms.

2. Which one of the following is NOT a high landform?
   ___ (*a*) plain
   ___ (*b*) mountain
   ___ (*c*) plateau

3. The measuring of altitude starts
   ___ (*a*) at the foot of a mountain.
   ___ (*b*) at sea level.
   ___ (*c*) below sea level.

4. Different altitudes on a relief map are

____ (*a*) always shown by colors.

____ (*b*) shown by patterns or colors that are explained in the key.

____ (*c*) shown by patterns but are not explained in the key.

5. A landform 4,500 feet above sea level would often be shown on a relief map by the pattern

____ (*a*) ▤ 0 to 1,000 feet.

____ (*b*) ▨ 1,001 to 2,000 feet.

____ (*c*) ▧ 2,001 to 5,000 feet.

6. Green on a relief map usually stands for

____ (*a*) land at low altitudes.

____ (*b*) trees and grass.

____ (*c*) mountainous land.

7. If the relief map on page 235 were in color, the highest mountains would be shown in

____ (*a*) light green.

____ (*b*) yellow.

____ (*c*) dark brown.

8. The phrase "below sea level" means

____ (*a*) underneath the sea.

____ (*b*) lower than the surface of the oceans.

____ (*c*) below the level of any body of water.

9. A plateau is

____ (*a*) a high, flat landform.

____ (*b*) low, flat land.

____ (*c*) a volcano.

10. Explain in two or three sentences why a relief map would be helpful to the pilot of a small airplane.

_____

_____

_____

_____

_____

_____

B. Study the following map of South Asia.

South Asia

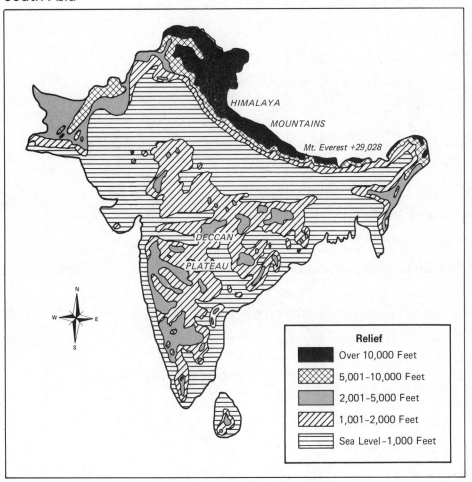

Place a check mark next to the correct answer to questions 1 to 10.

1. The relief map shows

___ (*a*) how many people live in South Asia.

___ (*b*) the altitudes of landforms in South Asia.

___ (*c*) the boundaries of countries in South Asia.

2. The altitudes on the map are shown by

___ (*a*) symbols.

___ (*b*) boxes.

___ (*c*) patterns.

3. The key on the map explains

___ (*a*) the difficult words on the map.

___ (*b*) the meanings of the patterns on the map.

___ (*c*) how to use an index.

4. The pattern ▆▆▆▆ stands for an altitude

_____ (a) under 1,000 feet.

_____ (b) between 2,001 and 5,000 feet.

_____ (c) over 10,000 feet.

5. The altitude of a landform on the map is measured from

_____ (a) the bottom of the landform.

_____ (b) the top of the landform.

_____ (c) sea level.

6. The center of South Asia is a vast

_____ (a) mountain range.

_____ (b) plain.

_____ (c) plateau.

7. The Himalaya Mountains at the top of the map have an altitude

_____ (a) less than 1,000 feet.

_____ (b) between 5,001 and 10,000 feet.

_____ (c) over 10,000 feet.

8. Mount Everest in the Himalaya Mountains has an altitude of

_____ (a) 10,000 feet.

_____ (b) 22,300 feet.

_____ (c) 29,028 feet.

9. The lowest areas in South Asia are

_____ (a) mostly in the north.

_____ (b) mainly in the south.

_____ (c) only in the east.

10. The highest areas in South Asia are

_____ (a) in the south.

_____ (b) in the north.

_____ (c) on the island.

C. Study the relief map of Russia on page 241.

Place a check mark next to the correct answers to questions 1 to 6.

1. The relief map of Russia shows

___ (a) heights of landforms.

___ (b) major seaports.

___ (c) population density.

Russia

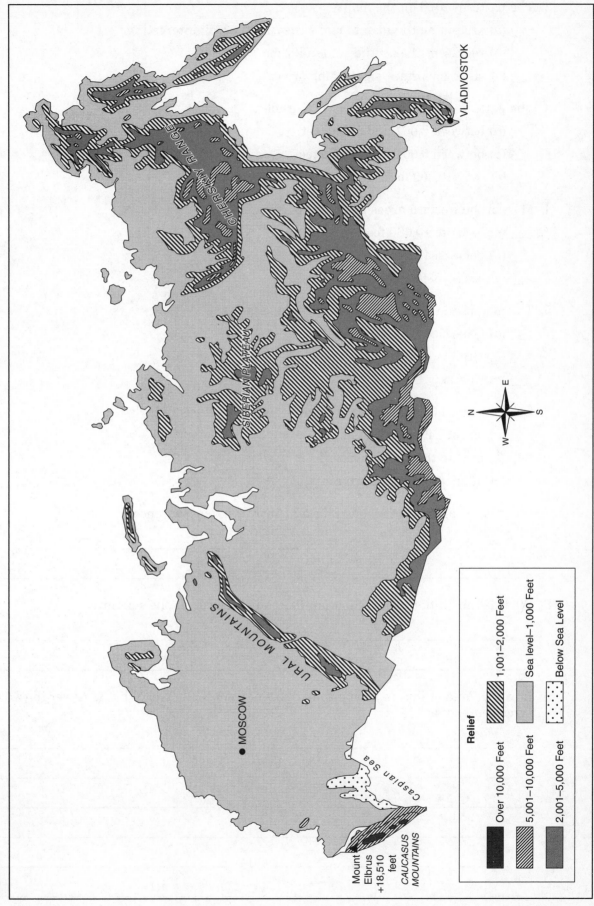

VLADIVOSTOK

CHERSKY RANGE

SIBERIAN PLATEAU

URAL MOUNTAINS

MOSCOW

Caspian Sea

Mount
Elbrus
+18,510
feet
CAUCASUS
MOUNTAINS

Relief

Over 10,000 Feet	1,001–2,000 Feet
5,001–10,000 Feet	Sea level–1,000 Feet
2,001–5,000 Feet	Below Sea Level

2. The patterns used on the map

___ (a) are put on the map to make the country look interesting.

___ (b) represent the altitude of landforms.

___ (c) show important sightseeing areas.

3. The pattern ■■■ stands for an altitude

___ (a) between 2,001 and 5,000 feet.

___ (b) between 5,001 and 10,000 feet.

___ (c) over 10,000 feet.

4. Most of the western areas on the map are

___ (a) 5,001 to 10,000 feet.

___ (b) below sea level.

___ (c) sea level to 1,000 feet.

5. The mountain range nearest the Caspian Sea is the

___ (a) Caucasus.

___ (b) Ural.

___ (c) Cherskiy.

6. On the map, there is an area of land below sea level located

___ (a) on the Siberian Plateau.

___ (b) next to the Caspian Sea.

___ (c) all along the northern coast.

7. What is the altitude of Mount Elbrus? (Answer in one sentence.)

_____

_____

8. What is the altitude of the Siberian Plateau? (Answer in one sentence.)

_____

_____

9. In which area of Russia do you think most of the people live? Why? (Answer in two or three sentences.)

_____

_____

_____

_____

_____

_____

10. How does the map on page 241 show that it must have been difficult to build the Trans-Siberian Railroad between Moscow and Vladivostok? (Answer in one or two sentences.)

_____

_____

_____

_____

_____

Chapter 28
Rainfall and Climate Maps

Rainfall

Rain is a major source of water for humans, animals, and plants. It influences the way people dress and the kinds of houses they live in. Rain also affects the production of food and the kinds of work people do.

Some areas of the world have almost no rain all year long. Other areas have rain almost every day of the year. In many countries, the amount of rainfall differs from one area of the country to another.

Maps can be drawn to show how much rain a country receives over a period of time. They are called *rainfall maps.*

Look at the rainfall map of Israel on page 245.

This map shows the average amount of rain different areas of Israel receive during a year. By using the key, you can see how much rain each area receives. One large area of the country receives 0 to 10 inches of rain a year. The pattern [ ] covers this area. Areas receiving 11 to 20 inches of rain a year have this pattern [||||||] . Another area of the country receives 21 to 40 inches of rain and is shown by the pattern [ ] .

Answer the following questions using the rainfall map of Israel.

1. The rainfall map shows that

_____ (*a*) Israel receives no rain at all.

_____ (*b*) Israel receives the same amount of rain in every area of the country.

_____ (*c*) not every area of Israel receives the same amount of rain in a year.

Which answer did you choose? The key shows that Israel receives three different amounts of rainfall in a year. This map uses patterns to show the different areas of Israel where three different amounts of rain fall. Therefore, the answer to question 1 is (*c*).

2. The rain on this rainfall map is given in

_____ (*a*) inches.

_____ (*b*) feet.

_____ (*c*) buckets.

Which answer did you choose? At the top of the key you can see the words "(in inches)." This means that the rainfall on the map is given in inches. Therefore, the answer to question 2 is (*a*).

_____ 3. True or False: The area of Israel that receives the least amount of rain in a year is southern Israel.

What was your answer? The key shows that the area with the pattern [ ] receives the least amount of rainfall (0 to 10 inches) per year. On the map, the area with this pattern covers the southern part of Israel. Therefore, the answer to question 3 is True.

Sometimes a rainfall map is called a *precipitation map.* Precipitation is water that falls as rain or snow. It is just as important to measure snowfall as it is to measure rainfall. (About 10 to 12 inches of snow—melted—are equal to one inch of rain.) On a precipitation map, the inches of precipitation may stand for snow or rain or both.

Climate

A map can also show *climates* in different areas of the world. Climate is the kind of weather each area of the world has over a long period of time. Weather is different

Israel

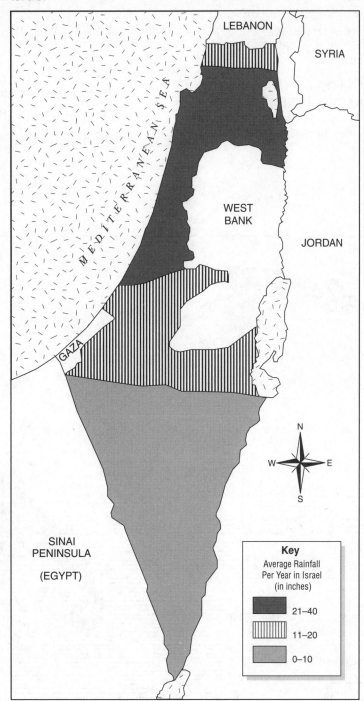

from climate because weather is the day-to-day changes in temperature, wind movements, and precipitation. Climate is the result of these changes over many years.

Different areas of the world have different climates. The following are some of the main reasons for these differences:

1. *Latitude.* A country located in the low latitudes usually has a warm climate.

One located in the high latitudes usually has a cold climate. Countries in the middle latitudes usually have a mild climate.

2. *Elevation,* or altitude (height above sea level). Land at a high elevation has colder temperatures than land at a low elevation.

3. *Landforms.* High landforms, such as mountains, block the movement of wind and clouds carrying precipitation. As a

result, the region on the side of a mountain facing the wind may get all the rain or snow and have a wet climate. The region on the other side of the mountain may have a dry climate.

4. *Ocean breezes and ocean currents.* Such movements bring cooler temperatures in the summer and warmer temperatures in the winter. These help create a mild climate in an area.

A map that shows climates in different areas of the world is called a *climate map.* Look at the following map of Africa and study its key.

1. The map shows

_____ (*a*) how much rain Africa receives.

_____ (*b*) the different climates of Africa.

_____ (*c*) that all of Africa is a desert.

Africa

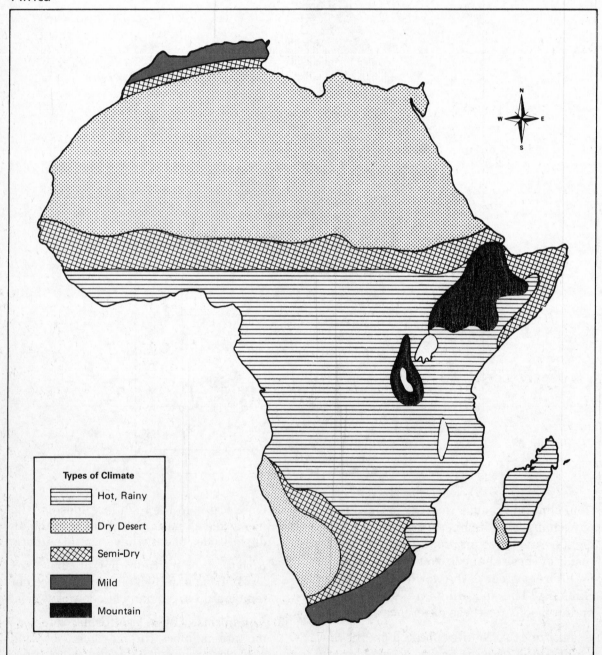

Types of Climate

Hot, Rainy
Dry Desert
Semi-Dry
Mild
Mountain

Which answer did you choose? The key shows that different patterns on the map stand for different climates. Because the map shows the different climates in Africa, the answer to question 1 is (b).

2. Which kind of climate is represented by the pattern ▮▮▮▮ ?

_____ (a) dry

_____ (b) mild

_____ (c) mountain

Which answer did you choose? The key shows you that the pattern ▮▮▮▮ stands for a mountain climate. Therefore, the answer to question 2 is (c).

Mountain climate has this name because it is the climate found around mountain areas. At the bottom, or foot, of a mountain, the climate is usually warm enough for food to grow. But as you go higher up a mountain, the climate becomes colder, making it more difficult to grow food.

3. Why do you think few people live in the climate area with the pattern ▦▦▦ ?

(Answer in two or three sentences.)

_____

_____

_____

_____

_____

_____

_____

_____

_____

What did you write? The map does not give you the answer to question 3. But sometimes you can use information on the map to help you learn something that is not on the map. The key shows that the area on the map with the pattern ▦▦▦ has a dry desert climate. Since water is needed to grow food, it is difficult to live in the dryness of the desert. Most likely, few people live in an area with this kind of climate. If these ideas were contained in your answer, you wrote a good answer to question 3.

By studying rainfall and climate maps, you can see how areas of the world are affected by different weather conditions and climates. Rain, heat, cold, and wind are important weather conditions. They influence what you wear, what you do, and sometimes how you feel. Climate in an area affects the kinds of crops that can be grown and how buildings are heated and cooled. Both weather and climate have a great influence on our daily lives.

Being able to understand and use rainfall and climate maps is an important Social Studies skill. The following exercises will give you practice in using these two important kinds of maps.

USING WHAT YOU HAVE LEARNED

A. True or False: If every part of the statement is true, write **T**.
If any part of the statement is false, write **F**.

_____ 1. Climate is the weather for a certain area over a long period of time.

_____ 2. If you say it rained on Monday and was sunny on Tuesday, you are talking about the climate.

_____ 3. If you say it is hot in Florida in the summers, you are talking about climate.

_____ 4. A rainfall map shows how much rain a country or area of land receives over a long period of time.

_____ 5. A climate map shows how people are affected by different climates.

_____ 6. Rainfall and climate have no effect on the kind of food a country grows.

_____ 7. Precipitation is any water that falls, including rain and snow.

_____ 8. In this chapter, precipitation on the rainfall maps is usually given in feet.

_____ 9. One inch of rain is equal to 10 to 12 inches of snow.

_____ 10. Rainfall and climate are always the same all over a country.

B. List and explain four reasons why different areas of the world have different climates.

_____

_____

_____

_____

_____

_____

_____

_____

_____

_____

_____

C. Study the following map of North Africa.

North Africa

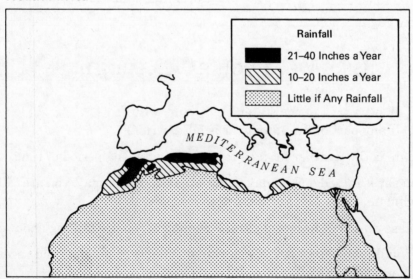

Place a check mark next to the correct answers to questions 1 to 5.

1. The map shows

___ (a) the population of North Africa.

___ (b) the altitudes of landforms in North Africa.

___ (c) how much rain different areas of North Africa receive during the year.

2. The rainfall on the map is measured in

___ (a) inches.   ___ (b) feet.   ___ (c) degrees of temperature.

3. The pattern ⬛ stands for

___ (a) little if any rainfall.

___ (b) rainfall between 10 and 20 inches a year.

___ (c) rainfall between 21 and 40 inches a year.

4. An area of North Africa receiving a rainfall of 25 inches a year is shown by this shading or pattern:

___ (a) ⬛

___ (b) ⬛

___ (c) ⬛

5. The best way to describe the land in the areas of North Africa covered by the pattern ⬛ is to say it is

___ (a) desert.

___ (b) good land for growing crops.

___ (c) covered with mountains.

D. Study the following map of Japan.

Place a check mark next to the correct answers to questions 1 to 8.

1. The map shows

___ (a) population density in Japan.

___ (b) the altitudes of landforms in Japan.

___ (c) how much rain different areas of Japan generally receive during a year.

2. The pattern ⬛ stands for rainfall

___ (a) between 20 and 40 inches a year.

___ (b) between 41 and 60 inches a year.

___ (c) between 61 and 80 inches a year.

Japan

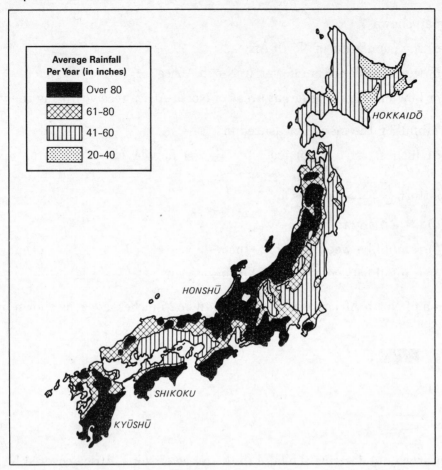

3. An area of Japan receiving 90 inches of rain a year would be shown on the map by which pattern?

_____ (a) ▮▮▮

_____ (b) ▨▨▨

_____ (c) ▦▦▦

4. Which island in Japan has the least rainfall in a year?

_____ (a) Hokkaidō

_____ (b) Honshū

_____ (c) Kyūshū

5. How much of the precipitation that falls in Japan is in the form of snow?

_____ (a) 10 percent

_____ (b) 50 percent

_____ (c) Impossible to tell from the information given.

6. Plants that need a lot of water would most likely be grown in an area covered by this pattern

_____ (a) ▮

_____ (b) ▨

_____ (c) ▨

Look at the map on page 227 that shows the population of some cities in Japan. Using the population map and the rainfall map, answer these questions:

7. Which of these cities generally receives the least amount of rainfall in a year?

_____ (a) Kyōto

_____ (b) Sapporo

_____ (c) Nagasaki

8. Which of these cities generally receives the most rainfall in a year?

_____ (a) Sapporo

_____ (b) Kōbe

_____ (c) Kitakyūshū

9. Look at the rainfall map. What does it tell you about when most of the precipitation falls in Japan? (Answer in one or two sentences.)

_____

_____

_____

_____

10. Why do you think it is important to know how much rainfall parts of Japan receive during a year? (Answer in one or two sentences.)

_____

_____

_____

_____

E. Study the following map of China.

Place a check mark next to the correct answers to questions 1 to 5.

1. The map shows

___ (a) how much rainfall China receives each year.

___ (b) the altitudes of landforms in China.

___ (c) the different climates of China.

China

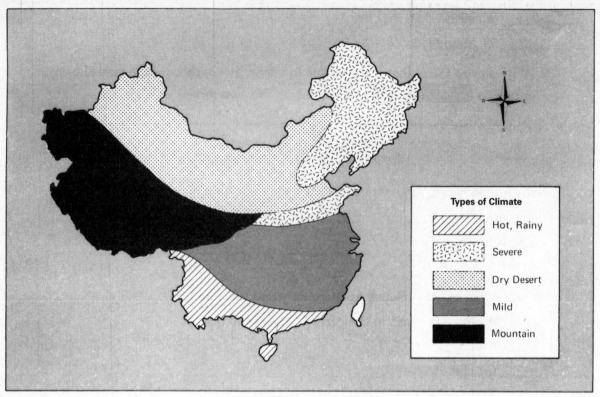

Types of Climate

- /// Hot, Rainy
- Severe
- Dry Desert
- Mild
- Mountain

2. The different kinds of climates are

___ (a) explained in the key.

___ (b) explained in the title.

___ (c) not explained at all.

3. The climate on the map shown by the pattern [⬚] is

___ (a) hot and rainy.

___ (b) dry desert.

___ (c) mild.

4. Severe climate (cold winters and hot summers) is shown on the map by which pattern?

___ (a) ///

___ (b) [severe pattern]

___ (c) ▬

5. Which one of the following climates changes as the altitude changes?

___ (a) severe

___ (b) mild

___ (c) mountain

6. Why do you think that most people in China live in the climate area shown like this

[____] ? (Answer in two or three sentences.)

_____

_____

_____

_____

_____

F. Study the maps of South America on pages 254 and 255.

Place a check mark next to the correct answers to questions 1 to 10.

1. Map A is a
   ___ (*a*) climate map.
   ___ (*b*) population map.
   ___ (*c*) political map.

2. Map B is a
   ___ (*a*) climate map.
   ___ (*b*) population map.
   ___ (*c*) political map.

3. Which map shows the boundary lines and capital cities of the countries of South America?
   ___ (*a*) Map A
   ___ (*b*) Map B
   ___ (*c*) both Map A and Map B

4. Use Map A and Map B to determine which one of the following countries has a mostly mild climate.
   ___ (*a*) Brazil
   ___ (*b*) Venezuela
   ___ (*c*) Uruguay

5. Which one of the following countries has a dry desert climate?
   ___ (*a*) Bolivia
   ___ (*b*) Argentina
   ___ (*c*) Uruguay

6. Brazil has a mostly

___ (a) hot, rainy climate.

___ (b) mild, rainy climate.

___ (c) dry desert climate.

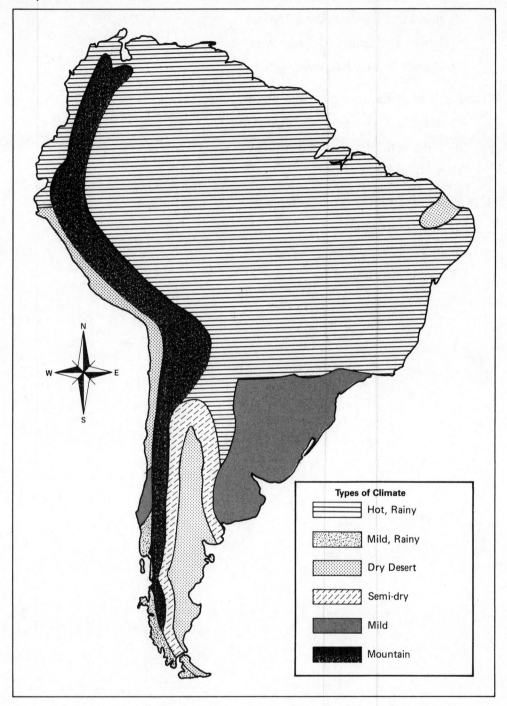

7. Which type of climate is NOT found in Chile?

___ (*a*) mountain

___ (*b*) mild, rainy

___ (*c*) hot, rainy

8. Which three capital cities are in a hot, rainy climate?

_____ (*a*) Santiago, Buenos Aires, La Paz

_____ (*b*) Brasília, Caracas, Georgetown

_____ (*c*) Bogotá, Lima, Asunción

9. Which of these climates does Peru have?

_____ (*a*) mountain, dry desert, and hot, rainy

_____ (*b*) mild, semi-dry, and hot, rainy

_____ (*c*) mild and mountain

10. Most of South America tends to have a

_____ (*a*) dry desert climate.

_____ (*b*) hot, rainy climate.

_____ (*c*) mountain climate.

Chapter 29
Vegetation, Land Use, and Product Maps

As you have learned, rainfall and climate have a lot to do with the way land is used. An area with plenty of rain can be good for growing valuable crops. But an area that does not have much rain will have little *vegetation* (natural plant life, such as flowers, grass, and trees) and may also be poor for growing crops.

Cold, heat, wind, and other climate conditions also affect the plant life in a country. These climate conditions play a part in deciding what kinds of crops can be grown. For example, there is little plant life near the South Pole. No crops are grown there because of the extremely cold climate and the snow and ice that cover the land.

Maps can be drawn to show what types of vegetation are found in a country. Maps can also show what the land is used for and what products (things made or grown) are found in an area.

Natural Vegetation Maps

The map on page 258 shows plant life found in Russia. This kind of map is called a *natural vegetation map* because it shows plants that grow naturally and not those set out by people. By studying the map and its key, you will see that different areas have different kinds of natural vegetation.

1. The natural vegetation map shows

   _____ (*a*) what crops are grown by people.

   _____ (*b*) where different kinds of natural plant life can be found.

_____ (*c*) what food is most popular in Russia.

Which answer did you choose? Natural vegetation means plant life grown by nature and not by people. The plant life differs from area to area, depending on altitude, rainfall, and other climate conditions. Natural vegetation maps show where different kinds of plant life grow in a country or region. On the map, large areas of land are covered by patterns that stand for different kinds of natural plant life found in Russia. Therefore, the answer to question 1 is (*b*).

_____ 2. True or False: Most of Russia has a natural vegetation of grassland.

What was your answer? The key explains the patterns used on the map to represent different kinds of vegetation. The pattern covering the largest area of Russia is ▨. It stands for forests and not for grassland. Therefore, most of Russia has a natural vegetation of forests. The answer to question 2 is False.

By studying a natural vegetation map, you can see how a country might make use of its land. Land that has a natural vegetation of trees could be used for *forestry* (growing and caring for trees). Grassland with enough rainfall could be used for growing crops. Grassland that does not receive much rainfall might be used for *grazing* (feeding grass to) animals. Sometimes land that has many mountains or lacks enough rainfall to be used to grow anything might be an area where useful minerals are found.

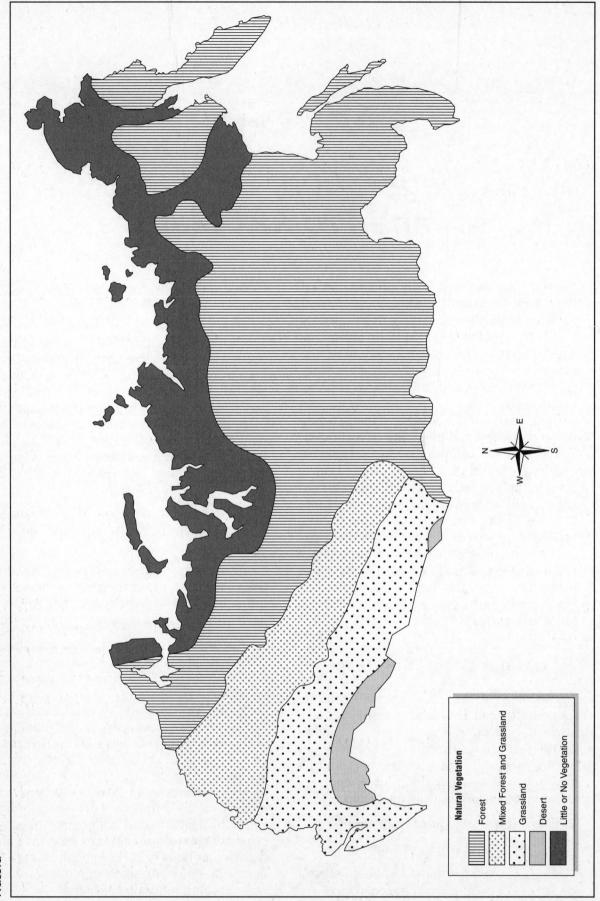

Natural Vegetation

Forest

Mixed Forest and Grassland

Grassland

Desert

Little or No Vegetation

Land Use Maps

Maps can be drawn to show how people make use of the land they live on. These maps are called *land use maps*. Look at the land use map of Russia on page 260.

Notice that this map is different from the natural vegetation map of the same area of the world, which shows plant life that grows naturally (is not planted by humans). A land use map shows how people use the land.

1. This land use map shows

    _____ (a) natural vegetation.

    _____ (b) how large areas of land are used by people.

    _____ (c) the kinds of machines used on farms.

Which answer did you choose? The four patterns on the land use map of Russia are explained in the key. These patterns stand for farming, grazing, forestry, and little-used land. They show how large areas of land are used by people. Therefore, the answer to question 1 is (b).

Look at both the natural vegetation and land use maps of Russia to answer the following questions.

2. An area of Russia appears on the natural vegetation map as having desert vegetation. This same area on the land use map is used for

    _____ (a) forestry.

    _____ (b) farming, some grazing.

    _____ (c) grazing, some farming.

Which answer did you choose? Find the pattern for desert vegetation in the key of the natural vegetation map. It is ▨ . Then find the area on the natural vegetation map where this pattern appears. Now look at the same area on the land use map. The pattern on it is ▨ . The key for the land use map shows that this pattern stands for land that is used for grazing and some farming. Therefore, the answer to question 2 is (c).

3. An area of Russia that is used mainly for farming appears on the natural vegetation map as

    _____ (a) grassland and forest.

    _____ (b) desert and forest.

    _____ (c) grassland and desert.

Which answer did you choose this time? Find a large area of land on the land use map that is used for farming. Now find the same area of land on the natural vegetation map. The area on the vegetation map is shared by two different kinds of vegetation. One kind of vegetation is grassland ▨ . The second is mixed forest and grassland ▨ . Therefore, the answer to question 3 is (a).

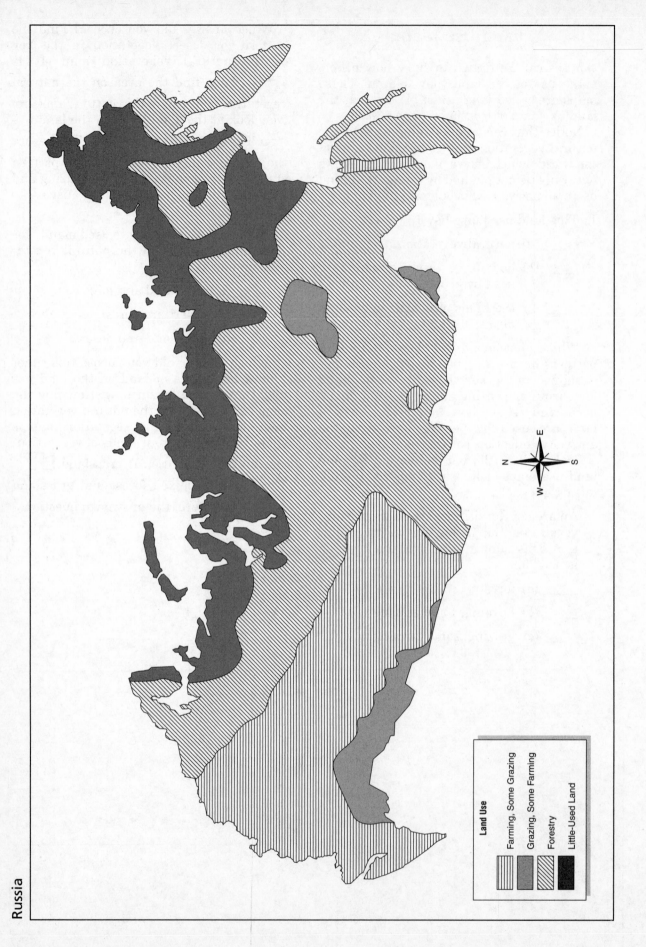

Russia

Land Use

Farming, Some Grazing

Grazing, Some Farming

Forestry

Little-Used Land

Product Maps

A map can be drawn to show the agricultural and mineral products of a country. Agricultural products are the crops grown or the animals raised in a country. Mineral products are the valuable resources found in the Earth, such as coal, oil, iron ore, and gold. A map that shows the agricultural and mineral products of a country is called a *product map*. Look at the product map of Russia on page 262.

This map shows where certain crops are grown and animals are raised. The map also shows where important minerals are found.

On the map, picture symbols stand for crops, animals, and minerals. The key explains what each symbol represents. For example, the symbol 🌾 stands for oats. A product map may have many pictures of oats, but this does not always mean that great amounts of oats are grown in the country. It may mean only that oats are grown in many different areas of the country. Each area of the country that grows oats is shown on the map with a picture of oats. The amount of oats grown in an area may be small or large.

The sections shaded gray on the map stand for industrial areas where mills and factories are located. Agricultural and mineral products are made into different goods in these mills and factories.

Use the product map of Russia to answer the following questions.

1. The map shows

   _____ (a) how much wheat is grown.

   _____ (b) the major agricultural and mineral products and where they are located.

   _____ (c) which products are grown in the greatest amount.

Which answer did you choose? The key shows that pictures on the map stand for the major agricultural and mineral products found in Russia. The map does not tell you which products are produced in the greatest amount. It shows only the different products and where they are located. Therefore, the answer to question 1 is (b).

2. Which symbol is NOT correctly matched with the mineral product it represents?

   _____ (a) 🥟 gold

   _____ (b) 🛒 coal

   _____ (c) ⛏ oil

Which answer did you choose? By looking at the key, you can see that 🥟 is the symbol for gold. The symbol for coal is 🛒. But the symbol for oil is not ⛏, as stated in choice (c). The symbol for oil in the key is ♟. The symbol ⛏ is the one for copper. In question 2, the symbol ⛏ is not correctly matched with its product. Therefore, the answer to question 2 is (c).

Minerals may be found in almost any area of a country. But very often minerals are found in mountainous areas. Compare the product map in this chapter with the relief map on page 241. You can see that much of the mineral wealth of Russia is found in areas of high altitude.

Look at both the land use and product maps of Russia to answer the following question.

3. Why is this statement true? "The product and land use maps of Russia show that agricultural products are found on land that is used for farming and grazing." (Answer in three or four sentences.)

   _____

   _____

   _____

   _____

   _____

   _____

   _____

   _____

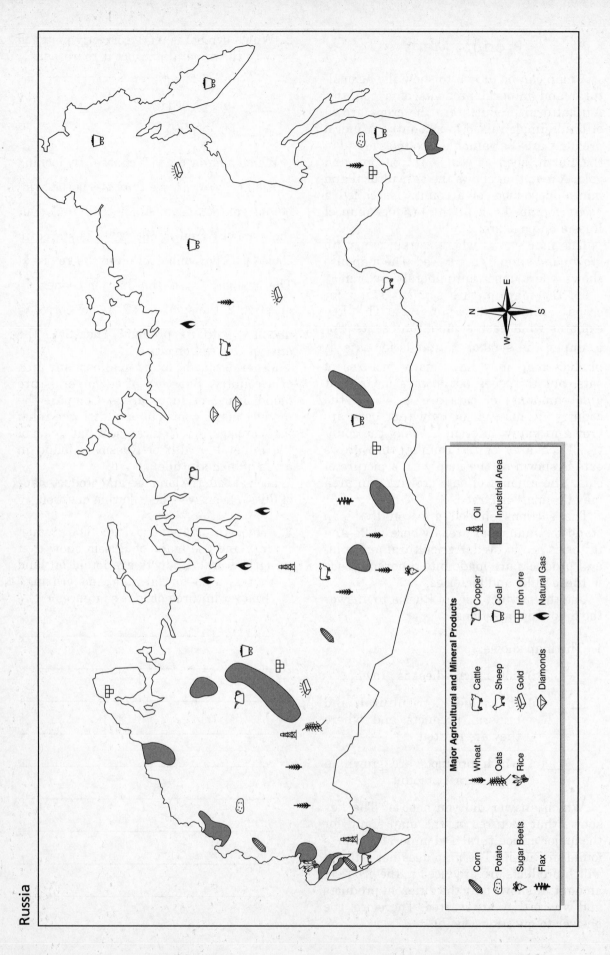

Russia

Major Agricultural and Mineral Products

Corn	Wheat	Cattle	Oil
Potato	Oats	Sheep	Coal
Sugar Beets	Rice	Gold	Iron Ore
Flax		Copper	Natural Gas
		Diamonds	Industrial Area

What did you write in your answer? Symbols are used on the product map to show the different agricultural products of Russia. On the product map, many of these symbols are in the western and southwestern areas of the country. The land use map shows that the western and southwestern areas are used for farming ▤ and grazing ▨. It makes sense that the areas used for farming and grazing would have the most agricultural products. If you included these ideas, you wrote a good answer.

By studying natural vegetation, land use, and product maps, you can learn a great deal about a country. They show you what people may do for a living, what kinds of trade may be carried on, and the types of natural resources a country has. The following exercises will give you more practice in using these three important kinds of maps.

USING WHAT YOU HAVE LEARNED

A. True or False: If every part of the statement is true, write **T**.
If any part of the statement is false, write **F**.

_____ 1. A natural vegetation map shows where different kinds of natural plant life are found in a country.

_____ 2. A land use map shows what kinds of food are grown in a country.

_____ 3. A product map shows what agricultural and mineral products a country has and where they are located in the country.

_____ 4. Different patterns on a land use map show how large areas of land are used by people.

_____ 5. Products are usually shown on a map by symbols.

_____ 6. Growing and caring for trees is called grazing.

_____ 7. Agricultural products are crops, animals, and minerals.

_____ 8. Rainfall, cold, heat, wind, and altitude have an influence on plant life and the growth of crops.

_____ 9. The natural vegetation of an area has nothing to do with the way the land is used.

_____ 10. The symbols on a product map show where products are grown, raised, or made, not what quantities are produced.

B. Study the maps of South America on pages 264 and 265.

Place a check mark next to the correct answers to questions 1 to 9.

1. Map A shows

___ (*a*) how much land in South America is used for farming.

___ (*b*) where different kinds of natural vegetation are found in South America.

___ (*c*) what products can be found in South America.

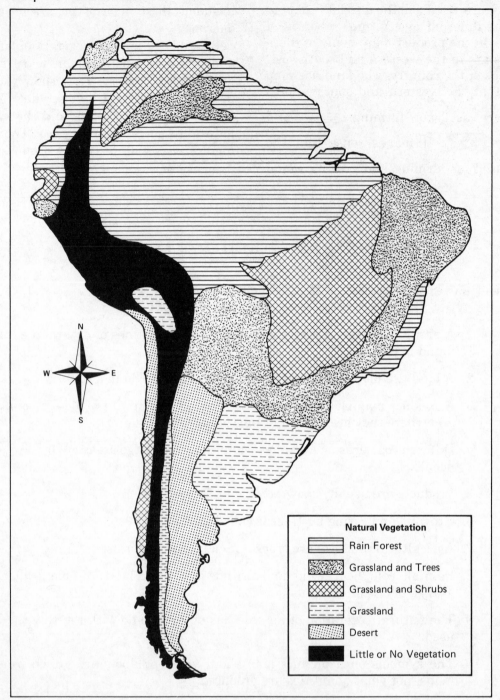

Natural Vegetation

	Rain Forest
	Grassland and Trees
	Grassland and Shrubs
	Grassland
	Desert
	Little or No Vegetation

2. Map B shows how

___ (a) much land in South America is covered by desert.

___ (b) much farming is done in South America.

___ (c) large areas of South America are used.

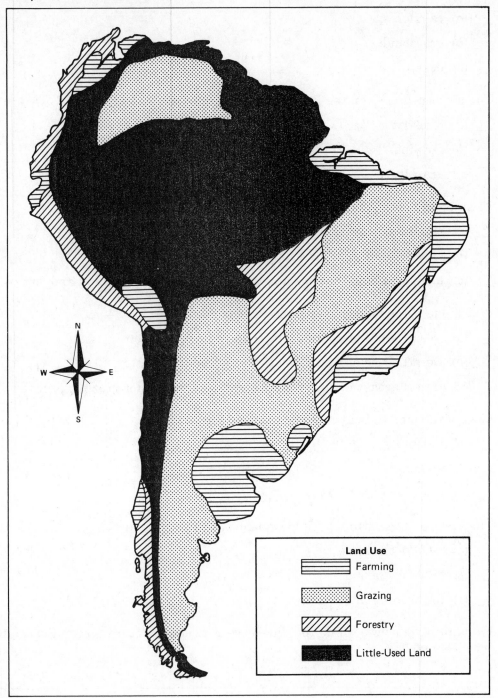

Land Use

Farming

Grazing

Forestry

Little-Used Land

3. Which is the pattern on the natural vegetation map for grassland?

___ (a)

___ (b)

___ (c)

4. Most of the northern areas of South America have a natural vegetation of

___ (a) rain forest.

___ (b) grassland.

___ (c) desert.

5. The pattern [▦] on the land use map stands for

___ (a) forestry.

___ (b) farming.

___ (c) grazing.

6. Farming in South America is done

___ (a) on land with various kinds of natural vegetation.

___ (b) only on land that has a natural vegetation of grassland.

___ (c) mostly on land that has a natural vegetation of grassland and shrubs.

7. Which one of the following statements is true?

___ (a) Desert areas of South America have no vegetation.

___ (b) Desert areas of South America are good for forestry.

___ (c) Desert areas of South America are used mostly for grazing animals.

8. Most of the land in South America is used for

___ (a) forestry.

___ (b) farming.

___ (c) grazing or very little.

9. The areas on the natural vegetation map with the pattern [▨] are used

___ (a) only for farming.

___ (b) only for grazing.

___ (c) for farming and forestry.

10. Explain in your own words the difference between a natural vegetation map and a land use map.

_____

_____

_____

_____

_____

_____

_____

C. Study the following map of South Asia.

South Asia

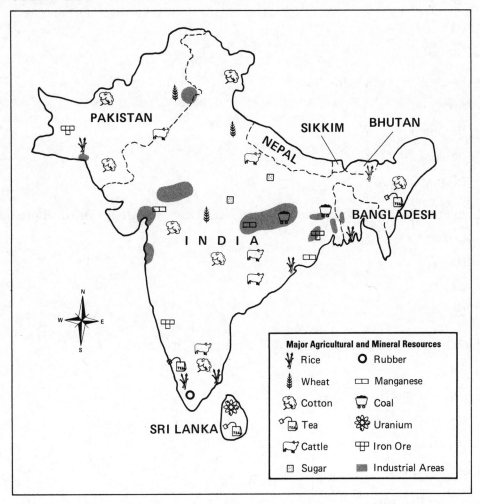

Place a check mark next to the correct answers to questions 1 to 9.

1. The map shows

___ (a) only the agricultural products of South Asia.

___ (b) only the mineral products of South Asia.

___ (c) the major agricultural and mineral products of South Asia.

___ (d) all of the agricultural and mineral products of South Asia.

2. Rubber is shown on the map by which symbol?

___ (a) 🐏

___ (b) ⊞

___ (c) ●

___ (d) 🛒

3. Manganese is shown on the map by which symbol?

___ (a) ⊏⊐

___ (b) ▮

___ (c) ⛏

___ (d) ✿

4. The symbol ▫ stands for

___ (a) cotton.

___ (b) sugar.

___ (c) coal.

___ (d) manganese.

5. Which one of the following symbols does NOT stand for an agricultural product?

___ (a) ⅄

___ (b) ⊛

___ (c) ⊶

___ (d) ⊞

6. Which mineral is mined in the island country of Sri Lanka?

___ (a) coal

___ (b) uranium

___ (c) iron ore

___ (d) manganese

7. The areas on the map colored ▩ are

___ (a) large farms.

___ (b) mines.

___ (c) industrial areas.

___ (d) seaports.

8. Which minerals can be found in the largest industrial area of India?

___ (a) uranium, iron ore

___ (b) coal, uranium

___ (c) iron ore, manganese

___ (d) coal, manganese

9. In India, rubber is produced mainly in the

___ (a) north.

___ (b) south.

___ (c) east.

___ (d) west.

10. India is more an agricultural country than an industrial country. How does the map show this to be true? (Answer in two or three sentences.)

_____

_____

_____

_____

_____

_____

D. Study the maps of China below and on page 270.

Place a check mark next to the correct answers to questions 1 to 8.

1. Map A shows

___ (*a*) where different kinds of natural plant life are found in China.

___ (*b*) what crops are grown in China.

___ (*c*) how large areas of China are used by people.

Map A—China

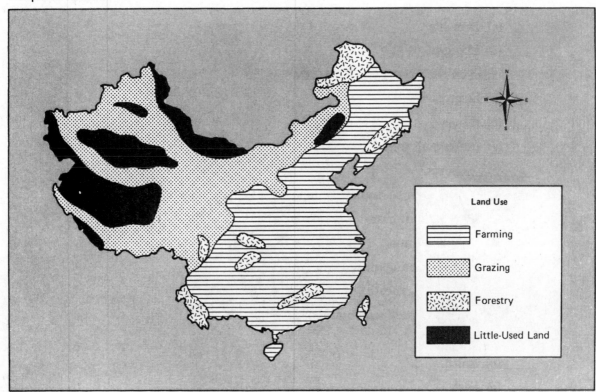

2. Map B shows

___ (a) the major agricultural products of China and where they are found in the country.

___ (b) which agricultural products in China are found in the greatest quantity.

___ (c) the major agricultural and mineral products of China.

3. The area of China that is used mainly for farming is in the

___ (a) north.   ___ (b) east.   ___ (c) west.

4. Soybeans are shown on the product map by which symbol?

___ (a) 🌽

___ (b) 🍃

___ (c) 🍵

5. The symbol 🌾 on the product map stands for

___ (a) rice.

___ (b) cotton.

___ (c) millet.

6. Forestry is carried out

___ (a) only in southern China.

___ (b) only in northern China.

___ (c) in many different areas of China.

Map B—China

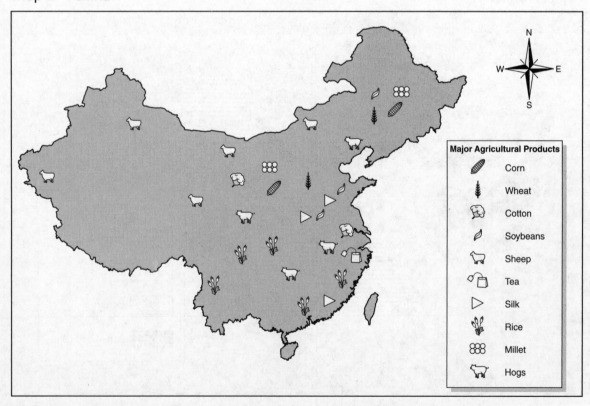

7. There is only one picture representing tea on Map B. This means that

___ (a) the people in this area are the only Chinese who like to drink tea.

___ (b) the government allows tea to be grown in only this area.

___ (c) tea is grown mainly in this area of China.

8. Which statement is supported by the information on both maps?

___ (a) Some farming is done in the grazing areas of China.

___ (b) Silk is produced in the grazing areas of China.

___ (c) Hogs are raised mainly in the grazing areas of China.

9. Why are the following pattern and symbol found in the same areas of China? ▦ 🐏 (Answer in two or three sentences.)

_____

_____

_____

_____

_____

10. How does the product map show that western China has relatively little farming? (Answer in one or two sentences.)

_____

_____

_____

_____

E. Study the maps of Africa on pages 272, 273, and 274.

Place a check mark next to the correct answers to questions 1 to 14.

1. Map A shows

___ (a) where minerals are found in Africa.

___ (b) where different kinds of natural plant life are found in Africa.

___ (c) how much land in Africa is used for farming.

2. Map B shows

___ (a) where different kinds of natural vegetation are found in Africa.

___ (b) the important agricultural and mineral products of Africa.

___ (c) how large areas of land in Africa are used by people.

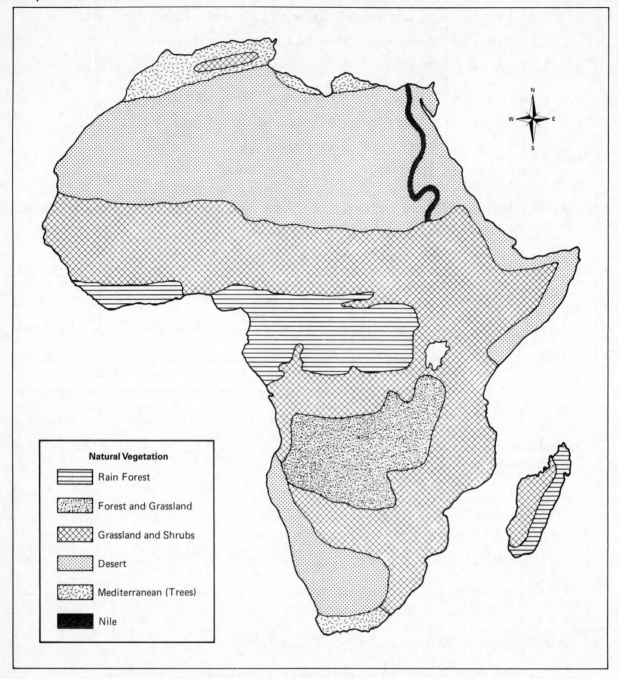

Natural Vegetation

Rain Forest

Forest and Grassland

Grassland and Shrubs

Desert

Mediterranean (Trees)

Nile

3. Map C shows

___ (*a*) the major agricultural and mineral products of Africa and where they are found.

___ (*b*) how much coffee and cotton are grown in Africa.

___ (*c*) the countries of Africa and their capital cities.

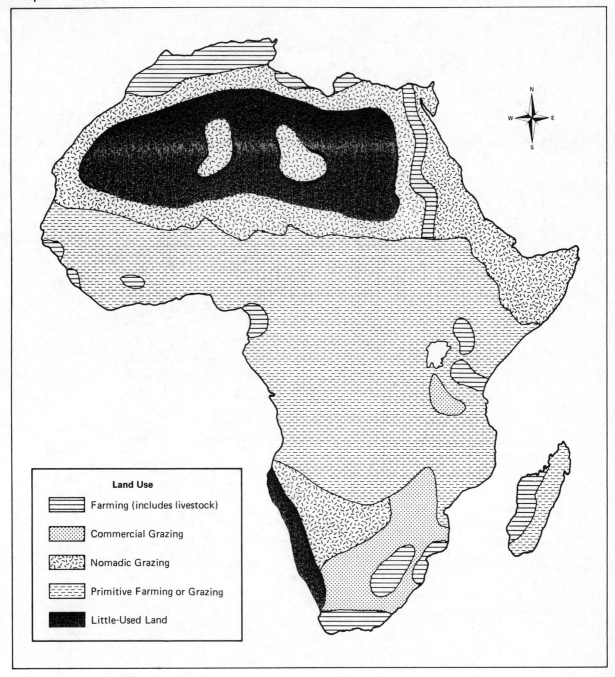

Land Use

Farming (includes livestock)

Commercial Grazing

Nomadic Grazing

Primitive Farming or Grazing

Little-Used Land

4. Most of northern Africa is covered with

___ (*a*) grassland vegetation.

___ (*b*) rain forest vegetation.

___ (*c*) desert vegetation.

5. Rain forest vegetation is found mostly in

___ (*a*) northern Africa.

___ (*b*) central Africa.

___ (*c*) southern Africa.

Map C—Africa Today

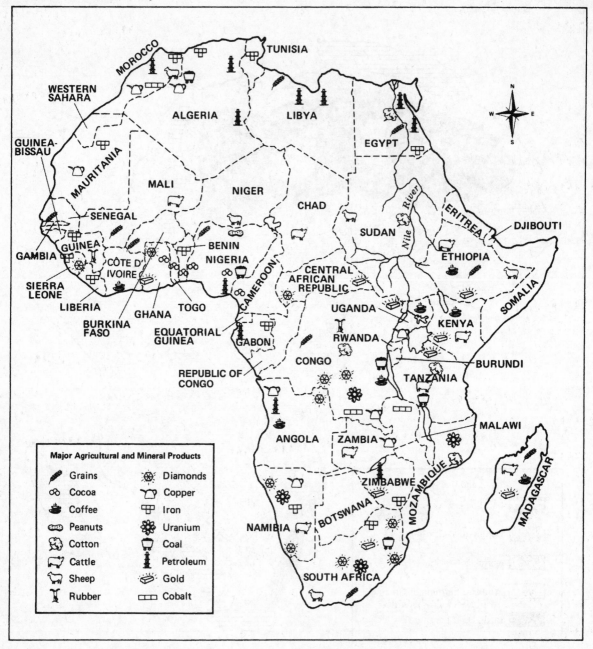

Major Agricultural and Mineral Products

🌾	Grains	💎	Diamonds
∞	Cocoa		Copper
☕	Coffee		Iron
⌇	Peanuts	✳	Uranium
🐑	Cotton		Coal
🐄	Cattle		Petroleum
🐑	Sheep		Gold
	Rubber	▭	Cobalt

6. The area on the land use map with the pattern ▮▮ is shown on the natural vegetation map by the pattern

   ___ (a) ▤

   ___ (b) ▩

   ___ (c) ▨

7. Most of the land in Africa is used for

   ___ (a) commercial grazing.

   ___ (b) nomadic grazing.

   ___ (c) primitive farming or grazing.

8. The Nile River Valley is used mostly for

___ (a) farming.

___ (b) commercial grazing.

___ (c) nomadic grazing.

9. Which area of natural vegetation is NOT used for primitive farming?

___ (a) grassland and shrubs

___ (b) rain forest

___ (c) Mediterranean

10. Rubber comes from an area of Africa with

___ (a) grassland vegetation.

___ (b) desert vegetation.

___ (c) rain forest vegetation.

11. The land in the Nile River Valley is used to grow

___ (a) cotton.

___ (b) peanuts.

___ (c) cocoa.

12. Coffee is grown in

___ (a) Algeria.

___ (b) Nigeria.

___ (c) Côte d'Ivoire.

13. Uranium is found in

___ (a) Egypt.

___ (b) Namibia.

___ (c) Libya.

14. Which one of the following countries has mostly desert vegetation?

___ (a) Libya

___ (b) Kenya

___ (c) Nigeria

15. How does the product map (Map C) show that South Africa must be a very rich country? (Answer in two or three sentences.)

_____

_____

_____

_____

_____

_____

F. Study the maps of mainland Southeast Asia on pages 276, 277, and 278.

F-1. Describe in your own words what each map shows.

MAP A _____

_____

_____

_____

MAP B _____

_____

_____

_____

MAP C _____

_____

_____

_____

Map A—Mainland Southeast Asia

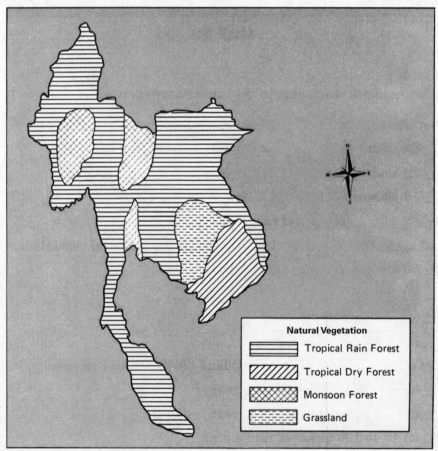

Natural Vegetation

Tropical Rain Forest

Tropical Dry Forest

Monsoon Forest

Grassland

Map B—Mainland Southeast Asia

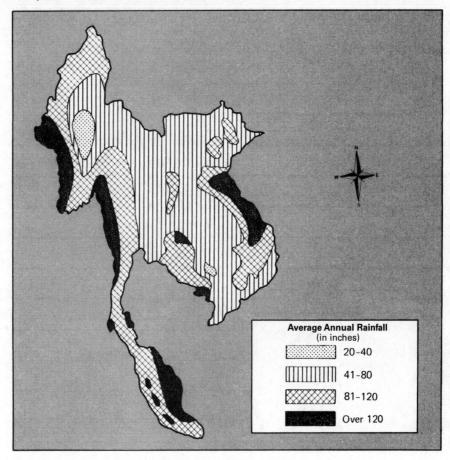

F-2. Place a check mark next to the correct answers to questions 1 to 10.

1. Most of mainland Southeast Asia receives

  ___ (*a*) under 40 inches of rain a year.

  ___ (*b*) under 81 inches of rain a year.

  ___ (*c*) between 41 and 120 inches of rain a year.

  ___ (*d*) over 120 inches of rain a year.

2. Most of mainland Southeast Asia is covered by a natural vegetation of

  ___ (*a*) tropical rain forest.

  ___ (*b*) tropical dry forest.

  ___ (*c*) monsoon forest.

  ___ (*d*) grassland.

3. Most of the grassland area of mainland Southeast Asia receives

  ___ (*a*) 20 to 40 inches of rain a year.

  ___ (*b*) 41 to 80 inches of rain a year.

  ___ (*c*) 81 to 120 inches of rain a year.

  ___ (*d*) over 120 inches of rain a year.

Map C—Mainland Southeast Asia

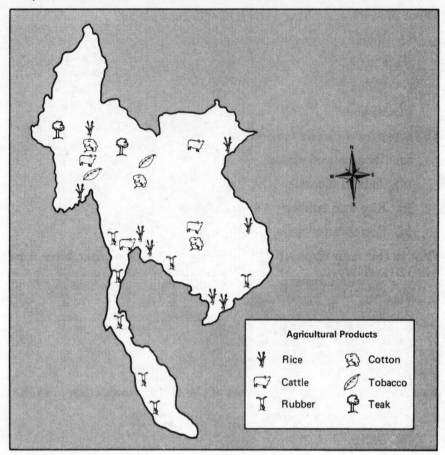

4. Which one of the following symbols is NOT matched with its product?

___ (a) ⚘ rice

___ (b) ✎ tobacco

___ (c) 🐑 cotton

___ (d) ⊥ teak

5. The grassland area of mainland Southeast Asia is used

___ (a) to grow rice and tobacco.

___ (b) to produce rubber and teak.

___ (c) to grow cotton and to raise cattle.

___ (d) for hunting animals.

6. Most of the rubber is produced in areas with a yearly rainfall of

___ (a) under 20 inches.

___ (b) between 20 and 40 inches.

___ (c) between 41 and 80 inches.

___ (d) over 80 inches.

7. Which product is produced in eight different places?

___ (*a*) rice

___ (*b*) cotton

___ (*c*) tobacco

___ (*d*) rubber

8. Which products can be found in the tropical dry forest area?

___ (*a*) tobacco and cotton

___ (*b*) teak and cattle

___ (*c*) rice and rubber

___ (*d*) cotton and cattle

9. What is the main type of vegetation in the sections that have a rainfall over 120 inches?

___ (*a*) monsoon forest

___ (*b*) tropical rain forest

___ (*c*) tropical dry forest

___ (*d*) grassland

10. In mainland Southeast Asia, most of the rubber production is in the

___ (*a*) north.

___ (*b*) south.

___ (*c*) east.

___ (*d*) west.

Demonstrating What You Have Learned

Chapter 30

Test Taking and Constructed-Response Questions

Previously in this book, you studied a number of important Social Studies skills. Did you ever stop to think that taking a test requires skill? In this chapter, you will learn how to study for a test and how to take a test and do well on it.

Studying for a Test

Start studying several days before a test, not just the night before. It is a good idea to review (read over) the material you are to be tested on a few times each day. If you review something many times, you have a better chance of remembering it.

You will study better without a television or radio on. If possible, study in a quiet place where you can be alone. You will probably find that you study better sitting in a chair rather than lying down. A bed or a sofa may be more comfortable than a chair, but how much studying can you do if you fall asleep?

The most important material you can study is the notes you took in class. If your notes are not clear or complete enough, you may need to read over parts of your textbook.

If your teacher gives a review lesson before a test, pay close attention to what is said. The teacher will discuss the important topics that will most likely be on the test. Be sure to take notes of this review lesson.

Taking a Test

A good night's sleep before the test will help your mind to work better. Arrive at the test on time and bring a pencil and a pen. Any delay in starting the test will only hurt you.

The most important rule in taking a test is a simple one: READ THE DIRECTIONS AND THE QUESTIONS. Many students rush to answer test questions without first reading the directions and each of the questions carefully.

Tests use all kinds of questions. In this chapter, you will learn about multiple-choice, true-or-false, essay, and constructed-response questions.

Multiple-Choice Questions

In most multiple-choice questions, you are given three or four possible answers. You have to choose the best answer. One or two of the choices may be obviously wrong. You can immediately eliminate (get rid of) them. It is also possible that two choices seem correct. You must choose the one that is the BEST answer.

Here is an example of a multiple-choice question.

1. Africa is

_____ (a) an ocean.

_____ (b) a country.

_____ (c) a continent.

Which answer did you choose? First, is there any choice that can be eliminated, or left out? Certainly Africa is not an ocean. This eliminates choice (a). You know that a country and a continent are both land-masses. But in your Social Studies class, you have learned that Africa is a very large landmass and that it is a continent. So the best answer to question 1 is (c).

Most multiple-choice questions are like question 1, but some are more challenging because of the way they are worded.

Here are *three* examples of questions that you need to read very carefully.

2. Which one of the following was NOT a reason for the European takeover of Africa in the 19th century?

_____ (a) the desire for the mineral wealth of Africa

_____ (b) the desire to find new lands in which to live

_____ (c) the desire to become more like the Africans

_____ (d) the desire for adventure

Which answer did you choose? In this question, three of the four choices were reasons for the European takeover of Africa. But you have to pick the choice that was NOT a reason. From your studies, you should know that the Europeans did not go to Africa to become more like the Africans. Therefore, the answer to question 2 is (c).

The next example asks the same question but in different wording.

3. All of the following were reasons for the European takeover of Africa in the 19th century EXCEPT

_____ (a) the desire for the mineral wealth of Africa.

_____ (b) the desire to find new lands in which to live.

_____ (c) the desire to become more like the Africans.

_____ (d) the desire for adventure.

The important word in this question is EXCEPT. This word means that one of the choices was NOT a reason for the European takeover of Africa. The other three choices were reasons. As you know, the correct answer is (c).

The next example points out the importance of reading all the choices.

4. The European takeover of Africa in the 19th century is best explained by

_____ (a) the desire for the mineral wealth of Africa.

_____ (b) the desire to find new lands in which to live.

_____ (c) the desire for adventure.

_____ (d) all of the above.

Which answer did you choose? You can see that choice (a) gives a reason for the European takeover of Africa in the 19th century. But so do choices (b) and (c). Only choice (d) puts these three reasons together, making it the BEST explanation. Notice that you had to read all the choices to see that the best answer to question 4 is (d). Always read all the choices before deciding on an answer.

The next example also requires that you think carefully.

5. Which one of the following is caused by the other three?

_____ (a) cars

_____ (b) factories

_____ (c) pollution

_____ (d) garbage

What was your answer this time? This question is telling you that three of the choices bring about, or cause, the fourth choice. Look carefully at the choices. Does any one of them happen because of the other three? Yes, there is pollution because of cars, factories, and garbage. Choice (*c*) is caused by choices (*a*), (*b*), and (*d*). Therefore, the answer to 5 is (*c*).

You will have little trouble understanding a multiple-choice question if you read the question and all of the choices carefully. Remember: Always choose the BEST answer.

True-or-False Questions

There is a simple rule for true-or-false questions. A statement must be completely true to be true. If any part of the statement is false, the whole statement is false.

Read the following example of a true-or-false question.

_____ Japanese planes attacked Pearl Harbor on December 7, 1941.

Every part of this statement is true. Therefore, on a test, it should be marked true.

Here is another example of a true-or-false question.

_____ Christopher Columbus sailed from Spain to the Americas in 1472.

Christopher Columbus did sail from Spain to the Americas, but the date 1472 is wrong. He did not make his first voyage to the Americas until 1492. Because one part of the statement is false, the whole statement should be marked false.

In a true-or-false question, you also have to be careful about words that can be tricky. These tricky words include "some," "many," "most," "everyone," "no one," "never," and "always." What may be true of something may not be true of everything.

Example:

_____ Everyone in the United States likes to watch television.

In order for this statement to be true, every single person in the United States has to like watching television. Surely there is at least one person who dislikes watching television. Therefore, the statement is false.

It could be proved that "most people in the United States like to watch television." This second statement, then, would be true.

Here is another example of a true-or-false question.

_____ Periods of dry weather are always followed by periods of very wet weather.

The word "always" means "all the time." Weather Bureau records show that dry weather is not followed by very wet weather all the time. Therefore, the statement is false. If the word "always" were changed to "sometimes," the sentence would be true.

Essay Questions

You learned how to write essays in Unit Two. Let us now think about how to follow directions for answering essay questions. Many students rush to answer them without first understanding the requirements.

Read the following directions and the questions that go with them.

Directions: Answer *two* of the following questions.

1. (*a*) Give reasons why Mao Zedong was able to take control of China in 1949.
   (*b*) Describe the changes Mao Zedong brought about in China after 1949.

2. (*a*) Explain why the Europeans were interested in Africa in the 19th century.
   (*b*) Give reasons why so many African countries gained independence between 1960 and 1970.

3. (*a*) Why has the United States always had a special interest in the problems of South America?
   (*b*) Explain why the United States stopped trading with Cuba in the 1960s and 1970s.

How many questions should you answer in this essay part of a test? Some students would answer all the questions just because they are on the page. But the directions clearly tell you to answer two questions.

Some students would answer 1. (*a*) and (*b*) and think they answered two questions. But they would have answered only two parts of the same question. The directions tell you to answer two questions. So you would have to choose:

1. (*a*) and (*b*)   and   2. (*a*) and (*b*)

or

1. (*a*) and (*b*)   and   3. (*a*) and (*b*)

or

2. (*a*) and (*b*)   and   3. (*a*) and (*b*)

In the essays in the example, notice the words "why," "describe," and "explain." When you see them on a test, be sure to give full, complete answers, ones usually written in sentences.

Constructed-Response Questions

An essay question *may* contain parts. A constructed-response question (CRQ) *always* contains parts. It will come with a document and a series of questions that build from the simple to the complex.

The document may be a reading selection, photograph, cartoon, chart, graph, or map.

Most CRQs give three questions. The first question will ask you to find information that is in the document. The second question will ask you to do something with the information in the document. The third question usually requires an answer that relies on information you learned at another time.

Here is an example of a constructed-response question.

Directions: Please use your knowledge of Social Studies and this document (the table) to answer questions 1 to 3.

Countries With the Most Foreign Visitors in 2006		In millions
1.	France	79.1
2.	Spain	58.5
3.	United States	51.1
4.	China	49.6
5.	Italy	41.1
6.	United Kingdom	30.7
7.	Germany	23.6
8.	Mexico	21.4
9.	Austria	20.3
10.	Russia	20.2

1. Name the countries on the table that had more foreign visitors in 2006 than the United States.

2. How many foreign visitors did the ten countries in the table have in total for 2006?

3. Why do you think the table contains more countries from Europe than from any other continent?

Is question 1 simple? It is if you consider that the answer is right in the document. France and Spain had more foreign visitors in 2006 than the United States.

Question 2 is a little more difficult. It requires that you add up all the numbers in millions. The answer is 395.6 million.

Question 3 is more difficult than question 2. The answer is open-ended and not on the table. You may not know all the countries on the table that are in Europe. But you know there is a high number because the question tells you so. Here is where you will have to rely on information you learned at another time. If you know that France is in Europe and you know something about France, you may begin to think of an answer. You could do the same for the other countries that you know are in Europe. You may think of famous places in Europe that you read about or saw on television. You would search all the information on Europe you have stored in your mind to come up with a good answer to question 3.

You have seen in this chapter how careful you must be in answering questions on a test. Here is a list of things to do when you are taking a test. Try to remember them.

1. Read the directions and the questions carefully.

2. Plan your time so that you leave enough time to answer all of the questions.

3. Leave the more difficult questions to the end. Answer the questions you know first.

4. Do not leave any answer blank. An answer left blank is always wrong, but a good guess may be correct. (However, be sure that points are not taken off for incorrect answers.)

5. Answer exactly as many essay questions as the directions tell you to.

6. In each essay question, answer all parts unless the directions tell you differently.

7. Do not panic because the answer to question 3 in a CRQ is not given in the provided document. Let the information in the document lead you to search your mind for information to answer the question.

Learning how to take a test is an important skill. Whether you are in school or looking for a job, you will be asked to take many tests during your life. The following exercises will give you more practice in using this important skill.

USING WHAT YOU HAVE LEARNED

A. Place a check mark next to the correct answers to questions 1 to 5.

1. It is important to take good notes in class because

    ___ (*a*) it pleases the teacher.

    ___ (*b*) you can show them to a parent or guardian when you get home.

    ___ (*c*) notes will help you remember what you learned in class.

2. A review lesson is important because it

    ___ (*a*) teaches you new material.

    ___ (*b*) points out important things you learned in other lessons.

    ___ (*c*) takes the place of studying for a test.

3. The most important rule in taking a test is to

    ___ (*a*) read the directions and the questions carefully.

    ___ (*b*) work as fast as you can.

    ___ (*c*) answer all of the questions.

4. In answering a multiple-choice question, you will find that

    ___ (*a*) one or two choices can usually be eliminated immediately.

    ___ (*b*) the longest choice is most likely the correct answer.

    ___ (*c*) the first choice is most likely the correct answer.

5. When two choices are close to being correct in a multiple-choice question, you

    ___ (*a*) can pick either choice.

    ___ (*b*) look for another choice.

    ___ (*c*) must pick the choice that is better.

B. Mark each statement **T** for *true* or **F** for *false*. Remember the rules you learned in the chapter about answering true-or-false questions.

___ 1. A true-or-false question is false if any part of it is false.

___ 2. In a review lesson, you learn only new material for the next test.

___ 3. The most important rule in taking a test is to work quickly and finish as soon as possible.

___ 4. The first student to finish a test always gets the highest mark.

___ 5. In a test, essay questions marked 1. (*a*) and 1. (*b*) always stand for two separate questions.

C. Place a check mark next to the correct answers to questions 1 to 3.

1. Which one of the following may be caused by the other three?

___ (*a*) failing a test

___ (*b*) not studying enough

___ (*c*) going to bed late the night before a test

___ (*d*) taking poor notes in class

2. All of the following will help you in taking a test EXCEPT

___ (*a*) arriving at the test on time.

___ (*b*) a good night's sleep.

___ (*c*) bringing a pen.

___ (*d*) leaving your studying to the last minute.

3. Look carefully at the following essay part of a test. Then answer questions A, B, and C.

Directions: Answer *two* of the following questions.

1. (*a*) Why did the Spanish come to the Americas?
   (*b*) Describe the influence Spain had on the countries of South America.

2. (*a*) Explain how apartheid began in South Africa.
   (*b*) How has apartheid affected the development of South Africa?

3. (*a*) Explain this statement: "Southeast Asia is blessed with natural resources."
   (*b*) Why was Thailand the only country in Southeast Asia able to withstand European colonization?

   A. How many questions do you have to answer in this essay part of a test?

   ___ (*a*) one

   ___ (*b*) two

   ___ (*c*) three

   B. How many questions are given on the above essay part of a test?

   ___ (*a*) three questions, each with two parts

   ___ (*b*) two questions

   ___ (*c*) six separate questions

C. Is the following statement true or false? "If I answer only 1. (*a*) and 1. (*b*), I have followed the directions correctly." (Explain your answer in two or three sentences.)

_____

_____

_____

_____

4. Which of the following statements is more likely to be *false*? Explain why. "Some countries in Africa have great trouble producing food." "A country with a large population is always a poor country." (Answer in two or three sentences.)

_____

_____

_____

_____

5. List *five* things you should think about when you take a test.

_____

_____

_____

_____

_____

D. Constructed-Response Questions

1. Directions: Use your knowledge of Social Studies skills and the document below to answer the questions that follow.

> A constructed-response question (CRQ) is made up of a document and a series of questions that build from the simple to the complex. The document may be a reading selection, photograph, cartoon, chart, graph, or map. Most CRQs give three questions. The first question will ask you to find information that is in the document. The second question will ask you to do something with the information in the document. The third question usually requires an answer that relies on information you learned at another time.

a. Name at least *five* kinds of documents used in constructed-response questions.

_____

_____

b. Why is it said that questions in a CRQ go from the simple to the complex?

_____

_____

_____

c. How might the information in the first and second questions of a CRQ help you to answer the third question?

_____

_____

_____

_____

2. Directions: Use your knowledge of Social Studies and the documents below to answer the following questions.

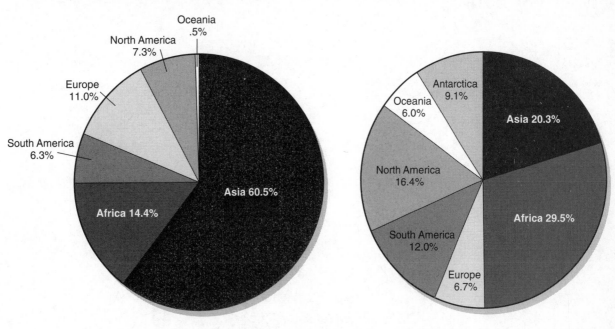

Population of the World's Largest Land Areas, by Percentage, 2006

Percentage of World's Land Areas, by Region, 2006

Note: Antarctica: no permanent residents

a. On which continent does more than half of the Earth's human population live?

_____

_____

_____

b. What two regions of the Earth together have 15.1 percent of the land area but only 0.5 percent of the population?

_____

_____

_____

c. Give and explain *two* reasons why some areas of the Earth are highly populated and other areas are much less populated.

_____

_____

_____

_____

_____

Chapter 31
Document-Based Questions (DBQs)

Throughout this book, you have been asked to answer questions based on a document. You have learned to answer the questions whether the document is a reading selection, a cartoon or picture, a chart or graph, or a map.

Some tests go beyond questions based on one document. They assess how well you can answer a question based on more than one document at the same time. To make this assessment, the tests use what is called a Document-Based Question, or DBQ. The goal of this type of question is to judge your ability to write a detailed and well-thought-out essay using various sources of information.

In this chapter, you will learn the skills needed to answer a Document-Based Question.

Using the Skills You Already Know

The DBQ requires the use of many skills. You have already learned most of them in this book. Let us review some of them:

1. Read all directions carefully so that you know what is expected of you.

2. Read the title of each document because it may quickly tell you the main idea.

3. Look for a date for each document. You want to know if the document is current or produced some time in the past.

4. Look to see if the author or source of the document is given. If the docu-

ment is about a past event, you want to know whether the author was present at the event. An eyewitness account of an event may be more accurate than an account written years later.

5. Examine everything in the document, including any chart, map key, caption, or explanation given in small print.

6. Examine any chart or graph so that you understand what each column and row are showing.

7. Be on guard for the accuracy of facts and details and for opinions that are offered as facts. Cartoons usually express an opinion.

The Parts of a DBQ

The word "scaffolding" is often used to describe the format of a DBQ. A scaffold is a structure with parts built on top of other parts. If you want to have a second floor in a scaffold, you must already have a first floor.

The DBQ uses a scaffolding approach to test your knowledge of a topic. Its goal is to have you write an essay based on various documents. But that essay question is on the scaffold's second floor. To get to it, you have to answer questions on the first floor.

The first-floor questions require short answers. They often involve interpreting the main idea or point of view expressed in the documents. There are one or two questions for each document. All of the questions have one purpose: to get you to focus on the documents. You must have a good understanding of each document if you are going to write a good essay.

After you answer the questions on the first floor, it is time to move to the second floor. In writing your essay, you will use all the knowledge you gained from the documents and all the knowledge relating to the topic that you have learned from any other source.

Writing a DBQ Essay

The DBQ essay tests how well you can express your knowledge and your thoughts in writing. In your essay, you will be required to do the following:

1. Accurately interpret the documents.

2. Decide on the importance and accuracy of the information in the documents.

3. Be aware of any conflicts or differences of opinion in the documents.

4. Combine what you learned from the documents with what you already know about the topic.

5. Use the documents and any outside source of information to support the view you are expressing.

6. Give examples that are on target in trying to support your point of view.

7. Use facts and details accurately.

8. Make sure your essay reads well and that it has a strong introduction and conclusion.

Let us see what you have learned about DBQs. Answer the following questions.

1. What is the main purpose of a DBQ? (Answer in one or two sentences.)

_____

_____

_____

_____

What did you write? The main purpose of a DBQ is to see how well you can write a detailed, well-thought-out essay based on various kinds of documents. If your answer contained this idea, you wrote a good response.

2. Why is the word "scaffolding" used to describe the format of a DBQ? (Answer in two or three sentences.)

_____

_____

_____

_____

_____

What did you write this time? You must build the first floor of a scaffold before you can build the second floor. In the DBQ, you must first answer questions based on each document. With the knowledge you gain from answering these questions, you are ready to move up the scaffold to the all-important essay. If you do not understand the documents, you will not do well on the essay. If your answer contained these ideas, you wrote a good response.

3. What does the following statement mean?

Your essay must not just repeat the information found in the documents.

(Answer in one or two sentences.)

_____

_____

_____

What did you write? The person who corrects your DBQ knows what the documents say. You do not have to repeat the information. If you restate part of a document, it should be done briefly and for only one purpose: to support your point of view. If your answer contained these ideas, you wrote a good response.

The following exercises will give you practice in answering Document-Based Questions. Remember: Read carefully, think through everything, and write with confidence.

USING WHAT YOU HAVE LEARNED

Document-Based Question 1

Directions: Your task is to write an essay on global warming based on the accompanying documents and your understanding of Social Studies issues. First, read the documents and answer the question or questions after each document. Each question is designed to focus your attention on the issue(s) in the document that relate to your essay. Then read the essay question that appears after the set of documents. Finally, write your essay.

Documents (A–D)

Directions: Read the documents, taking into account the source of each document and any point of view. Then answer the question or questions after each document. Be sure your answers are written in complete sentences.

Document A

Global Warming Fast Facts   **National Geographic News**
Updated June 14, 2007

Is It Happening? Yes. Earth is already showing many signs of worldwide climate change.

- Average temperatures have climbed 1.4 degrees Fahrenheit (0.8 degree Celsius) around the world since 1880, much of this in recent decades, according to NASA's Goddard Institute for Space Studies.
- Arctic ice is rapidly disappearing, and the region may have its first completely ice-free summer by 2040 or earlier. Polar bears and indigenous cultures are already suffering from the sea-ice loss.
- An upsurge in the amount of extreme weather events, such as wildfires, heat waves, and strong tropical storms, is also attributed in part to climate change by some experts.

Are Humans Causing It? "Very likely," the IPCC said in a February 2007 report.
The report, based on the work of some 2,500 scientists in more than 130 countries, concluded that humans have caused all or most of the current planetary warming.

Note: The Intergovernmental Panel on Climate Change (IPCC) was created in 1988 by the United Nations. It evaluates the risk of climate change caused by human activity.

Source: John Roach/National Geographic Image Collection. National Geographic Web site: *http://news.nationalgeographic.com/news/2004/12/1206_041206_global_warming.html*

1. What information does this document give to show that global warming is happening?

2. According to the IPCC, how much of the current global warming is caused by humans?

Where's the Global Warming   Jeff Jacoby, *Boston Globe*
March 8, 2009

The United States has shivered through an unusually severe winter, with snow falling in such unlikely destinations as New Orleans, Las Vegas, Alabama, and Georgia. On Dec. 25, every Canadian province woke up to a white Christmas, something that hadn't happened in 37 years. Earlier this year, Europe was gripped by such a killing cold wave that trains were shut down in the French Riviera and chimpanzees in the Rome Zoo had to be plied with hot tea. Last week, satellite data showed three of the Great Lakes—Erie, Superior, and Huron—almost completely frozen over. . . . 2008 was the coolest year of the past decade—global temperatures have not exceeded the record high measured in 1998, notwithstanding the carbon-dioxide that human beings continue to pump into the atmosphere.

None of this proves conclusively that a period of planetary cooling is irrevocably underway. . . . But considering how much attention would have been lavished on a comparable run of hot weather or on a warming trend that was plainly accelerating, shouldn't the recent cold phenomena and the absence of any global warming during the past 10 years be getting a little more notice?

Source: © 2009, *The Boston Globe*. Reprinted by permission.

1. What information in this story challenges the claim that global warming is getting worse?

2. Does Jeff Jacoby believe that news about global "warming" gets more attention than news about global "cooling"? Explain.

3. How does this article suggest that it may be difficult for the public to know all the facts about global warming?

Document C

© H. Payne, Detroit News/Dist. by United Feature Syndicate, Inc.

To what extent does this cartoon make it more difficult to get people to believe that there really is global warming?

How important is the issue of global warming to you personally: extremely important, very important, somewhat important, not too important, or not at all important?

Date of Poll	Extremely Important	Very Important	Somewhat Important	Not Too Important	Not at All Important
Jul. 23–28, 2008	16%	30%	32%	13%	9%
Apr. 5–10, 2007	18%	34%	30%	8%	9%
Mar. 9–14, 2006	17%	33%	32%	10%	8%

Source: http://www.pollingreport.com/enviro.htm
ABC News/Planet Green/Stanford University poll, July 23–28, 2008. N = 1,000 adults nationwide.

For someone who believes that people should be interested in global warming, there is good news and bad news in the above poll. What is the good news? What is the bad news?

Essay

Directions: Write a well-organized essay that contains an introduction, several paragraphs, and a conclusion. Be sure to include specific information from the documents you just read and additional information from your knowledge of Social Studies.

Task: Write an essay that both explains why global warming is a controversial issue and includes your recommendation on how to lessen the controversy.

Document-Based Question 2

Directions: Your task is to write an essay on human rights based on the accompanying documents and your understanding of Social Studies issues. First, read the documents and answer the question or questions after each document. Each question is designed to focus your attention on the issue(s) in the document that relate to your essay. Then read the essay question that appears after the set of documents. Finally, write your essay.

Documents (A–G)

Directions: Read the documents, taking into account the source of each document and any point of view. Then answer the question or questions after each document. Be sure your answers are written in complete sentences.

Document A

Eugene V. Debs, 1908 Speech
Five-time unsuccessful candidate for president of the United States

Now my friends, I am opposed to the system of society in which we live today, not because I lack the natural equipment to do for myself but because I am not satisfied to make myself comfortable knowing that there are thousands of my fellow men who suffer for the barest necessities of life. We were taught under the old ethic that man's business on this earth was to look out for himself. That was the ethic of the jungle; the ethic of the wild beast. Take care of yourself, no matter what may become of your fellow man. Thousands of years ago the question was asked: "Am I my brother's keeper?" That question has never yet been answered in a way that is satisfactory to civilized society. Yes, I am my brother's keeper. . . . What would you think of me if I were capable of seating myself at a table and gorging myself with food and saw about me the children of my fellow beings starving to death?

Why did Eugene V. Debs believe that it was his duty to help people who lack "the barest necessities of life"?

Document B

Universal Declaration of Human Rights (selected articles)
Adopted and Proclaimed by the General Assembly of the
United Nations on December 10, 1948

Article 1 of 30
All human beings are born free and equal in dignity and rights. They are endowed with reason and conscience and should act toward one another in a spirit of brotherhood.

Article 4
No one shall be held in slavery or servitude; slavery and the slave trade shall be prohibited in all their forms.

Article 5
No one shall be subjected to torture or to cruel, inhuman or degrading treatment or punishment.

Why do you think the United Nations felt a need to issue the Universal Declaration of Human Rights?

Document C

Global Trends in Freedom

Year Under Review	Free Countries	Partly Free Countries	Not Free Countries
1976	42 (26%)	49 (31%)	68 (43%)
1986	57 (34%)	57 (34%)	53 (32%)
1996	79 (41%)	59 (31%)	53 (28%)
2006	90 (47%)	58 (30%)	45 (23%)
2007	90 (47%)	60 (31%)	43 (22%)

According to the survey, 90 countries are free. There 3.0 billion inhabitants (47% of the world's population) enjoy a broad range of rights. Sixty countries representing just over 1.2 billion people (31%) are considered partly free. Political rights and civil liberties are more limited in these countries, in which corruption, dominant ruling parties, or, in some cases, ethnic or religious strife is often the norm. The survey finds that 43 countries are not free. The 2.4 billion inhabitants (22%) of these countries, nearly one-half of whom live in China, are denied most basic political rights and civil liberties.

Source: Freedom in the World, 2008, published by Freedom House.
www.freedomhouse.org/template.cfm?page=410&year=2008

1. To what extent do the survey statistics show an improvement in human rights?

2. What information in the comments below the table might explain why China was singled out for mention?

Document D

China Reports on U.S. Human Rights Violations

After all, it's China—the biggest country dedicated to communist ideals and for many in the world, the worst violators of human rights themselves. . . . Since China always seems to make the list in U.S. reports on global violators of human rights, China's stab at creating a government sanctioned document turning the tables on the U.S. is seen by everyone as nothing more than getting even with the U.S.

Yet, China's report, the Human Rights Record of the United States in 2007, is more than just a retaliatory document. . . . The report draws from FBI and census data and news sources in compiling a report built on facts to show the world that the U.S. has its own problems. The report goes as far as to bluntly say: "Racial discrimination is a deep-rooted social illness in the United States."

www.latinalista.net/palabrafinal/2008/03/china_reports_on_us_human_rights_violati.html

How does this article illustrate that countries like to point out human rights violations in other countries rather than in their own?

"A WOMAN IS ENDOWED WITH CERTAIN INALIENABLE RIGHTS, ALL OF WHICH SHE MUST FIGHT FOR."

© CartoonStock.com

1. What is meant by the expression "endowed with certain inalienable rights"?

2. The cartoonist chose to comment on women's rights. Describe a right that most women in the world have to fight for that most men do not.

Document F

U.S. Congress Acts to Prosecute Recruiters of Child Soldiers
No Safe Haven for Exploiters of Children

(New York, September 15, 2008)—New legislation adopted on September 15, 2008, will permit the United States to prosecute foreign military commanders who recruit child soldiers abroad, Human Rights Watch said today. The Child Soldiers Accountability Act passed the House of Representatives unanimously on September 8 and was adopted by the Senate today.

The law makes it a federal crime to knowingly recruit or use soldiers under the age of 15 and permits the United States to bring charges under the law against both U.S. citizens and non-citizens who are in the United States. The law imposes penalties of up to 20 years, or up to life in prison if death results, and allows the United States to deport or deny entry to individuals who have knowingly recruited children as soldiers.

Source: http://hrw.org/english/docs/2008/09/15/usdom19818_txt.htm

The law described in Document F permits the United States to prosecute foreign military commanders who recruit child soldiers abroad. It will be difficult for the United States to arrest such military commanders, especially when they are in a foreign land. So why do you think the U.S. Congress passed this law?

Human rights violations in cities around the world   **6 October 2008**

Caught in the crossfire: women's experiences of violence in shanty towns (Brazil)
Amnesty International has documented how, in the absence of protection from the state, women are vulnerable to violence within the home and from criminal gangs that dominate every aspect of life in the community. Women may be punished violently for breaking the "rules" set out by the gangs or factions or for their relatives having done so.

Lives in ruins—forced evictions of people living in poverty (Angola)
Amnesty International estimates that around 10,000 families have been forcibly evicted in Luanda, Angola, in the last seven years, without prior notification, information or consultation, legal protection, adequate alternative accommodation or an effective remedy. Between July and December 2007, hundreds of families were forcibly evicted from the Iraque neighbourhood of the Kilamba Kiaxi municipality in Luanda, in order to build a luxury housing complex in the area.

Source: www.amnestyusa.org/document.php?id=ENGNAU200810066096&lang=e

Every year, Amnesty International publishes a lengthy report on human rights violations around the world. What good does it do to publish this report?

Essay

Directions: Write a well-organized essay that contains an introduction, several paragraphs, and a conclusion. Be sure to include specific information from the documents you just read and additional information from your knowledge of Social Studies.

Task: Write an essay that explains why you agree or disagree with each of the following statements:

Progress has been made in recent years in expanding human rights.

The struggle for human rights never ends.

I have a role to play in improving human rights for all people.

Index